Mark

DOUGLAS R. A. HARE

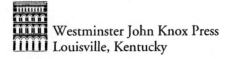
Westminster John Knox Press
Louisville, Kentucky

© 1996 Douglas R. A. Hare

Except where noted, the scripture quotations contained herein are from the New Revised Standard Version of the Bible, copyright © 1989 by the Division of Christian Education of the National Council of the Churches of Christ in the U.S.A., and are used by permission. All rights reserved.

Book design by Publishers' WorkGroup
Cover design by Drew Stevens

First edition

Published by Westminster John Knox Press
Louisville, Kentucky

This book is printed on acid-free paper that meets the American National Standards Institute Z39.48 standard. ♾

PRINTED IN THE UNITED STATES OF AMERICA

96 97 98 99 00 01 02 03 04 05 — 10 9 8 7 6 5 4 3 2 1

Library of Congress Cataloging-in-Publication Data

Hare, Douglas R. A.
    Mark / Douglas R. A. Hare. — 1st ed.
        p.   cm. — (Westminster Bible Companion)
    Includes bibliographical references.
    ISBN 0-664-25551-5 (alk. paper)
    1. Bible. N.T. Mark—Commentaries. I. Title. II. Series.
BS2585.3.H29   1996
226.3'077—dc20   96-397

Mark

Westminster Bible Companion

Series Editors

Patrick D. Miller
David L. Bartlett

Contents

Introduction

What was Jesus really like? This question, prompted by a very natural curiosity, has conferred on the Gospel according to Mark an importance it did not enjoy until fairly recent times. For most of Christian history, Mark was largely eclipsed by the longer Gospels. Lacking the Sermon on the Mount and other collections of Jesus' teachings found in Matthew, Mark was regarded as a truncated version of the First Gospel. In the nineteenth century, however, biblical scholars gradually came to a consensus that Mark, the shortest Gospel, was also the earliest; Matthew and Luke seem to have used Mark as the basis of their work and to have expanded on it by adding teaching material and stories that are not found in Mark. This conclusion suggested that it is in Mark that we are brought closest to the historical Jesus. It is not surprising, therefore, that thousands of modern Christians, hungering for a closer relationship to the church's Lord, have come eagerly to Mark in the hope of finding out what Jesus was really like.

In this regard, Mark has often been contrasted with the Fourth Gospel, John. Mark, it was claimed, is a *historical* Gospel, whereas John is a *theological* Gospel. In the past fifty years, however, scholars have come to recognize that Mark, too, is thoroughly theological. Although the author of Mark is writing history and not myth—that is, he writes about a real human being, Jesus of Nazareth—he is by no means an objective historian. What he gives us is not a photograph but a portrait in which Jesus' face is surrounded by a literary halo. He is not interested in telling us what Jesus was "really like" so as to satisfy our curiosity. Unlike biographers ancient and modern, he tells us nothing about what Jesus looked like, what his voice sounded like, how he presented himself to large crowds, and nothing about his childhood, family training and education, personal relationships, habits and idiosyncracies. From first verse to last, the Gospel according to Mark focuses on Jesus' meaning for faith.

It would not be inappropriate, therefore, to regard the Gospel according to Mark as a sermon. Because the book can be read in its entirety in about an hour, it seems likely that Mark was designed to be read aloud, probably to an audience consisting of both baptized Christians and inquirers. Like a sermon, it preaches Christ and calls for faith. Its primary intention is not to give us interesting information about Jesus but to challenge us to accept Jesus as God's saving deed.

It is not enough, however, to characterize the Gospel according to Mark as a sermon, for it differs dramatically from normal specimens of that literary form. After all, if Mark had intended to write only a sermon, the Gospel writer could have adopted a pattern closer to what we find in the Epistle to the Hebrews. Instead, he chose to write a gospel. But what is a gospel?

Clearly, it is unsatisfactory to treat the Gospels as biographies, historical chronicles, or martyrdom narratives, although they share features with each of these literary forms. The Gospels must be understood on the basis of their own peculiar form. The most satisfactory definition was suggested by the German scholar Martin Kähler a century ago: *A gospel is a passion narrative with an extended introduction.* That is, a gospel is a story about Jesus that focuses on his death and resurrection.

The validity of this definition can be tested by any reader. Take whatever Bible translation you are using and calculate the number of pages in Mark. Then count the number of pages devoted to the story of Jesus' last week (beginning at Mark 11:1). You will find that about one third of the Gospel consists of the passion narrative.

The ancient Gnostic library found in 1945 near Nag Hammadi in the Nile valley includes three writings known as the Gospel of Thomas, the Gospel of Philip, and the Gospel of Mary. (For information about Gnosticism and the Nag Hammadi Library, consult the articles in *The Interpreter's Bible* or *The Anchor Bible Dictionary*.) The latter two are Gnostic documents that claim to contain the secret teaching of Jesus. The Gospel of Thomas, although modified at certain points to make it more acceptable to Gnostic Christians, appears to be an early collection of Jesus' sayings, many of which are paralleled in the New Testament. None of these three is a gospel in the sense defined above, because none of them recounts a story that climaxes in Jesus' death and resurrection. No collection of Jesus' teachings, no matter how authentic, would qualify as a gospel.

It is important to observe that a gospel tells the story about *God's* activity in the life, death, and resurrection of Jesus. This is, of course, the reason why the name *gospel* is given to the first four books of the New Testament. Our English word *gospel* derives from two Old English words meaning "good" and "tale." It is thus a very accurate rendering of the Greek word *euaggelion* (the origin of our words *evangel* and *evangelism*), which literally means "good news."

When the Gospel according to Mark was first published—that is, when handwritten copies were provided for interested churches—it was probably not known as "a gospel," for Mark seems to have created the literary form. It is easy to understand, however, why this title soon became attached to the book, in view of Mark's opening words: "The beginning of the good news (*euaggelion*) of Jesus Christ, the Son of God" (Mark 1:1). By these words the author makes it clear to the readers that he is going to tell a story, and that this story constitutes good news about what God has done in and through his Son, Jesus the Messiah.

Mohandas Gandhi, the great Indian spiritual and political leader, felt greatly drawn to Jesus through the teachings of the Sermon on the Mount (Matthew 5—7). On the basis of these sayings he developed his successful strategy of nonviolent resistance. A host of others have likewise been inspired by Jesus' Golden Rule and his words about nonresistance and love for enemies, about not judging one another, and about feeding the hungry and visiting the sick and those in prison. Because all these are found in Matthew but are omitted from Mark, some are disappointed by the shorter Gospel, in which Jesus' moral passion seems to be inadequately represented. Mark's omissions, however, should help us see more clearly why Jesus is important to Christians. Although we gladly acknowledge Jesus as our great moral teacher, this is not why he is central to our faith (Israel's prophets were also great moral teachers). Jesus is important to us primarily because he is the window through which we see God; in the life, death, and resurrection of Jesus, God's love for us becomes visible. The Second Gospel is not an ethical handbook; it is good news about God. Although the story as Mark tells it has clear implications for our daily lives, Mark's main purpose is not to tell us how to live but how to worship. Our response to his story should be "How great thou art!"

WHO WROTE THE GOSPEL
ACCORDING TO MARK?

To many modern Christians this question sounds as foolish as the old teaser, "Who was the father of Zebedee's children?" From earliest times, perhaps as early as the beginning of the second century, Christian testimony has been unanimous in ascribing our Gospel to Mark. Although *Markos* (Greek) and *Marcus* (Latin) were very popular names in the contemporary world, early tradition is again unanimous in associating the Gospel with John Mark, about whom we read in Acts 12:12, 25; 13:13; and 15:37–39. Perhaps the same Mark is alluded to in Colossians 4:10, 2 Timothy 4:11, Philemon 24, and 1 Peter 5:13, although it is impossible to be certain about this. If all these statements refer to the same individual, the author of the Gospel was a Jewish Christian who grew up in a wealthy family in Jerusalem; his mother, Mary, had a home spacious enough to accommodate a large prayer group (Acts 12:12). His cousin was Barnabas, a landowner who became Paul's collaborator (Acts 4:36–37; Col. 4:10).

The earliest nonscriptural testimony concerning Mark's composition of the Gospel comes from a second-century Christian named Papias, who maintained, on the basis of an earlier witness, that Mark, the author of the Gospel, was the "interpreter" of Peter; Mark wrote accurately what he remembered Peter saying, but not "in order," meaning perhaps that he presented some incidents in a sequence different from that found in Matthew, or that he wrote in an anecdotal fashion rather than as a historian would write.

Despite the unanimity of early tradition that the author was John Mark, modern scholars are not confident that this was in fact the case. The Gospel itself gives little evidence that the author was personally familiar with Jesus' ministry in Jerusalem. Although the Fourth Gospel provides details concerning many visits of Jesus to the Holy City, Mark reports only the final visit. Moreover, it appears to many scholars that the anecdotal material collected in Mark reflects the shaping of the oral tradition (orally transmitted stories and sayings) in the church rather than the testimony of a single eyewitness, Peter. Despite Papias's declaration, the author never cites Peter as his source, nor reports an incident from Peter's perspective. He never writes: "Peter used to say, 'One sabbath, when we were with Jesus in the Capernaum synagogue, a man . . .'"

Whether or not the early tradition is correct, the Gospel itself is strictly anonymous. The title found in the earliest manuscripts is simply "According to Mark." This title was supplied at the time the four Gospels were combined into a single book, *The Gospel*, consisting of four large chapters, beginning with "According to Matthew." Apart from the heading "According to Mark," nothing in the Second Gospel itself points to its author. On the basis of the content alone, it is even disputed whether the author was a Jew or a Gentile (a scholarly consensus favors the former). That is to say, the author very successfully hides his identity instead of witnessing in his own name. Why? We must assume that he regarded anonymity as particularly appropriate to his task; it was not Mark's good news that he was reporting but God's. It is fitting, therefore, that his work became known as "The Gospel according to Mark," not "The Gospel of Mark."

Although the book is properly anonymous, we will regularly refer to author as "Mark," without thereby assuming his identity with John Mark.

WHEN AND FOR WHOM WAS MARK WRITTEN?

Some early testimony suggests that the Gospel was written in Rome while Peter was still alive. This would place the composition of Mark in the early sixties of the first century. Support for such an early date is found by some in the fact that Mark 13, in which Jesus prophesies the destruction of Jerusalem, seems not to reflect what actually happened in A.D. 70. Others argue that the author may not have been inclined to emend the tradition he received, and that it is as likely that the Gospel was written shortly after the fall of Jerusalem as before it. It is unlikely that Mark was published much later than the early seventies, in view of its probable use by Matthew and Luke.

The tradition that associates the Gospel with Rome is not at all impossible, but it must be noted that none of the book's content favors Rome above any other Greek or Roman city. The author clearly envisions a Gentile audience; at various points he feels it necessary to explain Jewish customs and to translate Aramaic expressions (Aramaic was the language most used by Jews in Palestine). If Mark was written in Rome after the martyrdoms of Peter, Paul, and scores of other Christians in Nero's persecution, it is strange that martyrdom and persecution are not given more attention in this Gospel. Such an argument from silence, however, is very weak. The inescapable truth is that we do not know for certain where, when, or by whom the Gospel according to Mark was written. We must seek to interpret it, therefore, from the text itself rather than on the basis of unverified traditions concerning its origin.

WHY DID MARK WRITE?

The authors of Luke and John supply reasons for their writing (Luke 1:1–4; John 20:30–31). Hiding in his anonymity, Mark gives no such reason. Many have speculated about his motive. It is often proposed that Mark wrote after a number of the apostles, including Peter, had died, when it seemed imperative to preserve the oral tradition in writing lest it be lost. Against this is the second-century witness of Papias that he himself still preferred the living and abiding voice of the oral tradition to written records.

Another proposal is that Mark was troubled by one or another heresy confronting the church; he wrote to provide a correct theology. This may well have been the case, but Mark is so subtle in his critique that scholars cannot reach any consensus concerning the nature of the heresy being attacked.

Robert H. Gundry argues that Mark's intention was to write an apology for the cross (see Gundry, *Mark*, 1993). Crucifixion was such a shameful form of death that many pagans who might otherwise have been attracted to Christianity were put off; how could they acknowledge the validity of a religion founded by a man who had been *crucified?* (The martyrdom of Socrates, who was executed by poisoning, seemed much more dignified!) Mark wrote to present the crucifixion as a success story instead of a miserable failure. Gundry's proposal is an attractive one. I regard it as improbable, however, that Mark's main reason for writing was to present the gospel to unbelievers. Mark takes Jesus' ethical teaching largely for granted. This suggests that he writes primarily for Christians who have already been instructed regarding the ethics of Christian living.

Taken as a whole, the Gospel itself suggests that Mark retold the passion narrative, supplying it with an extended introduction, in order to proclaim that in the ministry, death, and resurrection of Jesus, God had been active for our sake. Good news indeed!

THE STRUCTURE OF MARK

Because Mark is a seamless story, not a scholarly dissertation with sections and subsections, we must be cautious about imposing on it a structure that reflects our perspective more than the author's intention. Nevertheless, the author provides clues that the material has been ordered in accordance with a certain theological perspective.

It is apparent that the author does not intend to give us a simple chronological narrative of Jesus' ministry. The primary evidence for this fact is provided by the Fourth Gospel, which is undoubtedly accurate in reporting that Jesus made many trips to Jerusalem and conducted a ministry in Judea. This is what we would have expected, for male Jews were supposed to attend the ceremonies in the temple at least three times a year (Deut. 16:16). Mark has streamlined his story by having Jesus go to Jerusalem only in order to die. He has omitted many interesting details (such as Jesus' baptizing activity in Judea; see John 4:1–3) because they are unnecessary for his story line. His primary intention in the first ten chapters is to prepare for the passion and resurrection, which are recounted in the concluding chapters. A major division thus falls naturally at Mark 11:1 with Jesus' arrival in Jerusalem to die.

The "extended introduction" can likewise be divided into two main sections. Peter's confession that Jesus is the Messiah (8:29) is not just one incident among many; the author presents it as the major turning point in his story (contrast the low profile given to the similar declaration by Andrew in John 1:41). Its narrative importance is accented by the verb "began" in Mark 8:31: "Then he *began* to teach them that the Son of Man must undergo great suffering." Scholars refer to 8:31 as the "First Passion Announcement," because it is followed by two parallel predictions at regular intervals (9:31; 10:33–34). Immediately after each passion announcement is a brief scene in which the disciples demonstrate that they have seriously misunderstood or failed to hear what Jesus has said. In each case this is followed by teaching from Jesus concerning the meaning of discipleship in the light of his forthcoming passion. The passion announcements and the accompanying discipleship material thus provide the basic structure for the second half of the "introduction." The author has bracketed this literary complex with two miracle stories in which Jesus restores sight to blind persons—the only two stories about blindness found in Mark (8:22–26; 10:46–52). We are surely justified in regarding this placement of the two stories as intentional: The blind men symbolize for Mark the spiritual blindness of the disciples that can be removed only by a miracle, the miracle of the resurrection.

The first half of the "introduction" does not appear to have been so carefully structured. Indicative of this is the fact that there is little consensus among scholars concerning where the turning points are located. I treat 1:1–20 as the preface to Jesus' public ministry (1:21–8:26). Mark 1:21–8:26 is divided into four segments: Jesus' healing ministry begins (1:21–39); Jesus' ministry provokes controversy (1:40–3:12); Jesus prepares twelve apprentices for mission (3:13–6:13); Jesus' immense popularity prompts antagonism (6:14–8:26). This outline is merely to simplify study. Many of the passages do not fit neatly under the suggested section headings, presumably because Mark's selection and arrangement were not guided by our topics! If his story appears to ramble up until 8:27, it is surely because this reflects the itinerant nature of Jesus' ministry.

The passion narrative itself does reflect careful structuring. The opening section treats Jesus' arrival and his "cleansing" of the temple (11:1–25). This is followed by a long series of public disputes (11:27–12:44) and a private discourse about the future (Mark 13). Chapter 14 carries the story from the murderous plot of Jesus' enemies to his condemnation by the high priest's council. Chapter 15 reports Pilate's sentence, the shameful treatment of Jesus by the soldiers, his crucifixion and burial. The Gospel concludes in chapter 16 with the brief resurrection narrative of the empty tomb.

There are various ways of reading Mark. The most common, unfortunately, is to read it at home just as it is read in church—in bits and pieces. The most unhappy consequence of this approach is that the individual passages are divorced from the story line. Mark is first and foremost a story, not "religious instruction." We know how much is lost when we read a modern novel in such a disjointed way. We do the Gospel an injustice when we fail to appropriate it as a connected whole.

Although we have been conditioned to read the Gospels slowly, always searching for the deeper meaning hidden in the text (and, of course, this book will attempt to do this), there is much to be said for a swift "surface" reading of the story, which can be accomplished in about an hour.

A second useful approach would be to read the passion narrative first (chapters 11–16) and then read the "extended introduction" (chapters 1–10), for it seems probable that Mark was composed "backwards," beginning with the passion. Such a reading would encourage us to focus on the question, How do chapters 1–10 prepare us for the denouement?

If we read the Gospel in accordance with the author's intention, it will become clear to us that this is not just another story about far away and long ago. *The story addresses us!* Its function is not to entertain or inform but to summon a response. Like the cry "Fire!" in a crowded theater, the Gospel expects us to react not with "Isn't this interesting?" but with "What must I do?"

Because I have written this interpretation of Mark primarily for Christians without a theological education, I have ignored many of the issues discussed in scholarly studies. Some readers may be disappointed that their questions regarding various interesting details are not addressed. The For Further Reading list will direct these readers to technical commentaries and other studies that may provide help with such questions.

Specific reference to important scholarly discussions is not made except in rare instances. Because most readers will have neither the inclination nor the opportunity to consult ancient sources, references to statements of early authors, such as Josephus and Eusebius, are given without citation of book, chapter, and section. In most cases readers will be able to obtain such information by examining one of the technical commentaries provided in the For Further Reading list.

This book has a limited purpose. My intention for each section is to focus on the passage as a unit and to grasp its meaning in relation to the Gospel as a whole. Appropriating the text requires that there be a dialogue between the Gospel writer and the modern reader; otherwise, the Gospel will remain an archaic document, not a living voice. Hopefully this book will facilitate the dialogue by bringing the reader into Mark's time and Mark into the reader's time. The reader's responsibility is to approach the study expectantly, believing that God has yet more light to shine forth through the Word.

1. Beginnings

Mark 1:1–20

1. The Beginning of the Good News
Mark 1:1–20

Mark 1:1–20 constitutes a prologue to the public ministry of Jesus. Although this ministry is announced in verses 14–15, it begins in earnest only with verses 21–28, where Jesus' first demonstration of supernatural power is reported. Each of the five brief units in the prologue—concerning John the Baptist, the baptism of Jesus, the testing in the wilderness, Jesus' public appearance in Galilee, and the call of the first disciples—serves to define Jesus in anticipation of his manifestation of divine authority in the Capernaum synagogue.

JOHN THE BAPTIST PREPARES
FOR THE MESSIAH
Mark 1:1–8

1:1 **The beginning of the good news of Jesus Christ, the Son of God.**
 ² As it is written in the prophet Isaiah,
   "See, I am sending my messenger ahead of you,
     who will prepare your way;
   ³ the voice of one crying out in the wilderness:
     'Prepare the way of the Lord, make his paths straight,'"
 ⁴ John the baptizer appeared in the wilderness, proclaiming a baptism of repentance for the forgiveness of sins. ⁵ And people from the whole Judean countryside and all the people of Jerusalem were going out to him, and were baptized by him in the river Jordan, confessing their sins. ⁶ Now John was clothed with camel's hair, with a leather belt around his waist, and he ate locusts and wild honey. ⁷ He proclaimed, "The one who is more powerful than I is coming after me; I am not worthy to stoop down and untie the thong of his sandals. ⁸ I have baptized you with water; but he will baptize you with the Holy Spirit."

Because a gospel is a passion narrative with an extended introduction (see the Introduction), where should it begin? What would be lost if Mark's story began with Jesus' teaching in the Capernaum synagogue (1:21–28)? To some this might be acceptable, for John the Baptist does not seem to them to be *essentially* related to the good news about Jesus. Jesus' baptism and subsequent testing in the wilderness can be regarded (mistakenly) as superfluous in view of the belief in Jesus' sinlessness. The Gospel writers, however, agree unanimously that John the Baptist must be included. Although the three longer Gospels begin the story at an earlier point (Luke begins with the parents of John the Baptist, Matthew starts with Abraham, and John takes us back to the creation), they concur with Mark that John the Baptist is essential to the story. This early perspective is reflected in Acts 10:36–37, where Peter declares that the good news of peace through Jesus Christ began from Galilee "after the baptism that John announced."

This emphasis on John is surprising, in view of the fact that John's baptism of Jesus later became something of an embarrassment; it suggested that Jesus was inferior to John (see the defense presented in Matthew 3:14–15). Early Christian tradition preserved the memory of Jesus' association with John not only because it was historically true but also because it was theologically significant. It served as another reminder that Christianity was not a new religion but a development from Judaism. Whereas the second-century heretic Marcion represented Jesus as a visitor from heaven, Mark's Jesus is firmly anchored in the history of Israel. His public ministry is prepared for by God's prophet John. The Baptist's activity thus constitutes "the beginning of the good news concerning Jesus the Messiah, the Son of God" (Mark 1:1; "Christ" should be taken here as a title, not a second name).

John's status as the one who prepares the way of the Messiah is certified by a collage of three Old Testament verses (Exod. 23:20; Mal. 3:1; and Isa. 40:3). The fact that the composite quotation is attributed to Isaiah is to be regarded as due not to ignorance but to emphasis; the evangelist is suggesting that the allusions to Exodus and Malachi are best understood in the light of Isaiah's prophecy; the messenger promised in Exodus and Malachi is none other than the one whose voice is heard crying in the wilderness.

John does not preach repentance. What he *proclaims* or *announces* (see also Acts 10:37) is *baptism*. According to certain prophetic passages (Jer. 18:12; Hos. 5:4), repentance, or "returning" (to God), is not always a real possibility for Israel, but at some future point God will provide an opportunity for national repentance in preparation for the age of salvation

(Jer. 31:31–34; Hos. 3:5). In the ministry of John the Baptist, God created such an opportunity. Baptism in the Jordan was thus a sacrament of God's grace. Its function was not only sacramental cleansing (Ezek. 36:25–31), but a "sealing" (Rev. 7:3–8) in anticipation of the rapidly approaching Last Judgment. It may also have symbolized a new exodus "through the sea" (1 Cor. 10:1–2) by means of which one might enter a new promised land, the kingdom of God.

Mark stresses that there was a massive response to John's announcement. Although his language undoubtedly exaggerates (literally, "all the Judean countryside and all the Jerusalemites," v. 5), Herod Antipas was impressed by the number of those flocking to John. The Jewish historian Josephus reports that Herod became alarmed by the size of the crowds; fearing that John's movement might turn into a political revolution, he had John executed. Mark's point seems to be that John's ministry constituted not a minor incident in one small corner of Judea but a national event. In principle at least, John prepared the whole people for the coming of the Messiah.

The details concerning John's clothing and diet are probably intended to reinforce the reference to his wilderness habitat. In this case, "wilderness" refers not to a waterless desert but rather to an uninhabited area in the Jordan valley. "Wilderness" is stressed because of its symbolic power. It was in the wilderness that God had led and sustained his people (Deut. 8:16; Neh. 9:21; Hos. 13:5) and had judged them (Psalm 95:8–11; Ezek. 20:10–16). In accordance with a common idea that the last times shall be as the first, the prophets expected that God's future judgment would occur in the wilderness (Ezek. 20:35) and likewise that in the wilderness God would again show grace to Israel (Isa. 35:1–7; 43:19; 51:3; Hos. 2:14). Judgment and grace are thus combined in the wilderness baptism.

John's announcement of an eschatological (end-time) sacrament, a "one-time offer," implies that the end is near. His second announcement concerning the imminent arrival of "one who is more powerful than I" must therefore refer to the Messiah. The connection between the two announcements is clearer in Matthew and Luke, where the stronger one is presented as a judge who will thoroughly separate the wheat from the chaff (Matt. 3:12; Luke 3:17). That the Messiah was sometimes regarded as God's judge is evident from Isaiah 11:4.

According to Mark, John prophesied that the Messiah would baptize not with water but with the Holy Spirit. In Matthew and Luke, on the other hand, we are told that the coming one will baptize "with the Holy Spirit and fire" (Matt. 3:11; Luke 3:16). Because "fire" fits better with the attached saying about judgment by fire in the other Gospels, scholars suspect that the earliest form of the saying about the Messiah's baptizing referred to fire only. (The metaphor of baptism by fire may underlie Mark 10:38 and Luke 12:49–50.) Perhaps the presence of "tongues of fire" in the story of the gift of the Holy Spirit at Pentecost (Acts 2:3–4) explains the substitution. In any event, for Mark the coming of the Messiah means primarily grace rather than judgment. Just as John prepares the people for the Messiah by consecrating, or "sealing," them with baptismal water, so the Messiah will consecrate them for the glorious rule of God by bringing them into contact with God's Spirit.

THE BAPTISM OF JESUS
Mark 1:9–11

> 1:9 **In those days Jesus came from Nazareth of Galilee and was baptized by John in the Jordan. [10] And just as he was coming up out of the water, he saw the heavens torn apart and the Spirit descending like a dove on him. [11] And a voice came from heaven, "You are my Son, the Beloved; with you I am well pleased."**

Why was Jesus baptized? Why, if John announced a baptism of repentance for the forgiveness of sins, would Jesus participate unless he were a sinner? Christians later wrestled with this issue, as witnessed by the dialogue attributed to John and Jesus in Matthew 3:14–15. Mark is not troubled by the question. He assumes that his readers will regard it as perfectly appropriate that Jesus, a man of unblemished character, comes to be baptized by John.

There can be no doubt that the baptism actually occurred and that for Jesus it constituted a major turning point. It marked the great divide between his private life as a skilled handworker in an obscure village (Nazareth is never mentioned by Josephus or in the rabbinic writings) and the short but tumultuous public career that was terminated by his execution. It was undoubtedly his "call" experience, comparable in some respects to the experience of Amos (" The LORD took me from following the flock, and the LORD said to me, 'Go, prophesy to my people Israel,'" Amos 7:15). Jesus' call, however, was clearly distinctive; he was called not to be simply another prophet like John the Baptist but to be God's ultimate representative, the Messiah, God's Son. This awareness shaped his appointment of twelve apostles (3:13–19) and provides the only adequate explanation for Pilate's capital charge against him, "The King of the Jews" (15:26).

We do not have Jesus' own report of the experience. Mark's brief narrative has come to us from "the oral tradition"; that is, it was passed on by word of mouth and in the process was shaped by Christian reflection. We can assume that Jesus came to the Jordan to acknowledge in a public way the legitimacy of God's judgment on the sin of his people and to consecrate himself to God's sovereign rule by submitting to this sacrament of national renewal. We can assume also that his baptism was accompanied not only by a call to be God's Messiah but also by a strong sense of having been empowered for this role. Because of the way divine empowerment is conceived in the Hebrew scriptures, it would be natural for Jesus to speak of this experience in terms of the Spirit of God.

Mark's narrative speaks of this empowerment in visual terms: "He saw the heavens torn apart and the Spirit descending like a dove on him." The image of the heavens being split open is violently dramatic. It reflects the ancient Hebrew understanding of the sky as an inverted bowl separating the natural world from God's heavenly domain. Numerous scriptural passages refer to human visions of heaven that are made possible by an "opening" in the barrier. In Acts 7:56, Stephen announces, "I see the heavens opened and the Son of Man standing at the right hand of God!" Instead of employing the usual verb "opened," however, Mark chooses "torn apart." The verb torn recurs in the Gospel only at 15:38, where Mark reports that at Jesus' death the temple curtain was torn from top to bottom. In both instances Mark may have selected this violent verb in order to point to God's invasion of a sinful world. The barrier is breached at the baptism, not to allow Jesus a vision of God, but to permit God's transcendent power to become immanent in Jesus.

Israel perceived God's reality in his absence as well as in his presence: "Truly, you are a God who hides himself, O God of Israel, the Savior" (Isa. 45:15). A yearning for the manifestation of the elusive God is expressed forcefully in Isaiah 64:1, "O that you would tear open the heavens and come down." By using the same verb, Mark suggests that in Jesus this yearning has been answered.

In the first century there was a widespread expectation that the return of God's absent Spirit would be a sign that the end of the age was at hand and that God's kingdom was about to be inaugurated. The presence of the Spirit in Jesus' ministry was thus perceived by his followers as an eschatological sign (see Matt. 12:28). It could also be taken as a messianic sign, in view of such prophecies as Isaiah 11:2; 42:1; and 61:1. Indeed, it must have seemed self-evident that God's Messiah would be enabled to perform his tasks by the presence of the Spirit, the mediator of God's power.

Since others besides the Messiah were expected to be empowered by the Spirit in the last days (see the quotation of Joel 2:28–32 in Acts 2:17–21), the descent of the Spirit is not sufficient to identify who Jesus is. The narrative function of the voice from heaven is to permit the messianic status of Jesus to be affirmed by God.

At the transfiguration of Jesus in Mark 9:2–9, a voice from heaven will confirm Jesus' status in the presence of three disciples, "This is my Son, the Beloved," using third-person language. Here at the baptism the voice speaks directly to Jesus: "You are my Son, the Beloved." In this way Mark suggests that the baptismal experience is a private one. The heavenly voice is not heard by John or others.

It is likely that the report of the voice has been shaped by meditation on scripture. An echo can be heard here of Psalm 2:7, a verse much used in the early church (see Acts 13:33; Heb. 1:5; 5:5): "You are my son; today I have begotten you." This was originally a royal psalm, composed probably for the coronation of one of Israel's kings. Because of its reference to the Lord's anointed in verse 2, however, the psalm was inevitably treated in the first century as a messianic prophecy. From the Dead Sea Scrolls we know that the Messiah could be referred to as "God's Son" on the basis of 2 Samuel 7:14, where God, speaking through the prophet Nathan, makes a promise regarding David's royal offspring: "I will be a father to him, and he shall be a son to me."

Instead of including the psalm's adoption formula, "this day I have begotten you," the heavenly voice turns to another scriptural passage, Isaiah 42:1, "Here is my servant, whom I uphold, my chosen, in whom my soul delights; I have put my spirit upon him." The title "the Beloved," which is either a free rendering of "my chosen" or an echo of the Aramaic paraphrase of the psalm, served Jewish writers as a way of referring to the Messiah.

The final clause, "with you I am well pleased," confirms that Jesus has shown himself to be God's obedient Son by coming to John's baptism. However, because Mark's Greek verb is used in the past tense (literally, "in you I came to have pleasure"), it may mean more than this. Jewish tradition proposed that "the name of the Messiah" was one of the things that existed before the creation; that is, from the beginning God had already planned the Messiah's mission. Early Christians rejected the suggestion that Jesus of Nazareth was simply a good man whom God, on an impulse, "adopted" as his Son at the Jordan.

The baptismal narrative serves to identify Jesus as God's Son and thus to certify that the shameful death to which the story is leading will be in accordance with God's will, not a sign of divine displeasure.

Although the passage focuses primarily on Christ and his mission, early Christians undoubtedly found it relevant to their own baptism. Just as Jesus had been consecrated and empowered for his messianic role through baptism, so had they been commissioned through baptism to extend Jesus' ministry in lives of service. Whenever we affirm our baptism, we acknowledge God's right to rule, and we accept the commission to anticipate the kingdom of God by the way we live day by day.

THE TESTING OF GOD'S SON
Mark 1:12–13

1:12 **And the Spirit immediately drove him out into the wilderness.** [13] **He was in the wilderness forty days, tempted by Satan; and he was with the wild beasts; and the angels waited on him.**

It is difficult to read Mark's brief account of Jesus' forty days in the wilderness without being influenced by our recollections of the very different narrative presented in Matthew 4:1–11 and Luke 4:1–13. Matthew and Luke build on the tradition that Jesus went without food for forty days; Satan's threefold attack makes Jesus' hunger its starting point. Mark, however, makes no reference to fasting. Indeed, the verb he uses to describe the activity of the angels suggests that these heavenly visitors fed him repeatedly, just as an angel fed Elijah in the wilderness (1 Kings 19:5–8).

Mark emphasizes that Jesus was in the wilderness by divine compulsion—the Spirit *drove* him. Perhaps the forty days is reminiscent of Israel's forty years in the wilderness (Num. 14:33) or of Moses' forty days and forty nights on Mount Sinai (Exod. 24:18), but Mark develops neither of these possibilities. The number may simply be a stereotypical reference to an extended period of time. Although we are told that Jesus was undergoing testing, or tempting, by Satan, no stress is laid on this activity; we are left to assume that Jesus was victorious.

The references to Jesus' being "with the wild beasts" has given rise to two radically different interpretations. Some commentators see here a reference to the expectation that the Messiah will establish the "peaceable kingdom" envisioned in Isaiah 11:6–9, "The wolf shall live with the lamb, the leopard shall lie down with the kid." Mark is suggesting, they propose, that the wild animals live peaceably with Jesus in the wilderness in antic-ipation of God's kingdom, when Adam's peaceful relationship with the animals (Gen. 2:19–20) will be restored. Others, however, assume that the wild beasts are Jesus' enemies, who throughout the forty days threaten to destroy him. They may even represent the demonic forces that will at-tempt to abort the Messiah's mission. On this interpretation Jesus is vic-tor over the wild beasts in the same way that Daniel was victorious in the lions' den. The same Spirit that drove him into this hostile wilderness en-dowed him with supernatural power with which to control the beasts. The second proposal appears the more likely, but both must remain conjec-tural, since Mark gives no certain clue. The brief narrative suggests only that the Messiah learned in a hostile environment that he could depend on God's sustaining power.

JESUS BEGINS TO PREACH
Mark 1:14–15

> 1:14 **Now after John was arrested, Jesus came to Galilee, proclaiming the good news of God,** [15] **and saying, "The time is fulfilled, and the kingdom of God has come near; repent, and believe in the good news."**

Verse 15 has often been described as a "summary" of Jesus' preaching. This may well be accurate with respect to the historical Jesus, but it would not be accurate to say that it summarizes the teaching of Jesus as presented in this Gospel. Nowhere else in Mark does Jesus announce that the time is fulfilled or that the kingdom of God has drawn nigh. Nowhere does he call for repentance (except indirectly through the disciples, 6:12) or for faith in the good news. The message of verse 15 is implicit throughout the Gospel, however. For Mark, Jesus' entire ministry, including his death and resurrection, signifies that the time has come and that God's rule is at hand. His ministry in itself constitutes a call for repentance and faith.

Mark's language is so condensed that a literal translation can be mis-leading. "The time is fulfilled" does not mean "A set period of time has been completed," because the Greek word used here is not *chronos*, mean-ing extended time, but *kairos*, meaning "right time" for something to hap-pen (as in 11:13, "it was not the *kairos* for figs"). In the verse "fulfill" may therefore allude to the fulfillment or realization of prophetic promises, as in 14:49. Verse 15 can be paraphrased: "The time you have been waiting for, the time announced by the prophets, has finally arrived! The glorious new day of God's rule, in which God makes everything come out right, has just dawned!"

Mark's readers know that the context contains the end-time prediction of John the Baptist, the last of Israel's prophets, concerning the imminent arrival of God's Messiah (vv. 7–8). Implicit in verse 15 is thus the announcement that John's prophecy is being fulfilled in Jesus' public appearance.

Does "the good news of God" mean good news concerning God or good news from God? The Greek phrase permits both interpretations, but there is no essential difference. For Christians as for Jews there can be no good news about God that does not also originate with God. Although the content of the good news of verse 14 is provided in verse 15, Mark's readers know that Jesus himself is the essence of the gospel. There is no difference between "the good news of God" and "the good news of Jesus, the Messiah" of verse 1.

Interpreters debate whether the verb "has come near" (one word in Greek) implies that God's rule has already arrived or that it is still in the future. The Lord's Prayer indicates that Jesus regarded the coming of the kingdom as a future event for which prayer should be offered ("Thy kingdom come," Matt. 6:10; Luke 11:2; see also Mark 9:1; 14:25). Nevertheless, the context suggests something more than a future hope; the time of God's saving activity has arrived. There is thus truth on both sides of the debate. For Mark the kingdom of God has both present and future dimensions. Its full establishment remains the object of prayer and expectant waiting, but it is mysteriously present in Jesus' ministry (see comments on 4:10–12 regarding the mystery of the kingdom).

The narrative function of this brief passage is to provide the transition from anticipation to actualization. John proclaimed that God was about to act; Jesus announces that God's saving action has now begun. Because the passage is transitional only, no details are given concerning Jesus' hearers and their response. From verse 1 and verse 11 readers know that the inauguration of God's rule is realized in the single fact that Jesus is God's Son. The Messiah has been commissioned and empowered at the Jordan, tested in the wilderness, and is now ready to fulfill his role. Because Mark writes primarily for Christians (see the Introduction), they also know the end of the story; the inauguration of God's rule through the Messiah includes a cross. The time of salvation involves shameful suffering for the one who is the kingdom in person. Only gradually will this mystery be unfolded in the Gospel. It is foreshadowed, however, in the reference to John's being "delivered up" or "handed over" ("arrested" in v. 14 is not a literal translation); the same Greek verb will be used repeatedly with respect to Jesus' fate, beginning with 9:31, "The Son of man is delivered into the hands of men" (KJV). John's martyrdom will not be recounted until 6:14–29, but the enforced termination of his ministry anticipates Jesus' fate.

God's good news calls for decision: "Repent, and believe in the good news." At first glance these seem to be two very different activities. Often repentance is understood "atomistically" as remorse over itemized sinful acts, and belief is regarded as intellectual assent to specific truths of the faith. In Israel's prophetic tradition, however, individual sins were seen as symptoms of a turning away from God. The Hebrew verb underlying our English *repent* literally means "turn around"; repentance meant not merely turning away from specific sins but turning toward God in faith and obedience. When used with respect to God, "believe" is likewise a relational term. The announcement of the good news calls not for intellectual assent but confident trust and commitment. To believe in the good news means to wager one's future on the reality of God's involvement in the life, death, and resurrection of Jesus, despite the skepticism of the modern worldview. For us, as for Jesus' hearers, this means that we must turn and become like children (see 10:13–16).

JESUS CALLS FOUR FISHERMEN
Mark 1:16–20

> 1:16 As Jesus passed along the Sea of Galilee, he saw Simon and his brother Andrew casting a net into the sea—for they were fishermen. 17 And Jesus said to them, "Follow me and I will make you fish for people." 18 And immediately they left their nets and followed him. 19 As he went a little farther, he saw James son of Zebedee and his brother John, who were in their boat mending the nets. 20 Immediately he called them; and they left their father Zebedee in the boat with the hired men, and followed him.

This appears to be a story about discipleship. It is that, of course, but only secondarily. Primarily it is a story about Jesus. This is what we should expect in Mark's extended introduction to the passion. The story's primary function in the Gospel is to tell us something about the one whom the Romans will crucify.

The anecdote is tersely narrated (to appreciate this feature, compare this passage with the lengthy miracle stories of chapter 5). Although the four fishermen are identified by names (the names will recur together at 1:29; 3:16–18; and 13:3), no hint is given that these four have been called to special prominence in the post-Easter church. The title "apostle" is missing; even "disciple" is absent. No interest whatsoever is shown in what might have prepared the men to follow Jesus (had they heard him preaching the good news of God? had one or two of them encountered Jesus at the Jordan, as reported in John 1:35–40?). No words of response are attributed to them; mutely they abandon their nets. By paring away all superfluous details, Mark has laid all emphasis on Jesus' authoritative command, "Follow me!"

In the previous passage Jesus' authority was hidden in his message; he implicitly claimed the right to announce what God was doing. The following passage (vv. 21–28) will deal explicitly with the question of Jesus' authority. Here that authority is acted out; he commands, and four men leave everything behind to follow him. (It should be noted, however, that Simon Peter did not immediately dispose of his house, which is used by Jesus in 1:29 and 2:1; according to John 21:3, he kept his boat.)

Later these followers will be called "disciples" (2:15). The underlying Greek word means "learner" or "student." In 2:18 we hear about John's disciples and the disciples of the Pharisees. Ordinarily, discipleship was initiated by persons interested in learning from a religious leader. The Jewish historian Josephus, for example, tells us about choosing to be a disciple of a certain Bannus, a wilderness figure resembling the Baptist. All the more remarkable, therefore, is the fact that in this story the four express no interest in learning from Jesus. In fact, Jesus does not present himself as a teacher recruiting students. The only comparable situation is that of a king impressing people into his service. The fishermen are conscripts, not volunteers. They are called not simply to *learn* about the kingdom but to *participate* in the kingdom by serving the king.

The nature of this service is described in the promise attached to Jesus' command: "I will make you fish for people." Although the metaphor has a negative connotation in Jeremiah 16:16, it is surely intended positively here. The four are to capture men and women in their nets in order to include them in the kingdom, not for condemnation and punishment.

We often use the verb *fish* and the noun *fisherman* (*fisherwoman*) with reference to the sport of catching fish with line and hook. Jesus, however, was speaking of net fishing. Although some small nets were thrown and retrieved by individuals, fishing on the whole was a team effort, not a solo venture (Luke 5:4–7; John 21:6–8). Jesus is summoning followers to work together to capture people for the kingdom. Effective evangelism is a shared enterprise.

Notice the countercultural features of the story. Simon (he is not called Peter until 3:16), as we will learn in 1:30, was a married man, responsible for the support of a wife and children (unless he was widowed; but see 1 Cor. 9:5) and perhaps of his mother-in-law as well. His response to Jesus would have been regarded by his family, friends, and community as monumental irresponsibility. Because of the patriarchal structuring of society, the decision of James and John to leave their father's employment without securing his permission was a heinous violation of the cultural code. For Jesus, the urgency of the kingdom of God meant that normal expectations must be set aside. In response to the hesitation of another disciple, "Lord, first let me go and bury my father," Jesus imperiously replied, "Follow me, and let the dead bury their own dead" (Matt. 8:21–22).

Because Mark makes nothing of the fact that these four became "apostles" (see 3:13–19), we can assume that they here represent not church leaders as such but ordinary believers. All are summoned to the service of the king. Modern Christians can acknowledge the theological truth of the story. Although there is a sense in which we choose to follow Jesus by voluntary participation in a congregation where his name is proclaimed and his truth taught, we recognize that in our choosing we have been chosen; in our seeking we have been sought: "You did not choose me but I chose you. And I appointed you to go and bear fruit, fruit that will last" (John 15:16).

2. Jesus' Public Ministry

Mark 1:21–8:26

2. Jesus'
Healing Ministry Begins
Mark 1:21–39

JESUS DEMONSTRATES
HIS TEACHING AUTHORITY
Mark 1:21–28

> 1:21 **They went to Capernaum; and when the sabbath came, he entered the synagogue and taught.** 22 **They were astounded at his teaching, for he taught them as one having authority, and not as the scribes.** 23 **Just then there was in their synagogue a man with an unclean spirit,** 24 **and he cried out, "What have you to do with us, Jesus of Nazareth? Have you come to destroy us? I know who you are, the Holy One of God."** 25 **But Jesus rebuked him, saying, "Be silent, and come out of him!"** 26 **And the unclean spirit, convulsing him and crying with a loud voice, came out of him.** 27 **They were all amazed, and they kept on asking one another, "What is this? A new teaching—with authority! He commands even the unclean spirits, and they obey him."** 28 **At once his fame began to spread throughout the surrounding region of Galilee.**

Modern readers are apt to read this passage with some diffidence. Although it catches our interest by presenting Jesus as a teacher, the content of his teaching is entirely ignored. Mark includes not a single saying—not even the Golden Rule! Instead, at the heart of the narrative is an exorcism, which we can appreciate only with difficulty. Jesus' contemporaries attributed many misfortunes to evil spirits, including not only mental disorders but also physical maladies such as epilepsy (see 9:14–29), but modern science has rendered such diagnoses obsolete. Instead of rejecting the story as the product of primitive superstition, however, we should humbly acknowledge that our own knowledge of reality is lamentably incomplete, and that God meets us where we are, accommodating divine revelation to our limitations. God communicated through Jesus with people for whom demon possession was real. We can make the story our own by affirming that the same kind of powerful communication still occurs for us whose perceived reality does not include demons and exorcisms.

The placement of the story is important to Mark. As the very first anecdote concerning Jesus' public ministry, it sets the tone for the entire section extending to 8:26. It is the overture, whose themes are echoed and
developed in the ensuing chapters. Why does Mark choose this particular
story for the inauguration of Jesus' ministry? Presumably because it proclaims Jesus' authority in terms of both his teaching and his exorcistic activity. The authority that was implicit in the summary of his preaching in
verses 14–15, and acted out in the conscription of four fishermen, is now
a matter for explicit consideration.

Elsewhere in the Gospel, Jesus' public teaching occurs in the outdoors
(1:39 and 6:2 are exceptional). Here the setting in the Capernaum synagogue prepares for the contrast between Jesus and "the scribes." In Greek
and Roman society this term referred generally to professional clerks who
could be hired to write letters and other documents. Among Jews, however, the word designated persons who were knowledgeable about the
proper observance of the sabbath and the other requirements of the
Torah, the law of Moses. After A.D. 70 they became known as rabbis.
Many of these legal experts belonged to the party of the Pharisees, but
presumably some sided with the Sadducees, and others adhered to neither
party (the sect of the Dead Sea Scrolls also had their experts).

Because Mark does not tell us why the scribes taught without authority, we must infer it from the context. He is not referring to the style of
their teaching (the scribes appropriately supported their rulings by citing
precedents and earlier opinions, not by claiming unmediated authority)
but rather to the absence of eschatological power. Whereas the scribes occupied themselves with decisions about what was permitted and what was
not permitted in a business-as-usual world, Jesus was powerfully announcing the arrival of the kingdom of God. What is *new* (v. 27) about
Jesus' teaching is that it communicates the end-time power of God. It is
with authority because it is authorized by God.

We can now understand why an exorcism has been inserted into these
considerations of Jesus' teaching power. Any healing would have illustrated Jesus' God-given authority, but an exorcism had additional symbolic force. One of the most cherished hopes associated with the coming
of God's rule was the expectation that the forces of evil would be rendered
powerless. In this first miracle story Jesus is confronted by a demon ("unclean spirit" perhaps reflects the conviction that these spirits are totally
alien to the holiness of God) who speaks on behalf of all demons: "Have
you come to destroy *us*?" The demon attempts a self-defense by naming
and identifying Jesus, but before it can adjure Jesus to desist from the ex-

orcism (compare 5:7), Jesus' authoritative word silences and expels it. Because contemporary exorcisms normally included incantations, material items, and physical handling of the patient, the simple power of Jesus' command would have greatly impressed Mark's readers. "The Holy One of God," although not attested as a messianic title in Jewish sources, clearly has such a meaning here and in John 6:69. As God's all-powerful representative, the Messiah will destroy Satan's kingdom (see 3:20–30).

Because Jesus' teaching is characterized by eschatological power, he "teaches" the kingdom of God by expelling a demon. Mark wants us to know that Jesus' public ministry is of one piece; his healing activity is not subordinate to this teaching but part and parcel of it. His miracles reveal that his announcement of the kingdom of God is divinely authorized.

MANY ARE HEALED IN CAPERNAUM
Mark 1:29–34

1:29 **As soon as they left the synagogue, they entered the house of Simon and Andrew, with James and John.** [30] **Now Simon's mother-in-law was in bed with a fever, and they told him about her at once.** [31] **He came and took her by the hand and lifted her up. Then the fever left her, and she began to serve them.**

[32] **That evening, at sundown, they brought to him all who were sick or possessed with demons.** [33] **And the whole city was gathered around the door.** [34] **And he cured many who were sick with various diseases, and cast out many demons; and he would not permit the demons to speak, because they knew him.**

Although Mark is fond of using the adverb "immediately" (translated "as soon as" in v. 29 and "at once" in v. 30), sometimes where it makes little sense (NRSV ignores the adverb in v. 21; compare RSV), recent archeological excavation suggests that in verse 29 it is entirely appropriate. Simon Peter's house was situated immediately south of the synagogue, with its northern wall right under the synagogue balcony. The house was a large complex of clan dwellings with three shared courts, surrounded by a common exterior wall with a single entrance. It is possible, therefore, that Andrew too had his own dwelling in the complex. To the east of the house, just outside the entrance, was a large open area where a crowd could assemble, as suggested by verse 33 and 2:2 (*Anchor Bible Dictionary*, vol. 1:867).

The fact that the woman whom Jesus cured of a fever is given an explicit location (Simon's house) and identity (his mother-in-law) constitutes strong evidence in favor of historicity. The tradition, unfortunately, neglected to transmit her name. This is true of most of the women mentioned in Mark: the hemorrhaging woman (5:25), Jairus's daughter (5:40–42), Jesus' sisters (6:3), the Syrophoenician woman and her daughter (7:24–30), the widow in the temple (12:42), and the woman who anointed Jesus at Bethany (14:3). Even Jesus' mother is unnamed at her first appearance! (3:31; but see 6:3). Exceptional is the naming of the women who witnessed Jesus' death and burial and the empty tomb (15:40, 47; 16:1). Although many men healed by Jesus are also anonymous, it seems likely that sexism is responsible for the fact that Bartimaeus, son of Timaeus, is remembered by name and Peter's mother-in-law is not.

The previous narrative dealt with a demon-possessed person, that is, someone who from a modern point of view was mentally disturbed but physically healthy. This story concerns a person with a physical disease. In the absence of modern drugs, fevers were often fatal. Jesus does not function as a physician; he does not create a potion that will break the fever. Nor does he behave like many of the magical healers of his day; he does not "exorcize" the fever by means of incantations and manipulation of the woman's body. He does not even pray audibly. His supernatural power is exhibited in the simplicity of the healing; he merely takes the patient by the hand and raises her from her bed. It is not surprising that Mark later reports that people regard his body and clothing as power-filled (the hemorrhaging woman is sure she can be healed by touching his cloak, 5:27–28).

The modern scientific worldview makes it difficult for some to accept such stories as historical. Although it is not necessary to regard every New Testament miracle story as authentic, two arguments count in favor of the recollection that Jesus was a miracle worker. First, Jesus was honored after the resurrection as the Messiah, yet nothing in Jewish tradition suggested that the Messiah would function as an itinerant healer. There was thus no motive for early Christians to make up stories about Jesus as a faith healer. Second, Jesus was remembered as a magician in later Jewish literature. If this is not simply a hostile reaction to the Gospels themselves, it corroborates the Christian recollection of Jesus' career. Moreover, although demonstration is difficult, scientists now concede that the relationship between mind and matter is far more sophisticated than previously assumed. There is no good reason for denying the tradition that Jesus attained fame as a healer.

At sundown—that is, when the sabbath is over and it is again permissible to carry burdens—the people of Capernaum bring their sick and demon-possessed to Peter's house for Jesus to heal. The narrative suggests that many came just as spectators ("the whole city"). This serves to emphasize that Jesus' activity as a healer is now a matter of public record (see v. 28).

What do the "miracles" mean? Whereas modern skeptics will regard them as strange instances of the power of mind over matter, early Christians, like Jesus himself, viewed the healings and exorcisms as manifestations of God's saving power (see Matt. 11:4–6, 20–24; 12:28). They remembered Jesus as one who "went about doing good and healing all who were oppressed by the devil, for God was with him" (Acts 10:38). Jesus is never represented as using his healings as a means of magnifying himself; the response he asks of those healed is to give glory to God (5:19).

The final note of the passage is ambiguous. Why does Jesus muzzle the demons? One possibility is that these, like the unclean spirit of verse 24, want to use their knowledge of Jesus' identity as a weapon of self-defense. Scholars are inclined, however, to a second possibility. Running through Mark is a theme referred to as "the messianic secret motif," according to which the messiahship of Jesus is a secret that must not be divulged prematurely (see especially 3:12 and 8:30). As supernatural beings, the spirits recognize Jesus as the Messiah, but they are strictly forbidden to reveal this fact. The narrative function of the motif is to remind the readers that Jesus is in fact the Messiah even though he is not conforming to expectations normally associated with the role. Even if the motif appears rather artificial at some points (see especially 5:43), it need not be viewed as totally unhistorical. If Jesus did in fact regard himself as the Messiah (as this book will assume), he probably thought it inappropriate for his identity to be announced by any except God. Did he not teach, "All who exalt themselves will be humbled, and all who humble themselves will be exalted" (Matt. 23:12)?

A PREACHING AND HEALING TOUR
Mark 1:35–39

> 1:35 **In the morning, while it was still very dark, he got up and went out to a deserted place, and there he prayed.** [36] **And Simon and his companions hunted for him.** [37] **When they found him, they said to him, "Everyone is searching for you."** [38] **He answered, "Let us go on to the neighboring towns, so that I may proclaim the message there also; for that is what I came out to do."** [39] **And he went throughout Galilee, proclaiming the message in their synagogues and casting out demons.**

The preceding passages present Jesus as an overwhelming, unqualified success. News of his charismatic power has spread like wildfire (v. 28). The "whole city" of Capernaum, gathered at his door, watched intently as he healed the sick and exorcized demons (vv. 33–34). Jesus is a sensation! How will he handle success? Will he bask in the adulation of the crowd, or will he remember Satan's testing in the wilderness and hold to the course set for him by God?

Jesus rises long before dawn and goes out to "a deserted place" to pray. This is not the normal morning prayer of pious Jews. The unusual time is presumably dictated by the need to evade his "public" (fortunately, he did not have to worry about reporters and photographers!). Especially significant is Mark's description of the prayer site. Underlying the word "deserted" is the same Greek word that earlier was translated "wilderness" (vv. 12–13). Since there was no "wilderness" in the vicinity of Capernaum, "wilderness place" is probably intended to be reminiscent of the testing by Satan.

Like all religious Jews, Jesus undoubtedly prayed regularly, at least three times each day. Because Mark makes no mention of Jesus' normal prayer life, we should probably assume that each of the few references to prayer holds some special significance in his story (see 6:46; 14:32–39). Here the predawn prayer is apparently a response to the public success he has achieved in Capernaum. Like the prayer in Gethsemane, it seeks conformity with God's will.

The problem faced by Jesus involves the ambiguity of miracles. He meant them to be perceived as signs of the kingdom of God. They were intended to arouse repentance and faith (see vv. 14–15). The grave danger was that people, seeing his acts of healing merely as spectacular feats of magic, would not alter their relationship to God in the slightest. From much later in his ministry comes a saying reflective of Jesus' great disappointment with the people of Capernaum: "And you, Capernaum, will you be exalted to heaven? No, you will be brought down to Hades. For if the deeds of power done in you had been done in Sodom, it would have remained until this day" (Matt. 11:23).

When Simon and his companions track Jesus down, bringing further news of his success, Jesus shows that he has not been swayed from his task of widely proclaiming the kingdom of God. He goes on to repeat in other synagogues what he has done in Capernaum—preaching the gospel with authority and providing visible signs of God's rule by exorcizing Satan's minions.

3. Jesus' Ministry
   Provokes Controversy
   Mark 1:40–3:12

Up to this point Mark has portrayed Jesus' ministry as an unqualified success. Because an important function of his "extended introduction" (see the Introduction) is to prepare readers for the passion, he now begins to present the negative reaction to Jesus on the part of Israel's religious leaders in a series of controversies (2:1–3:6). These are bracketed by two further "success stories" about Jesus' healing (1:40–45; 3:7–12).

JESUS DARES TO TOUCH A LEPER
Mark 1:40–45

> 1:40 **A leper came to him begging him, and kneeling he said to him, "If you choose, you can make me clean."** [41] **Moved with pity, Jesus stretched out his hand and touched him, and said to him, "I do choose. Be made clean!"** [42] **Immediately the leprosy left him, and he was made clean.** [43] **After sternly warning him he sent him away at once,** [44] **saying to him, "See that you say nothing to anyone; but go, show yourself to the priest, and offer for your cleansing what Moses commanded, as a testimony to them."** [45] **But he went out and began to proclaim it freely, and to spread the word, so that Jesus could no longer go into a town openly, but stayed out in the country; and people came to him from every quarter.**

The supplicant in this passage is called a leper, but it is unlikely that he was suffering from the horrible disease we call leprosy (which was referred to in Greek literature by a different name). "Leprosy" covered a variety of skin rashes, most of which were not life threatening and perhaps not even physically debilitating. The suffering experienced by Jewish lepers was primarily social and religious, not physical. Leviticus 13:45–46 specifies that a person identified by the priest as leprous "shall wear torn clothes and let the hair of his head be disheveled; and he shall cover his upper lip and cry out, 'Unclean, unclean.' He shall remain unclean as long as he has the disease; he is unclean. He shall live alone; his dwelling shall be outside the camp." Such persons were not only isolated from family and friends but were excluded also from public worship. Anyone who came in contact with a leper was rendered temporarily unclean and required ritual cleansing. Note that the leper does not ask to be healed but to be made ritually pure by the removal of his rash, presumably so that he can again live and worship with others.

Because the news of Jesus' authority has reached the leper in his isolation, he does not for a moment doubt that Jesus can purify him. He is not as certain that Jesus will want to. The reason for this uncertainty may derive from the fact that leprosy is frequently viewed in the Old Testament as punishment for sin (Num. 12:9–10; 2 Kings 5:27; 15:5; 2 Chron. 26:19–21). There was a natural analogy between ritual impurity, which separated a person from the worship of God, and sin, which separated one from God in a profounder sense. If this is the basis for the words "If you choose," the leper is implicitly requesting forgiveness of his sins. Such an understanding would explain why Mark places the story here; it anticipates Jesus' pronouncement of forgiveness of the paralytic's sins in 2:1–12.

The most famous instance in the Old Testament of a leper being cleansed involved Naaman the Syrian (2 Kings 5:1–14; Luke 4:27). Although nothing in Mark's narrative is reminiscent of this earlier story, it is probable that many of his Gentile readers saw a connection and found here comforting evidence that Jesus chose to make them "clean" and render them fit to share with Jewish Christians in the worship of the God of Israel.

Particularly striking is the boldness of the leper. In Luke's story about Jesus cleansing ten lepers, the men call out to him from a distance (Luke 17:12–13). Here the man ignores the restrictions imposed by Leviticus and comes so close that Jesus can touch him. Mark undoubtedly perceived the man's boldness not as callous disregard of the Torah or as disrespect of Jesus but as an expression of intense faith. He coveted for his readers the same boldness of faith (see 11:24).

It is significant that Jesus touches the leper. In the story in Luke 17 there is no touching; Jesus' authoritative word is sufficient. Here Jesus' touch overcomes the man's isolation. Jesus has no fear of incurring defilement; his power to cleanse eclipses leprosy's power to defile.

No explanation is given of Jesus' stern requirement of silence. Perhaps it is intended as a reminder that Jesus is not seeking glory for himself. Another proposal is that Jesus wants the man to go immediately to the priest instead of stopping constantly to report his experience. In any event, the command is ignored, and the leper's story adds to Jesus' fame, so that he is forced to stay outside the towns in "wilderness places." Even here he cannot remain hidden, and people flock to him from everywhere.

JESUS DEMONSTRATES HIS RIGHT TO FORGIVE SINS
Mark 2:1–12

2:1 **When he returned to Capernaum after some days, it was reported that he was at home.** [2] **So many gathered around that there was no longer room for them, not even in front of the door; and he was speaking the word to them.** [3] **Then some people came, bringing to him a paralyzed man, carried by four of them.** [4] **And when they could not bring him to Jesus because of the crowd, they removed the roof above him; and after having dug through it, they let down the mat on which the paralytic lay.** [5] **When Jesus saw their faith, he said to the paralytic, "Son, your sins are forgiven."** [6] **Now some of the scribes were sitting there, questioning in their hearts,** [7] **"Why does this fellow speak in this way? It is blasphemy! Who can forgive sins but God alone?"** [8] **At once Jesus perceived in his spirit that they were discussing these questions among themselves; and he said to them, "Why do you raise such questions in your hearts?** [9] **Which is easier, to say to the paralytic, 'Your sins are forgiven,' or to say, 'Stand up and take your mat and walk'?** [10] **But so that you may know that the Son of Man has authority on earth to forgive sins"—he said to the paralytic—**[11] **"I say to you, stand up, take your mat and go to your home."** [12] **And he stood up, and immediately took the mat and went out before all of them; so that they were all amazed and glorified God, saying, "We have never seen anything like this?"**

This is perhaps the most dramatic of all the miracle stories in Mark. Jesus has returned secretly to his Capernaum home, probably Simon Peter's house (for a description, see my comments on 1:29–35). Soon his presence is discovered, and he is again confronted by a huge crowd. While he is "speaking the word" to them—that is, proclaiming the good news of God's dawning kingdom (see 1:14–15)—he is suddenly interrupted. The roof above him is being demolished! Four men, unable to bring their paralyzed friend to Jesus through the crowd, have lifted him onto the flat roof. After digging through the mud and branches covering two beams, they lower their friend with ropes into Jesus' presence.

No word is spoken by the men, but their daring action renders their faith visible. At one level their faith may be no more than confidence that Jesus is an effective healer. Mark probably has something more in mind: The men dare to believe that God's victory over evil, including the evil of physical disability, is being actualized in Jesus' ministry.

Mark does not tell us whether or not the paralyzed man shares his friends' faith. Jesus' reaction suggests the possibility that he does not. Instead of responding to a mute cry for healing, Jesus declares, "Child, your sins are forgiven!" (*teknon*, designating a child of either gender, is not intended here as a demeaning but as a kindly form of address). Since a declaration of this kind occurs nowhere else in the Gospel, we are probably to assume that it is particularly apt in this case. With his head the man believes that it belongs to God's nature to forgive (Exod. 34:6–7), but he cannot believe in his heart that God wills to forgive *him*. Jesus has preached repentance, but repentance requires faith (see my comments on 1:14–15). The good news proclaimed to all must now be addressed to one needy individual in a form he can appropriate: "*Your* sins are forgiven" (the Greek word order stresses "your").

The man's disability is powerfully symbolic. Guilt is a crippler. It hinders our worship of God and handicaps our relationships with family and friends. Indeed, there are documented cases in which paralysis has been caused by feelings of guilt (a dramatic instance of a psychiatric cure of guilt-induced paralysis is reported by Morna Hooker, *Mark*, 85). Mark does not present this as such a case, however. The man's paralysis is not cured by Jesus' word of absolution. Perhaps he needs Jesus' second word, "I say to you, stand up, take your mat and go to your home," for the first word to become fully effective; the cure of his paralysis finally convinces him that God really has forgiven him.

All this is conjectural, of course, because the response of the handicapped man is not reported. Instead, the story suddenly takes an ugly turn. In this passage we encounter for the first time a negative response to Jesus. Up to this point Mark has presented Jesus' ministry as an overwhelming success. At his first appearance in Capernaum he was received enthusiastically as one who taught with authority "and not as the scribes" (1:22). Now some of these scribes appear in the audience and silently accuse Jesus of vile heresy. He has committed blasphemy in their eyes by arrogating to himself the divine prerogative of forgiving sins. (Anyone found guilty of blaspheming, that is, intentionally insulting God, was to be stoned to death according to Leviticus 24:10–23.) Their unspoken question, "Who can forgive sins except One, God?" is reminiscent of the Shema, Israel's basic creed: "Hear, O Israel, the Lord our God, the Lord is One" (Deut. 6:4; Mark 12:29). Is "this fellow" subverting monotheism, claiming to be God by forgiving sins?

Aware of their hostile reaction, Jesus first challenges their theology with a conundrum: "Which is easier, to say to the paralytic, 'Your sins are forgiven,' or to say, 'Stand up and take your mat and walk'?" This puzzling question admits of no simple answer because the significance of "easier" is uncertain. Its general intent, however, is indicated by the similar question posed by Jesus to critics who later demand of him the source of his authority (11:27–33). In both cases Jesus invites his opponents to acknowledge that God has been present and active in his ministry. If he heals by the power of God, then surely his authority to forgive comes from the same source.

Jesus' next response to the scribes presents us with the first instance of the expression "the Son of Man." The meaning of this phrase is far from clear. For most of Christian history it was taken as a way of referring to the human nature of the Son of God as distinguished from his divine nature. In the past century, scholars have tended to regard it as the title for a heavenly Messiah. Recently the scholarly pendulum has been swinging back in the direction of the earlier view. With very few exceptions (none in Mark), the phrase is always used as Jesus' self-designation. It never prompts a reaction from the narrative audience; no one reacts either positively or negatively to his use of this name. That is, his application of the phrase to himself makes no theological claim. Mark apparently regards it as a mysterious name that Jesus uses when he wants to speak indirectly (modestly) about his present vocation, anticipated suffering, and future glory. In what sense Mark associated the phrase with Daniel 7:13 will be discussed in the comments on 13:26.

For Mark the charge of blasphemy, although unjustified, is understandable. Jesus' claim to divine authority exceeds all precedents in Judaism. As the one in whom God's rule is being actualized, he asserts a right that prophets and high priests did not exercise. It is inevitable that Jesus' lofty claims will meet stern resistance among those responsible for maintaining religious order. In the accusation "It is blasphemy!" we have the first foreshadowing of the passion; it will be on the charge of blasphemy that Jesus will be condemned to death by the high priest's council (14:64).

The people of Capernaum do not concur with the scribes. Even though they have already witnessed other healings at Peter's house (1:32–34), they now *glorify God* as a result of the paralytic's double liberation from sin and paralysis. God's honor has not been impugned by Jesus' behavior but exalted.

JESUS CALLS A SOCIAL OUTCAST
TO DISCIPLESHIP
Mark 2:13–17

> 2:13 Jesus went out again beside the sea; the whole crowd gathered around him, and he taught them. 14 As he was walking along, he saw Levi son of Alphaeus sitting at the tax booth, and he said to him, "Follow me." And he got up and followed him.
>
> 15 And as he sat at dinner in Levi's house, many tax collectors and sinners were also sitting with Jesus and his disciples—for there were many who followed him. 16 When the scribes of the Pharisees saw that he was eating with sinners and tax collectors, they said to his disciples, "Why does he eat with tax collectors and sinners?" 17 When Jesus heard this, he said to them, "Those who are well have no need of a physician, but those who are sick; I have come to call not the righteous but sinners."

This "call" story is similar to the one involving the four fishermen (1:16–20), except that it contains no promise ("I will make you fish for people," 1:17). A major difference, however, is suggested by the fact that "Levi son of Alphaeus" does not appear in the list of twelve apostles in 3:16–19. It is usually argued that Levi had another name, "Matthew," which does appear in the list, or that he is there referred to as "James son of Alphaeus." Because Mark is careful to note Simon's alternate name, other scholars maintain that Mark did not think of Levi as one of the twelve (James son of Alphaeus may be his brother). In this case Levi represents a wider circle of followers, from which the twelve were eventually selected (see 2:15; 3:13). Presumably most of these other followers remained in Galilee with their families and pursued their vocations. They may have belonged to the group of "more than five hundred" who saw the risen Christ (1 Cor. 15:6).

Levi was not a representative of the Roman tax system but an employee of Herod Antipas. His job was collecting customs duties on goods coming from the tetrarchy of Philip, which lay north and east of the Sea of Galilee (Capernaum was near the border). Customs officers were despised as little better than thieves and swindlers because they often charged too much.

In the Gospels, tax collectors are often associated with sinners. The latter term seems to refer to people whose sins are notorious, like those of the tax collectors. It may include people whose very professions involve breaking the law, such as bankers and moneylenders (the Torah strictly prohibits the charging of interest on loans; see Exod. 22:25; Deut.

23:19–20). Probably the term also designates people who are careless or indifferent respecting the practice of religion and who are therefore looked down upon as unpatriotic or "un-Jewish" by religiously observant persons. They may be compared to people in a modern Christian community about whom church members say, "They'll never come to church, and if they did they just wouldn't fit in."

Jesus greatly shocked good, religious people by associating with such riffraff. He not only recruited a tax collector as a follower, but he dined sumptuously with other tax collectors and "sinners" at Levi's home. Jesus and his companions did not "sit" at table, as many translations suggest, but *reclined*; the verbs indicate that this was not a normal meal but a banquet, at which the guests reclined as Romans did. In accordance with Palestinian village culture, such banquets were often semipublic events; an entrance to the courtyard was left open so that villagers could enter and observe how important guests like Jesus were being entertained. It was Jesus' participation in events like this that prompted the hostile comment: "Look, a glutton and a drunkard, a friend of tax collectors and sinners!" (Matt. 11:19; Luke 7:34).

In this passage the critics are identified as "the scribes of the Pharisees." This is Mark's first reference to the Pharisees (in 2:1–12 the opponents were referred to simply as "the scribes"). The Pharisees were the most important religious party in Judaism. After the disappearance of the Sadducees with the fall of the temple in A.D. 70, the Pharisees dominated the synagogues and reconstituted the religion in accordance with their own principles. Modern Judaism has evolved from the Pharisaic movement. In the Gospels, the Pharisees are generally portrayed in very negative terms because of their opposition to Jesus and his followers. Lamentably, the term *pharisee* has come into English usage as a synonym for "hypocrite," one who is "censorious" and "self-righteous." Undoubtedly there were Pharisees in Jesus' day who deserved such epithets (they are castigated in Jewish literature, too), but on the whole the movement attracted people who were serious about religion and eager to please God by obeying the law of Moses more completely. Their opposition to Jesus in this passage must be seen in relation to their goals; while they campaign for greater conformity with the law, Jesus (in their view) encourages laxity by hobnobbing with unreligious scofflaws.

Jesus defends himself with a proverbial saying and a vocational statement. As the physician sent by God to Israel, he must concern himself primarily with those who leave God out of account. A similar thought is expressed with a different metaphor in Matthew 15:24, "I was sent only to the lost sheep of the house of Israel." Jesus' ministry to tax collectors and sinners is presented by Mark as evidence that Jesus personifies the good news of God. In Jesus God's grace is brought near to those whose faith in God has been too weak to permit them to repent (see my comments on 1:14–15).

Jesus is still the friend of sinners. Many a drug or alcohol addict, bedeviled by low self-esteem and a history of failure, has found in Jesus empowerment to leave the past behind and make a new beginning.

A DISPUTE OVER FASTING
Mark 2:18–22

> 2:18 Now John's disciples and the Pharisees were fasting; and people came and said to him, "Why do John's disciples and the disciples of the Pharisees fast, but your disciples do not fast?" [19] Jesus said to them, "The wedding guests cannot fast while the bridegroom is with them, can they? As long as they have the bridegroom with them, they cannot fast. [20] The days will come when the bridegroom is taken away from them, and then they will fast on that day.
> [21] "No one sews a piece of unshrunk cloth on an old cloak; otherwise, the patch pulls away from it, the new from the old, and a worse tear is made. [22] And no one puts new wine into old wineskins; otherwise, the wine will burst the skins, and the wine is lost, and so are the skins; but one puts new wine into fresh wineskins."

Occasional abstinence from food was highly valued among Jews as an expression of religious devotion. Individuals fasted in order to demonstrate repentance for specific sins and thus to win God's favor (2 Sam. 12:16–17). Communities combined fasting with prayer as a means of averting a disaster (Ezra 8:21–23). The Day of Atonement is the only fast required by Torah (Lev. 16:29), but the postexilic period saw the emergence of several additional fast days (see Zech. 7:5; 8:19). In Jesus' day it was customary for Palestinian Jews to engage in community fasting when the fall rains were delayed.

Mark supplies no details concerning the fasting of John the Baptist's disciples and the Pharisees, but we may assume that special practices are in mind, not the national or community fasts in which the general populace participated. John the Baptist was known for his abstemious lifestyle (Luke 7:33). Presumably his fasting was associated in some way with his announcement of imminent judgment and the urgency of repentance (1:4;

Matt. 3:7–12). In this case the fasting of his followers may be seen as an appeal to God for mercy on Israel (compare Jon. 3:5–7). The Pharisees' abstinence may have the same motive, or it may be an expression of personal devotion (Luke 2:37; 18:12).

As in the two preceding passages, Jesus shocks his challengers by departing from conventional religion. He justifies the nonfasting of his disciples by means of a parable: Would it be proper to fast at a wedding? The celebration must continue as long as the bridegroom is present! Those who had heard Jesus proclaim the good news concerning the arrival of God's rule would get the point. This is not a time to lament God's absence but to celebrate God's presence! In Jesus' ministry God is powerfully active.

Early Christians quickly adopted "the bridegroom" as a way of referring to the Messiah (Matt. 25:1–13; 2 Cor. 11:2; Rev. 22:17), but there is no evidence of an earlier Jewish use of this symbolism. Consequently, the parable does not divulge the secret of Jesus' identity. It does make a very bold claim, however; it suggests that Jesus himself is the focal point of the celebration.

The parable presents the first intimation of the passion. Jesus' followers will fast on the day when the bridegroom is taken away. There is no reason to doubt that Jesus foresaw his own violent death (see my comments on 8:31). It is possible that this expectation arose only later in his ministry, when opposition intensified. Perhaps Mark has placed this anecdote at an early point on his story line as preparation for the murderous response of the Pharisees at the conclusion of this series of disputes (3:6).

To the sayings about the bridegroom are attached the twin parables about patching an old garment with unshrunk cloth and pouring fermenting wine into fully stretched wineskins. Both parables stress the incompatibility of the new with the old and the irresistible power of the new (one cannot prevent new cloth from shrinking or new wine from expanding). The parables must not be taken broadly as suggesting that Christianity has rendered Judaism obsolete. The context suggests that their point is much more focused; the good news about God's active presence is incompatible with the gloomy stance of those who are continually waiting for God to do something.

Although modern Christians are not much inclined to fasting, they often exhibit the same mournful attitude. Although we should always mourn over greed, violence, and the abuse of the environment, we also ought to look around us and rejoice in the evidence that God is still at work in our world. Insane bombers may destroy buildings and lives, but thousands of volunteers in food pantries, shelters for the homeless, and other social programs render God's love for the poor visible and concrete.

TWO DISPUTES OVER SABBATH OBSERVANCE
Mark 2:23–3:6

2:23 One sabbath he was going through the grainfields; and as they made their way his disciples began to pluck heads of grain. 24 The Pharisees said to him, "Look, why are they doing what is not lawful on the sabbath?" 25 And he said to them, "Have you never read what David did when he and his companions were hungry and in need of food? 26 He entered the house of God, when Abiathar was high priest, and ate the bread of the Presence, which it is not lawful for any but the priests to eat, and he gave some to his companions." 27 Then he said to them, "The sabbath was made for humankind, and not humankind for the sabbath; 28 so the Son of Man is lord even of the sabbath."

3:1 Again he entered the synagogue, and a man was there who had a withered hand. 2 They watched him to see whether he would cure him on the sabbath, so that they might accuse him. 3 And he said to the man who had the withered hand, "Come forward." 4 Then he said to them, "Is it lawful to do good or to do harm on the sabbath, to save life or to kill?" But they were silent. 5 He looked around at them with anger; he was grieved at their hardness of heart and said to the man, "Stretch out your hand." He stretched it out, and his hand was restored. 6 The Pharisees went out and immediately conspired with the Herodians against him, how to destroy him.

It is difficult for Christians to appreciate the significance of the sabbath for Jews. In Jesus' day, as now, it was regarded as a great gift, the sign of God's special favor. It was a day of celebration as well as of worship and study. Even poor families were encouraged to reserve something special for the sabbath meal, in order to honor God. The most notable feature of sabbath observance, and prized as a visible mark of Jewish identity, was, of course, abstinence from workday activities, in obedience to the Fourth Commandment (Exod. 20:8–11). In support of rigorous observance, later rabbis proposed that the Messiah would come when Israel had perfectly observed two sabbaths.

Nevertheless, it was not easy to determine whether certain actions violated the Fourth Commandment. Were Jesus' disciples guilty of violating the sabbath when they plucked a few heads of grain as they made their way through a field? The Pharisees in the story insist that they are guilty.

Modern Jewish scholars, however, point out that there was great diversity of opinion on such matters in the first century, and that "plucking" is not included among the thirty-nine classes of prohibited labor listed in the Mishnah, a collection of the oral law from about A.D. 200.

From Jesus' response it is not possible to determine whether or not he agrees with the Pharisees, for he does not defend the disciples' action by denying the accusation. Instead, he appeals to a historical precedent, the case of David's illegal consumption of the bread of the Presence (1 Sam. 21:3–6). Because this narrative precedent has nothing to do with the sabbath as such, its function is not to prove that the disciples are innocent of sabbath breaking but rather to demonstrate that their violation (if such is the case) is justified by reference to a higher obligation. That higher obligation, however, is not the mere satisfaction of personal hunger; Jesus is not represented as arguing that anyone who is hungry can transgress the sabbath law. The focal point of the historical precedent is David. His violation of the law is permissible only because of his special place in God's plan for Israel. Jesus is implying that something greater than David is here (compare Matt. 12:6). As the one who both announces and embodies the arrival of God's rule (1:14–15), Jesus takes precedence over the sabbath.

We must be careful, therefore, not to read more into verse 27, "The sabbath was made for humankind, and not humankind for the sabbath," than is justified from the context. This saying does not abrogate the sabbath by suggesting that people can do whatever they want on the seventh day; it reaffirms the conviction that the sabbath is God's gift. Nor does it suggest that how one observes the sabbath is a matter of personal interpretation. It merely states as a general principle that sabbath observance must sometimes be subordinated to humanitarian concerns (a principle found also in early rabbinic literature).

This general principle is further restricted by the attached saying about Jesus' authority, "so the Son of Man is lord also of the sabbath." As the one commissioned by God to inaugurate the kingdom of God, Jesus has the authority not only to forgive sins (2:10) but also (preferable to NRSV "even") to subordinate sabbath observance to the work of the kingdom. As kingdom workers, his disciples bear no guilt for "harvesting" on the sabbath.

Mark intimates that the second sabbath dispute occurs later on the same day. The "again" suggests that the scene is the Capernaum synagogue, where Jesus' authority was exhibited in an exorcism (1:21–28; in that passage, however, no exception is taken to the fact that he exorcizes on the sabbath). The anonymous "they" who lie in wait for Jesus in the expectation that he will heal on the sabbath are undoubtedly the Pharisees of 2:24, who are mentioned again in verse 6. They intend to "accuse" him, that is, bring formal charges before a court (see 15:3–4).

At first glance, Jesus' question, "Is it lawful to do good or to do harm on the sabbath, to save life or to kill?" is puzzling. His opponents would naturally agree with him that it is not lawful to do harm or to kill, whether on the sabbath or on any other day. The issue, they would insist, is whether the sabbath is properly observed by a healer who plies his trade when work is prohibited. Why does Jesus not simply point out that, because he mixes no potions and applies no poultices but only speaks, he is in fact not working, and therefore their unspoken accusation is groundless? Because he has no intention of defending himself! Instead, he turns the tables on his opponents by challenging *their* behavior. How are they honoring the sabbath? By planning to do evil and take life!

The upshot of the healing is that the Pharisees immediately arrange a meeting with the Herodians, people who exercised secular power through their ties with Herod Antipas. This indicates that the Pharisees do not plan to bring formal charges against Jesus as a sabbath-breaker (he has not been guilty of any flagrant violation). Indeed, it is not his sabbath behavior as such that upsets them but rather his unabashed usurpation of authority in religious affairs. Who does he think he is?

The plot to destroy Jesus thus concludes the series of disputes about his authority that began in 2:1–12, and anticipates the passion, when religious leaders will seek the support of political forces (the Romans) in order to get rid of Jesus.

JESUS ATTRACTS
AN ENORMOUS CROWD
Mark 3:7–12

> 3:7 Jesus departed with his disciples to the sea, and a great multitude from Galilee followed him; 8 hearing all that he was doing, they came to him in great numbers from Judea, Jerusalem, Idumea, beyond the Jordan, and the region around Tyre and Sidon. 9 He told his disciples to have a boat ready for him because of the crowd, so that they would not crush him; 10 for he had cured many, so that all who had diseases pressed upon him to touch him. 11 Whenever the unclean spirits saw him, they fell down before him and shouted, "You are the Son of God!" 12 But he sternly ordered them not to make him known.

With this passage we reach the conclusion of the section that began at 1:40. In this segment of the Gospel, Mark begins the process of preparing for the passion by presenting a series of stories in which Jesus provokes a negative response from scribes, Pharisees, and Herodians. The climax has just been reached in a murder plot (3:6).

This passage serves as a bright foil to that dark scene. Whereas a few leaders react with murderous opposition to Jesus, the people as a whole press around him in unprecedented numbers, threatening to crush him in their enthusiasm. The significance of the crowd is enhanced by a list of areas from which people have been drawn to Jesus. The list is counterclockwise, beginning with Jesus' own territory, Galilee. Judea and Jerusalem come next, perhaps because of their special importance to Jews. Idumea lay south of Judea. It had been taken over by non-Jews following the fall of Judea to the Babylonians, but after the Maccabean revolt it came under Jewish dominance once again and was home to many Jews in the first century. "Beyond the Jordan" was a common way of referring to Perea, a Jewish territory east of the Jordan, which was included with Galilee in the tetrarchy of Herod Antipas. Tyre and Sidon, Phoenician cities on the Mediterranean coast north of Galilee, included significant numbers of Jewish inhabitants, both in the urban centers and in the rural territories under their control. It has been proposed that Mark lists areas containing Christian churches in his day. It is true that Christian communities in Tyre and Sidon are mentioned in Acts 21:3–4 and 27:3. This explanation is unsatisfactory, however, because the list omits Samaria and the Decapolis. Acts 8 reports the early establishment of the gospel in Samaria, and from other sources we surmise that there were Christians in the Decapolis in Mark's time. It is probable, therefore, that the list is meant to refer simply to Jewish populations in various parts of Palestine. Jesus' fame is such that he draws Jews from far and near. In this respect he outshines his forerunner, John the Baptist, who is represented by Mark 1:5 as attracting crowds only from Judea and Jerusalem.

Homage is paid to Jesus not only by the vast multitude but by demon-possessed persons who prostrate themselves and cry out, "You are the Son of God!" Similar confessions are uttered by demons in 1:24 and 5:7. In each instance the narrative audience totally ignores the information provided by the unclean spirits; the spectators neither accept nor reject the identification. When Jesus later asks his disciples what opinion people hold concerning him, the answer provided by the disciples suggests that the public has paid no attention to the demoniacs (8:27–28). Jesus' silencing of the demons, therefore, is not a case of closing the barn door after the horse has escaped. It is Mark's way of reminding his readers that the public revelation of Jesus' identity must await his crucifixion. At his death a Roman centurion will confess: "Truly this man was God's Son" (15:39).

By commanding the demons not to divulge his identity, Jesus acknowledges the truth of their announcement; he *is* the Son of God. This reminder of what was announced by the narrator in 1:1 and by the voice from heaven in 1:11 is strategically placed as the sequel to the plot of the Pharisees and Herodians. The one whose death is being planned by religious and secular leaders is none other than the Messiah, the Son of God.

4. Jesus Prepares
   Twelve Apprentices
   for Mission
   Mark 3:13–6:13

The next segment of the Gospel, 3:13–6:13, contains diverse material, including another controversy narrative (3:19b–30), a collection of parables (4:1–34), and three important miracle stories (4:35–5:43). Because it begins with the appointment of the twelve and concludes with their preaching and healing mission, we can regard it as held together loosely by the theme of preparing the twelve to represent Jesus.

THE APPOINTMENT OF THE TWELVE
Mark 3:13–19a

> 3:13 **He went up the mountain and called to him those whom he wanted, and they came to him. ¹⁴ And he appointed twelve, whom he also named apostles, to be with him, and to be sent out to proclaim the message, ¹⁵ and to have authority to cast out demons. ¹⁶ So he appointed the twelve: Simon (to whom he gave the name Peter); ¹⁷ James son of Zebedee and John the brother of James (to whom he gave the name Boanerges, that is, Sons of Thunder); ¹⁸ and Andrew, and Philip, and Bartholomew, and Matthew, and Thomas, and James son of Alphaeus, and Thaddaeus, and Simon the Cananaean, ¹⁹ and Judas Iscariot, who betrayed him.**

Jesus' selection of twelve men for a special relationship to him is one of the most certain things we know about him. It is sometimes proposed that "the twelve" is a fiction created after Easter, but it is entirely improbable that such a pious fabrication would include the betrayer, Judas Iscariot. Moreover, the eleven seem not to have played the kind of role in the early church that would call forth a legend of this sort (Luke reports stories about only three of them in Acts). Confirmation of the historicity of Jesus' appointment of twelve is provided by Paul, who reports that the risen Christ appeared "to Cephas, then to the twelve" (1 Cor. 15:5).

Why did Jesus choose *twelve?* Mark gives no hint. In his telling of the story, Jesus might just as well have chosen ten or fourteen. The symbolism was obvious to early Christians, however, who understood Jesus' role as Messiah to include the restoration of the twelve tribes of Israel (see Rev. 21:12–14). In Luke 22:28–30, Jesus promises these closest followers a special role in the messianic kingdom: "You will sit on thrones judging the twelve tribes of Israel" (compare Matt. 19:28).

Many ancient manuscripts omit the phrase "whom he also named apostles" (the words are omitted from the KJV), but it is probably authentic (see 6:30). To modern ears "apostle" sounds like a title, that is, an indication of status, but in Jesus' use it was the designation of persons with a specific function. The Greek word *apostolos* means someone who is sent. Jesus probably used *shaliach*, from the Hebrew verb "send." In Judaism this term pointed not simply to the fact that the person so designated was being sent on a specific mission (for example, to negotiate a marriage or a sale of property) but especially to the *authorization* conferred by the one who sent him. The *shaliach* was legally empowered to act on behalf of the sender. The concept is clearly reflected in this passage, where twelve are selected to be sent out to preach, that is, to extend Jesus' message of 1:14–15 and to have *authority* to cast out demons. God has conferred on Jesus authority to proclaim the good news of God's rule and to act out the good news by attacking the forces of evil (see my comments on 1:21–28). The twelve commissioned representatives receive delegated authority to participate in Jesus' kingdom ministry.

Both before and after their being sent out, however, the apostles are to be "with him." One could understand this as referring primarily to the need for instruction. Indeed, such an understanding is encouraged by the term "disciple" ("learner") by which these followers are normally identified. The British scholar T. W. Manson proposed, however, that the term used by Jesus for his followers was not a word meaning "student" (suggesting rote learning and the study of books) but "apprentices." Followers were to learn from him by observing carefully and imitating what they saw, just as if they were apprentices of a master carpenter (Manson, *The Teaching of Jesus*, 239–40). All Christians are called to be "with Jesus" in this sense—not simply to learn *about* him but to learn *from* him how to live as signs of God's rule by acting compassionately and resisting evil.

The twelve are named not only here but also in Matthew 10:2–4, Luke 6:14–16, and Acts 1:13. No two lists agree completely. The four fishermen are always listed first. Andrew is coupled with his brother Simon in Matthew and Luke, but here he is named after James and John, because they, with Peter, constitute an inner circle of the twelve (5:37; 9:2; 14:33;

but in 13:3 Andrew is included, again in fourth place). All four lists have Philip, Bartholomew, Matthew, Thomas, James son of Alphaeus, and Judas Iscariot. Variations occur for the remaining two. A second Simon is identified as "the Canaanite" here and in Matthew, but as "the Zealot" in Luke and Acts. Thaddeus (Matthew and Mark) is replaced by a second Judas (son of James) in Luke's works (also John 14:22). The fact is that these members of the twelve are shadowy figures about whom we know nothing else; they seem not to have made any impression on any of the writers of the New Testament.

Simon is mentioned first in all four lists, undoubtedly because of his importance in the early church. Mark reports that Jesus gave him a new name—henceforth in this Gospel he will always be referred to as Peter except at 14:37—but the evangelist gives no hint of Jesus' motive (but see Matt. 16:18). The same is true of the nickname "Sons of Thunder" given to Zebedee's sons. A possible explanation for the latter is provided by the anecdote about them in Luke 9:51–56.

In all these lists Judas Iscariot is included, despite the embarrassment that Jesus selected a man who would prove to be his betrayer. The identification of Judas by reference to his future role serves as another foreshadowing of the passion.

JESUS' TRUE FAMILY
AND THE BEELZEBUL CHARGE
Mark 3:19b–35

3:19b Then he went home; 20 and the crowd came together again, so that they could not even eat. 21 When his family heard it, they went out to restrain him, for people were saying, "He has gone out of his mind." 22 And the scribes who came down from Jerusalem said, "He has Beelzebul, and by the ruler of the demons he casts out demons." 23 And he called them to him, and spoke to them in parables, "How can Satan cast out Satan? 24 If a kingdom is divided against itself, that kingdom cannot stand. 25 And if a house is divided against itself, that house will not be able to stand. 26 And if Satan has risen up against himself and is divided, he cannot stand, but his end has come. 27 But no one can enter a strong man's house and plunder his property without first tying up the strong man; then indeed the house can be plundered.

28 "Truly I tell you, people will be forgiven for their sins and whatever blasphemies they utter; 29 but whoever blasphemes against the Holy Spirit can never have forgiveness, but is guilty of an eternal sin"— 30 for they had said, "He has an unclean spirit."

31 Then his mother and his brothers came; and standing outside, they sent

to him and called him. [32] A crowd was sitting around him; and they said to him, "Your mother and your brothers and sisters are outside, asking for you." [33] And he replied, "Who are my mother and my brothers?" [34] And looking at those who sat around him, he said, "Here are my mother and my brothers! [35] Whoever does the will of God is my brother and sister and mother."

In this passage we encounter a literary technique of which Mark is particularly fond; he sandwiches one narrative between the first and last parts of another (for other examples, see 5:21–43, 11:12–25; 14:53–72). His intention, it seems, is to let each story illuminate the other. Here an anecdote about Jesus' rejection by his own family (vv. 21, 32) is paralleled by one in which he is rejected by religious leaders (vv. 22–30).

Following the appointment of the twelve Jesus goes home, presumably to Peter's house in Capernaum (see 1:29; 2:1), where he is again surrounded by a crowd. The note about not being able to eat suggests that the crowd remains for an extended period of time, perhaps all day. His relatives get word of his whereabouts and determine to take charge of him, because they are convinced that he has become insane.

Mark gives us no hint concerning which aspects of Jesus' behavior prompt this response. Does his family think that he has reneged on his responsibility, as the eldest son, to support his widowed mother? (The omission of Joseph in 3:31 and 6:3 suggests that he has died.) Have they heard of the extravagant claims he makes on behalf of his itinerant ministry (Matt. 8:22)? Has his selection of twelve legal representatives suggested to them that he is bewitched by grandiose political dreams? Mark is not interested in their motives. What is of importance is simply that they are unable to acknowledge his ministry as evidence of God's activity, and therefore they must attribute his unusual conduct to madness.

The sandwiched story about religious leaders intensifies the theme of rejection. Whereas the family merely regard Jesus as crazy, the scribes from Jerusalem (foreshadowing the role they will take in Jesus' execution, 14:1) publicly declare that Jesus' success as an exorcist is due to a partnership with Satan. They do not attack the practice of exorcism as such; there were many other Jewish exorcists (9:38; Matt. 12:27; Acts 19:13). It is presumably Jesus' claim to unprecedented authority (2:7) that antagonizes them. Here Satan, Prince of Demons, is given the rare name "Beelzebul." There are many scholarly guesses concerning the origin and meaning of this name, but there is not enough evidence to confirm any of them.

Jesus makes three defensive moves against this slanderous charge. The first is logical; evil cannot undermine evil without negating its own character by becoming good. Although Satan can be credited with disguising himself as an angel of light (2 Cor. 11:14) and by working miraculous signs (2 Thess. 2:9; Rev. 13:13), he is incapable by definition of attacking evil.

The second and third defenses are identified as "parables," that is, instances of figurative language or analogies. If the opponents' charge were true (which is logically impossible), and Satan were using Jesus as a means of attacking his own evil empire, then his realm would be self-destructing! The second parable develops the notion of Satan's "house." Here we have not a contrary-to-fact picture but a realistic one. Satan, the strong man, thinks his house is impregnable; but one stronger than Satan has the power to bind him and plunder his property, that is, release those whom Satan has captured. Jesus' exorcisms are thus offered as evidence that the power exercised by Jesus is stronger than Satan's power.

The source of this stronger power is not specified, but readers know that Jesus, identified from heaven as "My Son," was empowered at his baptism with God's Holy Spirit (1:10–12). It is this implicit reference to the Spirit (explicit in the parallel at Matt. 12:28) that underlies the following saying about the unforgivable sin. By calling Jesus' exorcisms the devil's work, the opponents have committed blasphemy against God; they have maligned the power of God's Spirit by identifying it as evil.

The saying opens with the solemn phrase "Amen, I say to you" (the usual translation, "truly," is weak, obscuring the force of the original). Although it was common to conclude a statement with "Amen" as a word of confirmation ("So be it"), only Jesus, as far as we know, marked important utterances by beginning with "Amen." It functions as an implicit claim to authority.

The opening statement, "people will be forgiven for their sins and whatever blasphemies they utter," is by no means a promise of automatic forgiveness for unrepented sins. It merely affirms the traditional conviction that it is God's nature to forgive the penitent (Exod. 34:6–7). The general statement confers greater emphasis on the restriction provided in the second half of the saying: "whoever blasphemes against the Holy Spirit can never have forgiveness."

It is sometimes argued that there can be no such thing as an unforgivable sin, because this would deny God's nature as forgiving. Jesus' saying does not negate God's right to forgive; it recognizes the inability of some to receive ("have") forgiveness. People who persist in calling good evil renounce their God-given capacity for acknowledging the evil in themselves, and thus become incapable of penitence.

Many Christians have worried unnecessarily about the possibility of being guilty of the unforgivable sin. As has often been pointed out, those who worry about the unforgivable sin are least capable of such guilt. It is those who perceive no evil in themselves who should worry!

Following Jesus' refutation of the scribes' charge, his mother and brothers finally arrive to take charge of him. When news of their presence is brought to Jesus, he utters a shocking word. His natural family is no longer primary; his real family consists of those crowding about to hear him. "Whoever does the will of God" may involve ethics, but Mark does not develop this possibility. In this context, those who do the will of God are the people who respond in faith to Jesus' claim that God has authorized and empowered his ministry.

In every age this saying about Jesus' true family has been of enormous comfort to Christians who have been compelled to choose between their natural families and Jesus. Becoming an "apprentice" of Jesus by no means requires that we disassociate ourselves from our blood relatives. Indeed, Paul taught his converts *not* to separate from an unbelieving spouse if at all possible (1 Cor. 7:12–16). There are instances, however, in which dysfunctional families put great pressure on a believer to participate in their evil. In such cases a sharp break may be required. The intimacy of the family is then replaced by the intimacy of Christian fellowship.

Striking in the last line is the word "sister." This is undoubtedly an allusion to the participation of younger women in the Jesus movement (see 15:40–41) and in the early church. Unfortunately, we know almost nothing about the role these women played. Perhaps their prototype was Mary of Bethany, who sat, in the posture of an attentive student, at Jesus' feet (Luke 10:39).

PARABLES OF THE KINGDOM
Mark 4:1–34

In the last chapter Mark used the word "parables" with reference to Jesus' word pictures about a divided kingdom and a strong man's house (3:23–27). There was no suggestion that these parables would be difficult for the audience to understand. In every culture speakers employ figurative language to make a point. Later in the Gospel the meaning of a parable will be transparent to a hostile audience (12:12). In Mark 4, however, parables have a very different function. They are presented not simply as illustrations or extended metaphors but as puzzles.

In this special use, "parable" seems to be the translation of the Hebrew word *mashal*, which often means "riddle" or "enigmatic utterance." In

Ezekiel 17:2, for example, God tells the prophet, "Son of man, propound a riddle, and speak a *mashal* to the house of Israel." The *mashal* turns out to be an allegory, that is, an edifying story in which each detail has a special meaning that must be explained to the audience. The *mashal* is thus a form of indirect communication; its function is to tease the minds of the hearers, prompting deeper insight than would occur in response to direct communication. An analogy is provided by modern psychotherapy; the therapist's task is not to tell the patient what the problem is but to stimulate the kind of self-examination in which insight can occur.

The parables collected in Mark 4 are often called "parables of the kingdom" because they refer in one way or another to the "mystery" or "secret" of the kingdom of God (v. 11). The first parable (vv. 3–9) is followed by a brief discussion about the function of the parables (vv. 10–12) and then by an allegorical interpretation of the parable (as in Ezekiel 17). No interpretation is provided for the other parables in the collection, but the conclusion suggests that explanations were provided privately to the disciples (v. 34).

The Parable of the Six Seeds (Mark 4:1–9)

4:1 **Again he began to teach beside the sea. Such a very large crowd gathered around him that he got into a boat on the sea and sat there, while the whole crowd was beside the sea on the land. 2 He began to teach them many things in parables, and in his teaching he said to them: 3 "Listen! A sower went out to sow. 4 And as he sowed, some seed fell on the path, and the birds came and ate it up. 5 Other seed fell on rocky ground, where it did not have much soil, and it sprang up quickly, since it had no depth of soil. 6 And when the sun rose, it was scorched; and since it had no root, it withered away. 7 Other seed fell among thorns, and the thorns grew up and choked it, and it yielded no grain. 8 Other seed fell into good soil and brought forth grain, growing up and increasing and yielding thirty and sixty and a hundredfold."
9 And he said, "Let anyone with ears to hear listen!"**

Although this parable is known popularly as the parable of the Sower, the sower is not mentioned again after the opening statement. Sometimes it is called the parable of the Soils, but this seems to miss the point, since emphasis lies exclusively on the seeds and what becomes of them.

Most translations, including the NRSV, take "seed" as a collective term. Mark's Greek version, however, distinguishes between a singular in verses 4–7 and a plural in verse 8a, which is followed by three singulars in verse

8b. What we have, therefore, is a story about six individual seeds. Three fail to produce fruit for various reasons, and three produce differing quantities of grain.

Mark's placement of the parable may provide the clue to its original meaning. The preceding passages present two very different responses to Jesus. Whereas the twelve and other followers crowd around Jesus because they are confident that God's power is present in his ministry, the Pharisees, scribes, and his own family think that he is either crazy or in partnership with Satan. The two sets of seeds may thus symbolize productive and nonproductive reactions to his work. The parable may have been intended by Jesus to reassure his followers that, despite the negative responses of some, his work would bear an abundant harvest.

The Purpose of the Parables (Mark 4:10–12)

4:10 **When he was alone, those who were around him along with the twelve asked him about the parables.** [11] **And he said to them, "To you has been given the secret of the kingdom of God, but for those outside, everything comes in parables;** [12] **in order that**

'they may indeed look, but not perceive,
and may indeed listen, but not understand;
so that they may not turn again and be forgiven.'"

Most readers find these verses very troubling. It seems entirely out of character for Jesus to speak in riddles *in order that* those who have not responded positively to his ministry may not repent and be forgiven.

Various attempts have been made to remove this offense. It is often proposed that these verses derive not from Jesus but from the early church, as it wrestled with the problem that Israel had not accepted the gospel. In his struggle over this issue Paul concluded that God had temporarily "hardened" most Jews so that the Gentiles might have a chance to receive the gospel (Romans 9–11, especially 11:7–12). By quoting Isaiah 6:9–10, Mark maintains that the failure of many to understand Jesus' message was predetermined by God (for a similar use of the text, see Acts 28:25–28).

Another proposal suggests that in Jesus' Aramaic version of these verses the word translated "in order that" was ambiguous, indicating either purpose or result. Accordingly, it was not Jesus' intention to use parables as a tool for excluding anyone, but this was the result. Those who were unresponsive or hostile to him and his message were unable to benefit from the parables; they could hear them only at a superficial level without obtaining any insight (understanding) that would prompt the repentance necessary for forgiveness.

We must not ignore the positive half of the statement: "To you has been given the *mysterion* of the kingdom of God." In the New Testament this Greek word, translated as either "mystery" or "secret," usually refers to God's plan for the consummation of the ages (for another instance, see Rom. 11:25). Jesus' followers have not obtained insight into what God is doing by their own intellectual efforts; their insight is a matter of divine grace. "Those outside" have heard the same words from Jesus' mouth (1:14–15) and have observed the same healings, but have found them meaningless. The secret that God is inaugurating the new era in and through Jesus is hidden from them.

This passage must not be treated as support for the biblically questionable doctrine of "double predestination," according to which God has predestined some people to be damned before they are born. It belongs rather to the paradox of grace and free will. Humans must take responsibility for their evil actions (and their evil nonactions), but recognize that when they do what is good they have been moved by divine grace. This paradox makes little sense to the intellect, but enormous sense to the heart responsive to God.

An Allegorical Interpretation (Mark 4:13–20)

4:13 And he said to them, "Do you not understand this parable? Then how will you understand all the parables? [14] The sower sows the word. [15] These are the ones on the path where the word is sown: when they hear, Satan immediately comes and takes away the word that is sown in them. [16] And these are the ones sown on rocky ground: when they hear the word, they immediately receive it with joy. [17] But they have no root, and endure only for a while; then, when trouble or persecution arises on account of the word, immediately they fall away. [18] And others are those sown among the thorns: these are the ones who hear the word, [19] but the cares of the world, and the lure of wealth, and the desire for other things come in and choke the word, and it yields nothing. [20] And these are the ones sown on the good soil: they hear the word and accept it and bear fruit, thirty and sixty and a hundredfold."

Throughout Christian history the parables of Jesus were thoroughly allegorized by interpreters, following the example set by this passage; a spiritual meaning was attributed to each detail. In the twentieth century, scholars reversed this trend, arguing that parables should be carefully distinguished from allegories. Each parable has one main point, it was claimed; the details of the story must not be treated as significant in themselves. More recently the pendulum has begun to swing back toward a middle position. In view of the use of allegorical "parables" in the Old Testament (as in Ezekiel 17), there is no reason to deny such parables to Jesus. Nevertheless, there is good reason to think that the allegorical interpretation provided in these verses, at least in its present form, reflects Christian experience in Mark's own day. There is no evidence in the Gospels that Jesus' followers were persecuted during his life (v. 17). Nor do we hear of any disciple deserting Jesus because of the lure of wealth (v. 19). It is entirely possible, however, that Jesus employed allegory to speak of the falling away of some who had earlier been enthusiastic followers (see John 6:66).

At first reading the allegorical interpretation is confusing. In verse 14 we are told that the seed symbolizes Jesus' message. In verse 15 "the ones on the path" are apparently distinguished from "the word that is sown in them," yet there is nothing corresponding to this item in the parable except the seed that falls on the path. The distinction is further blurred in the following verses, where the sown seeds represent different people and their responses to the gospel. It is obviously a mistake to insist on precision. For example, it would be foolish to suggest that one's response to Jesus is simply a matter of luck, depending upon one's "soil." The main point is clear; people respond to the gospel in different ways, with differing results.

Modern Christians recognize the truth of the parable and its interpretation. Many who make an enthusiastic commitment to Jesus find their loyalty steadily eroded by pressures from family, friends, employers, and fellow workers. Although we do not fear physical persecution, we shrink from the scorn of those with whom we associate regularly. And the lure of wealth is a constant competitor of love for Jesus. Nevertheless, our faithfulness is not predetermined by external circumstances. We may choose a more productive soil in which to grow and produce fruit by planting ourselves in a healthy fellowship.

A Lamp Is Not to Be Hidden (Mark 4:21–25)

4:21 He said to them, "Is a lamp brought in to be put under the bushel basket, or under the bed, and not on the lampstand? 22 For there is nothing hidden, except to be disclosed; nor is anything secret, except to come to light.

²³ **Let anyone with ears to hear listen!"** ²⁴ **And he said to them, "Pay attention to what you hear; the measure you give will be the measure you get, and still more will be given you.** ²⁵ **For to those who have, more will be given; and from those who have nothing, even what they have will be taken away."**

The four sayings in this passage may have been uttered by Jesus on separate occasions (the first three are found in different settings in Matthew 5:15; 7:2; and 10:26). Mark has placed them together here, presumably because he regarded them as relevant to his collection of kingdom parables. Although the first and third sayings are not parables in the usual sense, they are "picture-words," employing a lamp and the act of measuring as the means of conveying truth. To each is attached a saying that is to be understood as interpreting or reinforcing the point of the parabolic saying.

Although it is obvious that a lamp is meant to give light, not to be hidden, it is by no means clear what the lamp symbolizes in this instance. In John 5:35, Jesus refers to John the Baptist as "a burning and shining lamp." Some interpreters, consequently, are inclined to regard Jesus himself as the lamp in this Markan saying. Despite the hostility that threatens to extinguish him (see 3:6), Jesus must shine by exercising his ministry in the most public way instead of hiding from his enemies. Such an interpretation, however, does not seem to suit this context.

When read with the following verse, the lamp saying appears to be speaking about something that is expected to shine but is in fact hidden. It is sometimes argued that the lamp symbolizes Jesus' messianic status; at the moment his messiahship is a secret, but at some point in the future it will become public knowledge. Because the theme of the parables collection is the kingdom of God (see vv. 11, 26, 30), it seems more likely that Mark understood these sayings as referring to the inauguration and consummation of God's rule (in which Jesus plays a central role). At the moment it is hidden, visible only to eyes of faith, but a time will come when it is fully revealed, both to the believing and to the unbelieving.

The second image is drawn from the marketplace. Commodities are sold by measure, either by volume or by weight. The seller can be generous or greedy in measuring out the desired quantity. "The measure you give will be the measure you get" appears to be a proverb, roughly equivalent to "Do as you would be done by." In Matthew 7:2 it serves as a warning against judging others harshly. In Mark's context, however, as the sequel to the warning "Watch out how you hear!" (Luke 8:18 understands Mark's Greek better than most modern translations), it refers not to conduct but to hearing. The spiritually lazy hear carelessly; they do not listen intently enough to get the point. Jesus urges them to listen "generously" instead of "stingily," measuring out their attentiveness in generous portions. Those who listen generously will receive generously in return; the secret of the kingdom will be theirs in full measure.

The paradoxical saying of verse 25 is probably the Palestinian equivalent of our proverb "The rich get richer, the poor get poorer." In this context it serves as further comment on the problem of spiritual laziness. Those who hold on to their insight that God is active in Jesus will find that their faith grows stronger and deeper. Those who refuse to take Jesus seriously will experience a diminishing of their capacity for responding to the spiritual dimension of life. Faith, like a muscle, must be exercised or it will atrophy.

Parable of Mysterious Growth (Mark 4:26–29)

> 4:26 He also said, "The kingdom of God is as if someone would scatter seed on the ground, 27 and would sleep and rise night and day, and the seed would sprout and grow, he does not know how. 28 The earth produces of itself, first the stalk, then the head, then the full grain in the head. 29 But when the grain is ripe, at once he goes in with his sickle, because the harvest has come."

Mark does not indicate whether this parable and the following one are addressed to the disciples alone (v. 10) or the large crowd of verse 1. In view of the conclusion (vv. 33–34), we can assume that the larger audience is in view. Although both parables begin with an explicit reference to the kingdom of God, this by no means suggests that the mystery of the kingdom (v. 11) is being divulged. Jesus has spoken openly about God's rule from the beginning of his ministry (1:14–15). Only those who respond in faith are able to incorporate his good news into their very being and thereby receive the mystery.

This is the only parable in Mark without any parallel in Matthew or Luke. Because no explanation is provided in the Gospel, the parable remains a puzzle. Some interpreters propose that the central point concerns the farmer. Accordingly, it has been understood variously as the parable of the Patient Farmer, the Unbelieving Farmer, and the Reaper. It is more likely, however, that the focus lies on the seed's mysterious growth. Without any help from the farmer, the seed germinates, greatly expands in size, and finally produces fruit to be harvested. The farmer's ignorance and passivity do not constitute significant elements of the parable, but simply reinforce the central point. Even though the strange phrase "sends in the sickle" (a more literal translation of v. 29) probably echoes Joel 3:13, where the same unusual expression is found, this vague allusion is not sufficient to prove that the parable focuses on the Last Judgment.

Jesus has announced the arrival of God's kingdom, but to skeptical eyes nothing has changed. In this parable he assures his followers that they are not to be misled by superficial observation. The implanted word advances with invisible power.

This parable has brought comfort to many a preacher, who has faithfully planted the good news without seeing much in the way of results. In some cases it takes years for the seed to germinate! The work of the Spirit is invisible. We must not assume that nothing is happening when no dramatic changes can be seen.

The parable also reminds us that it is foolish to think that we can build the kingdom of God on earth by our own efforts. Although we must strive constantly to be effective signs of the kingdom, its establishment can be accomplished by God alone. Our task is to pray for it ("Your kingdom come," Matt. 6:10; Luke 11:2) and wait faithfully.

The Mustard Seed (Mark 4:30–32)

4:30 **He also said, "With what can we compare the kingdom of God, or what parable will we use for it?** 31 **It is like a mustard seed, which, when sown upon the ground, is the smallest of all the seeds on earth;** 32 **yet when it is sown it grows up and becomes the greatest of all shrubs, and puts forth large branches, so that the birds of the air can make nests in its shade."**

The central point of this parable is unmistakable; attention is focused on the remarkable contrast between the tiny mustard seed (which was regarded proverbially as the smallest thing one could see) and the large plant it produces.

Our translations are misleading at two points. Mark's Greek does not suggest that the mustard plant is the largest of all shrubs, which would be untrue, but of all "vegetables" or "herbs." "Make nests" is also an unfortunate translation of a verb that means simply "dwell," "rest," or "settle." Because the plant is an annual, achieving a height of up to six feet only

when fully grown, it is not large enough during the spring nesting season
for even the smallest nests. When it is mature, small birds can rest on its
branches and larger birds can settle in its shade.

By this parable Jesus informs his audience that, although the begin-
nings of the kingdom of God in his ministry may appear infinitesi-
mally small, like the almost invisible mustard seed, its growth will be
phenomenal.

Conclusion (Mark 4:33–34)

4:33 **With many such parables he spoke the word to them, as they were able
to hear it;** [34] **he did not speak to them except in parables, but he explained
everything in private to his disciples.**

From the first three Gospels it is evident that Jesus was a master parable-
maker. Mark's summarizing conclusion suggests both that he told many
other parables that are not here included and that his parable telling was
in some way accommodated to the hearing of his audience. One guesses
that at an earlier stage of the tradition the words "as they were able to hear
it" referred to the fact that Jesus found his audience more attentive when
his message was communicated indirectly by means of parables. The failure of the Christian mission to Israel, however, has resulted in a more negative interpretation of Jesus' indirect communication. As verses 10–12 assert, Jesus' parables came to be viewed as obscure riddles whose meaning
could be obtained only through Jesus' own interpretation. Verse 34 reaffirms this view: Jesus spoke to "those outside" *only* in riddles. For Mark's
Gospel this is not strictly accurate, for Jesus will teach publicly without
parables on numerous occasions (for example, 6:1–2; 7:14–15; 8:34; 10:1).
Perhaps Mark means that Jesus spoke to the crowds about the nature of
the kingdom of God only in this indirect manner (open proclamation is
suggested in 1:15).

JESUS MASTERS A STORM
Mark 4:35–41

4:35 **On that day, when evening had come, he said to them, "Let us go
across to the other side."** [36] **And leaving the crowd behind, they took him
with them in the boat, just as he was. Other boats were with him.** [37] **A great**

windstorm arose, and the waves beat into the boat, so that the boat was already being swamped. [38] But he was in the stern, asleep on the cushion; and they woke him up and said to him, "Teacher, do you not care that we are perishing?" [39] He woke up and rebuked the wind, and said to the sea, "Peace! Be still!" Then the wind ceased, and there was a dead calm. [40] He said to them, "Why are you afraid? Have you still no faith?" [41] And they were filled with great awe and said to one another, "Who then is this, that even the wind and the sea obey him?"

Because of our scientific worldview, this story is troublesome to modern Christians. Advances in psychosomatic medicine have reduced our skepticism concerning the healing miracles, and psychiatric studies have rendered the exorcisms credible, but the "nature miracles" are beyond our comprehension. In some liberal circles it was fashionable to "explain" this incident as the result of a remarkable coincidence; the storm happened to pass on precisely at the moment Jesus uttered his commands. It is a mistake to emasculate the story in this way. Obviously, no one in the early church would have bothered to repeat the story if its origin was so easily understandable. Let us refrain from idle speculation about what really happened and enter into the spirit of the story.

The narrative is connected with the preceding parables' discourse by means of its introduction. At 4:1 we were told that Jesus was teaching a vast crowd from a boat. Now this same boat permits Jesus to leave the multitude ("just as he was" probably means that he is still in the boat). No indication is given concerning the significance of the fact that "other boats were with him." We may assume that these vessels carried other disciples, but they play no further role in the story. It is sometimes argued that the normal fishing boats on the Sea of Galilee were too small to carry Jesus and the twelve (hence the necessity for other little boats), but recent archeological studies maintain that larger boats were also used. The language of verse 38 points in this direction: Jesus is not simply at the back of a small boat but "in the stern," that is, in a raised area of a larger boat, either on the seat normally occupied by the steersman or, more probably, under the afterdeck. In either case he is protected from the waves. His sleeping reflects his confidence in divine providence. When the high waves begin to spill into the boat, the distraught disciples wake Jesus. It is not clear what they want him to do. Probably they expect him to pray. There is here a clear parallel with Jonah, who is awakened by the ship captain's reproachful question, "What are you doing sound asleep? Get up, call on your god! Perhaps the god will spare us a thought so that we do not perish" (Jon. 1:6). Jesus, however, does not pray. He arises and issues commands to the winds and the sea. The verb translated "rebuke" means far more than "criticize"; Jesus tells the wind to stop what it is doing. To the sea he says, "Be silent, be muzzled!"

Because the wind and sea are here addressed as if they were personal beings, it is sometimes proposed that this is an exorcism story in which Jesus expels the demons responsible for the storm. Although this may be reading a little too much into the story, it does seem likely that Jesus is here represented as attacking the powers of chaos that threaten to engulf his disciples.

The great storm is replaced by an equally great calm (the same adjective is used in v. 37 and v. 39). Now it is Jesus' turn to be reproachful: "Why are you so cowardly? Do you still have no faith?" The disciples have not yet been transformed by the awareness that God is actively present in Jesus' ministry. Their cowardice reflects their old world, which regards God as absent and uninvolved.

Because Jesus has not prayed for God's protection but has instead exhibited divine power in a direct way, Mark's readers are reminded of passages in the Psalms that attribute control of the chaotic sea to God, especially Psalm 107:29, "He made the storm be still, and the waves of the sea were hushed" (see also Psalms 104:7 and 106:9, where the verb "rebuke" is used, as in Mark 4:39). The disciples are filled with reverent fear at this awesome display of supernatural power and ask each other about Jesus' identity. It is clear to them that he is more than a holy teacher (v. 38) and more than a prophet like Jonah, but what is he? The answer to this question will be provided gradually and progressively in the latter half of the Gospel, beginning with Peter's confession in 8:29.

Even Christians who are apt to be skeptical about the event here reported can find comfort in the story. It affirms that the Creator of this vast universe, the power behind the "Big Bang," is not to be conceived of as a watchmaker who wound up the universe and abandoned it to run on its own, but as involved and interactive. For Mark this is a story about Jesus' messiahship; as Messiah, Jesus is vested with supernatural power (see Isa. 11:4). For us it is also a story about God, whose involvement with the world was given a unique focus in Jesus of Nazareth. This God does not abandon us to the storms that threaten to annihilate us. As Paul testifies, nothing in life or death can separate us from the love of God in Christ Jesus our Lord (Rom. 8:38–39).

JESUS EXORCIZES
A LEGION OF DEMONS
Mark 5:1–20

5:1 They came to the other side of the sea, to the country of the Gerasenes. ² And when he had stepped out of the boat, immediately a man out of the tombs with an unclean spirit met him. ³ He lived among the tombs; and no one could restrain him any more, even with a chain; ⁴ for he had often been restrained with shackles and chains, but the chains he wrenched apart, and the shackles he broke in pieces; and no one had the strength to subdue him. ⁵ Night and day among the tombs and on the mountains he was always howling and bruising himself with stones. ⁶ When he saw Jesus from a distance, he ran and bowed down before him; ⁷ and he shouted at the top of his voice, "What have you to do with me, Jesus, Son of the Most High God? I adjure you by God, do not torment me." ⁸ For he had said to him, "Come out of the man, you unclean spirit!" ⁹ Then Jesus asked him, "What is your name?" He replied, "My name is Legion; for we are many." ¹⁰ He begged him earnestly not to send them out of the country. ¹¹ Now there on the hillside a great herd of swine was feeding; ¹² and the unclean spirits begged him, "Send us into the swine; let us enter them." ¹³ So he gave them permission. And the unclean spirits came out and entered the swine; and the herd, numbering about two thousand, rushed down the steep bank into the sea, and were drowned in the sea.

¹⁴ The swineherds ran off and told it in the city and in the country. Then people came to see what it was that had happened. ¹⁵ They came to Jesus and saw the demoniac sitting there, clothed and in his right mind, the very man who had had the legion; and they were afraid. ¹⁶ Those who had seen what had happened to the demoniac and to the swine reported it. ¹⁷ Then they began to beg Jesus to leave their neighborhood. ¹⁸ As he was getting into the boat, the man who had been possessed by demons begged him that he might be with him. ¹⁹ But Jesus refused, and said to him, "Go home to your friends, and tell them how much the Lord has done for you, and what mercy he has shown you." ²⁰ And he went away and began to proclaim in the Decapolis how much Jesus had done for him; and everyone was amazed.

To modern readers this is one of the strangest stories in the Gospels. Its worldview is very different from our own. Even if we find comprehensible the idea of "alien evil" in a mentally disturbed person, the thought of thousands of demons inhabiting a single individual and then being transferred to a herd of pigs is totally foreign to us. Early Christians, however, must have regarded this as one of their most entertaining stories. Not only is it told with a great many picturesque details, but its denouement is full of humor, especially for Jewish Christians, for whom pork was unclean, forbidden, and pagan (pigs were regularly sacrificed to Zeus and other deities).

The narrative is not presented by Mark merely for its entertainment value, however. It is grouped with the storm miracle of 4:35–41 and the raising of Jairus's daughter (5:21–43) as evidence of the Messiah's mastery over the powers of chaos, the armies of Satan, and the seemingly invincible power of death.

The ancient manuscripts of the Gospels disagree on the site of this miracle, both here and at the parallels in Matthew 8:28 and Luke 8:26. The three candidates are Gerasa, Gadara, and Gergesa. Of these Gerasa appears the least likely, because the city was thirty-seven miles southeast of the Sea of Galilee. Gadara (the preferred reading in Matthew 8:28) was five miles from the sea, and the shoreline in that vicinity is low. The most appropriate site, therefore, is the obscure town of Gergesa (modern El Koursi), near which is the only steep cliff on the eastern shore.

The herd of pigs indicates that Jesus has entered Gentile territory, but we must not too quickly assume that the demoniac is a Gentile. At the conclusion of the story, we are told that the healed man proclaimed his story "in the Decapolis." This collective term, originally designating a league of ten city states, was applied to a number of Gentile cities in Transjordan, including Gerasa and Gadara. According to the Jewish historian Josephus, however, there were significant pockets of Jewish population in this largely Gentile area. Presumably Matthew is referring to Jews when he reports that many from the Decapolis came to Jesus (4:25), for in Matthew 15:24 Jesus tells the Syrophoenician woman, "I was sent only to the lost sheep of the house of Israel." Because Mark is careful to note that this woman whose daughter Jesus heals near Tyre is a Gentile (7:26), it is likely that he would have done the same here if he believed that the man was a non-Jew.

We should assume, therefore, that Jesus' command in verse 19, "Go home to your family" (a preferable translation) carefully directs the man to tell other Jews about what God is doing in and through Jesus. The man is not the first Gentile evangelist.

Paul and other Jewish-Christian missionaries to the pagan world may have found it a little embarrassing that Jesus interacted so seldom with Gentiles. Why had "the Savior of the world" restricted his attention so narrowly to Jews? One theological answer is provided in John 12:20–23. The request of Gentiles to see Jesus is the signal that the time for him to die has come. Only through his death and resurrection can Jesus speak saving words to the Gentiles.

One of the humorous features of this story is the attempt of the evil spirits in verse 7 to control Jesus by means of an oath invoking the name not of Satan but of God! This is especially funny, because the spirits have just recognized Jesus as the unique Son of God. Early readers must have found it humorously appropriate that these unclean spirits chose unclean animals as their next habitation. Even the demons' collective name will have seemed ironical. "Legion" is a Latin word, designating a Roman army of approximately five thousand soldiers. In view of Galilean hostility toward the occupying army, it will have been humorous to have a whole battalion of unclean spirits so named.

Interpreters differ concerning the next detail of the story. Does Mark think that the spirits invade the pigs in order to destroy them (and perhaps to embarrass Jesus in this way), or does he mean to suggest that the stupid spirits do not foresee that this transfer will lead to their own destruction (or, at the very least, eviction from their new homes)? The narrative provides no answer to this question. In any event, Jewish-Christian readers will have delighted at the destruction of the demon-infested swine.

It is occasionally objected that Jesus is here represented as showing little respect for property rights (the owners of the pigs suffer a severe economic loss). Is this the reason the local people beg Jesus to leave their area? We are not told, but Mark probably means that Jesus' spectacular power is regarded as too dangerous by the Gergesenes (see v. 15). Nothing in the story suggests that Jesus intends to destroy the pigs.

Jesus denies the man's request to "be with him," because this privilege is reserved to the twelve (3:14). The former demoniac joins the much larger group of followers, to which we also belong. Like him, we are commissioned to tell our family and friends how much God has done for us in and through Jesus.

A DEAD GIRL IS RESUSCITATED
AND A HEMORRHAGING WOMAN
IS HEALED
Mark 5:21–43

5:21 **When Jesus had crossed again in the boat to the other side, a great crowd gathered around him; and he was by the sea. 22 Then one of the leaders of the synagogue named Jairus came and, when he saw him, fell at his feet 23 and begged him repeatedly, "My little daughter is at the point of** death. Come and lay your hands on her, so that she may be made well, and live." [24] So he went with him.

And a large crowd followed him and pressed in on him. [25] Now there was a woman who had been suffering from hemorrhages for twelve years. [26] She had endured much under many physicians, and had spent all that she had; and she was no better, but rather grew worse. [27] She had heard about Jesus, and came up behind him in the crowd and touched his cloak, [28] for she said, "If I but touch his clothes, I will be made well." [29] Immediately her hemorrhage stopped; and she felt in her body that she was healed of her disease. [30] Immediately aware that power had gone forth from him, Jesus turned about in the crowd and said, "Who touched my clothes?" [31] And his disciples said to him, "You see the crowd pressing in on you; how can you say, 'Who touched me?'" [32] He looked all around to see who had done it. [33] But the woman, knowing what had happened to her, came in fear and trembling, fell down before him, and told him the whole truth. [34] He said to her, "Daughter, your faith has made you well; go in peace, and be healed of your disease."

[35] While he was still speaking, some people came from the leader's house to say, "Your daughter is dead. Why trouble the teacher any further?" [36] But overhearing what they said, Jesus said to the leader of the synagogue, "Do not fear, only believe." [37] He allowed no one to follow him except Peter, James, and John, the brother of James. [38] When they came to the house of the leader of the synagogue, he saw a commotion, people weeping and wailing loudly. [39] When he had entered, he said to them, "Why do you make a commotion and weep? The child is not dead but sleeping." [40] And they laughed at him. Then he put them all outside, and took the child's father and mother and those who were with him, and went in where the child was. [41] He took her by the hand and said to her, "Talitha cum," which means, "Little girl, get up!" [42] And immediately the girl got up and began to walk about (she was twelve years of age). At this they were overcome with amazement. [43] He strictly ordered them that no one should know this, and told them to give her something to eat.

The series of three miracle stories here reaches its climax. After mastering the powers of chaos in the storm scene (4:35–41) and overpowering a battalion of Satan's army in the exorcism of "Legion" (5:1–20), Jesus now demonstrates God-given power over death by resuscitating a dead girl.

This story is interwoven with one about a hemorrhaging woman. Perhaps two independent events have been combined by Mark or his source, but it is just as possible that they belonged together from the beginning. The setting is the western side of the lake, presumably in or near a town large enough to have a synagogue and where a large crowd can quickly gather. Although Capernaum is not mentioned, it is a likely site.

A major feature of the double story, whether conscious to the Gospel writer or not, is the contrast between Jairus on the one hand and the woman and the girl on the other. Whereas the male is named, the females are not. The man's social status as a synagogue ruler ("president") is stressed, but the fact that the woman has had significant wealth is merely implicit; it must be inferred from the fact that only well-to-do persons could afford the services of physicians, and she has paid extensively, perhaps for ten years or more. Whereas the man comes to Jesus directly and boldly requests help, the woman timidly approaches him from behind, wanting only to touch his clothing.

The woman's timidity is often attributed to her ritual uncleanness. Although she is technically unclean (presumably because of continual vaginal bleeding; see Lev. 15:25–30), and communicates uncleanness to anyone who touches her, this disability must not be exaggerated. Ordinary sexual intercourse also rendered the partners unclean. Such uncleanness was a problem only for those who wanted to participate in temple worship in Jerusalem. A much more serious problem is presented by the fact that her condition makes a normal marriage impossible, for intercourse with a menstruant constitutes a serious sin according to Leviticus 18:19 and 20:18.

It is likely, therefore, that the woman's timidity is due not to her uncleanness but to her role in a patriarchal society. Among Jews, women ranked only a little above children and slaves. They were not expected to study the Torah, and their role in worship was severely restricted. In some circles it was regarded as inappropriate for religious men to converse with women. The woman may have thought that Jesus would be offended if she approached him directly (like a man!) with a request for healing. Her fear and trembling (v. 33), however, derive not from anxiety that she has affronted Jesus, either by communicating uncleanness or by drawing on his power without permission, but from her experience of that awesome power.

Although Jesus, who according to Luke 3:23 was only about thirty years old, may well have been younger than the woman, his way of addressing her, "Daughter," should not be taken as paternalistic or demeaning but rather as affectionate and affirming. Whereas he must exhort faith in Jairus's case (v. 36), he praises the woman's faith. She has been made well not because of the magical properties of his clothing but because she firmly believed that God's power works through him. Accordingly, "Go in peace" is probably much more than a formal farewell; it implies peace with God.

The story about Jairus's daughter resumes with the arrival of news that she has just died. Jesus' response to the grieving father suggests that nothing has really changed; the power of God that was capable of curing the girl of a mortal illness can also restore her to life.

Interpreters puzzle over Jesus' statement to the mourners: "The child is not dead but sleeping" (v. 39). The simplest explanation, of course, is that the words are to be taken literally; Jesus declares that the diagnosis of death is mistaken. The laughter of the mourners supports such an understanding. In this case the story reports not a raising of the dead but the healing of a comatose patient. Most interpreters, however, follow Luke in treating this as the story of the resuscitation of a dead person (Luke 8:55). We must consequently take Jesus' words in a less literal way; he is claiming that she is not permanently dead, and therefore her temporary death is like a sleep.

One reason for the uniting of these stories is that they both concern females. In the Old Testament we read about two men being taken up into heaven (Enoch, Gen. 5:24; Elijah, 2 Kings 2:11) and about two boys and a man being raised from the dead (1 Kings 17:17–24; 2 Kings 4:18–37; 13:20–21). No woman or girl receives such treatment! This story about Jesus restoring a girl to life must have been especially meaningful to Gentile readers. In Greek and Roman society it was common practice to abandon female babies at birth. Christians refused to do this, claiming that their Lord Jesus taught them that females were of equal value in God's sight (1 Pet. 3:7).

JESUS IS REJECTED
IN HIS OWN VILLAGE
Mark 6:1–6a

6:1 He left that place and came to his hometown, and his disciples followed him. 2 On the sabbath he began to teach in the synagogue, and many who heard him were astounded. They said, "Where did this man get all this? What is this wisdom that has been given to him? What deeds of power are being done by his hands! 3 Is not this the carpenter, the son of Mary and brother of James and Joses and Judas and Simon, and are not his sisters here with us?" And they took offense at him. 4 Then Jesus said to them, "Prophets are not without honor, except in their hometown, and among their own kin, and in their own house." 5 And he could do no deed of power there, except that he laid his hands on a few sick people and cured them. 6 And he was amazed at their unbelief.

This passage provides significant information regarding Jesus' real humanity. There are Christians who regard Jesus primarily as a heavenly visitor having no essential connection to human life as we know it. There are also skeptics who take this a step further by arguing that Jesus never lived but was the figment of early Christian imagination. Both positions are countered by this report concerning Jesus' humble origins. It is entirely improbable that fabricators of a life of Jesus would have created such a story as this.

Although his hometown is not named, readers were informed in 1:9 that Jesus originated in Nazareth. The village is not mentioned in the Old Testament or in the writings of the historian Josephus, but its existence in the first century has been confirmed by archeology. Excavations indicate that in Jesus' day Nazareth was an agricultural village with a population of under five hundred.

Jesus is here identified as a *tekton*. Although "stone mason" and "wheelwright" are possible translations, the tradition that Jesus was a woodworker appears the most probable. He presumably made yokes, plows, and other instruments for farm and home. Although carpenters were not highly regarded in Greek or Roman society, in Jewish Palestine such craftsmen had local status and were comparatively well paid. We should not think of Jesus as coming from an impoverished family.

The designation "son of Mary" has often been regarded as an insult, for in that culture men were usually identified in terms of their fathers (compare John 1:45). It is proposed that this phrase reflects rumors of Jesus' illegitimacy. Others suggest that it is Mark's way of alluding to Jesus' birth from a virgin. Because Mark nowhere else refers to the tradition about Mary's miraculous conception, however, it is more likely that "son of Mary" is simply an informal way of identifying Jesus. It probably implies that Joseph has died.

The four brothers of Jesus are named after Israelite patriarchs: Jacob, Joseph, Judah, and Simeon. This suggests that the parents were pious Jews. The sisters (two or more) are not named, partly, no doubt, because they are less important in a patriarchal society. Because it was customary for Jewish women to marry at an early age, we can assume that they have families of their own. This probably explains why they are not included with their mother and brothers in Luke's description of the earliest church in Jerusalem (Acts 1:14).

From the second century until now, there have been divergent views about the brothers and sisters of Jesus. One view held that these were children of Joseph by a former marriage. No hint of this can be found in the New Testament. A second position maintained that "brothers" and "sisters," following Aramaic usage, here refer to cousins, not siblings. Because the Greek language carefully distinguished between siblings and cousins, however, it is likely that Mark intended the terms to be taken in their normal sense.

While we prize the story because it provides information regarding Jesus' origins, for Mark it is important primarily because it deals with the theme of Jesus' rejection by his own people. The series of controversy narratives in 2:1–3:6 portrays the hostility of the scribes and Pharisees toward Jesus. Here Jesus is rejected not by religious leaders but by ordinary people. They are astounded at his wisdom and deeds of power, yet they cannot acknowledge that these come from God, because they know that he is nothing special. They have watched him grow up and ply his trade, and they know his family well. Although they may not be willing to admit it, they agree with Nathanael's estimate of their village, "Can anything good come out of Nazareth?" (John 1:46). It is impossible that God should call one of them for unique service. Their lack of faith in Jesus thus turns out to be lack of faith in God.

In this respect the Nazarenes well illustrate the point made by Jesus in 4:12; they are "outsiders" who indeed look but do not perceive, who listen but do not understand. The evidence that God is at work in Jesus astounds them, and yet they resist the claim it makes upon them. "They took offense at him" is better rendered "they stumbled over him." The verb *skandalizō* (from which we get "scandalize") was used by Greek-speaking Jews with reference to falling into sin, as in 9:43, "If your hand causes you to stumble," or falling away from faith, as in 4:17 (see also 14:27, 29). Mark is suggesting not simply that the villagers were angry at Jesus but that he was the occasion of the sin of unbelief (v. 6).

In the conclusion it is noted that Jesus "could do no deed of power there" (v. 5) apart from a few healings. Mark carefully points out that Jesus is no wandering magician who overpowers skeptics with dazzling exhibitions of supernatural power. He is God's agent, as indicated by the phrase "by his hands" in verse 2. God's power is unlimited, but its expression is correlated with the response of faith. An imperfect but helpful analogy is provided by human relationships; love, to be fully experienced, must be returned. Conversely, those who expect nothing from God will not be disappointed.

THE MISSION OF THE TWELVE
Mark 6:6b–13

6:6b Then he went about among the villages teaching. ⁷ He called the twelve and began to send them out two by two, and gave them authority over the unclean spirits. [8] He ordered them to take nothing for their journey except a staff; no bread, no bag, no money in their belts; [9] but to wear sandals and not to put on two tunics. [10] He said to them, "Wherever you enter a house, stay there until you leave the place. [11] If any place will not welcome you and they refuse to hear you, as you leave, shake off the dust that is on your feet as a testimony against them." [12] So they went out and proclaimed that all should repent. [13] They cast out many demons, and anointed with oil many who were sick and cured them.

In 3:14–15 Mark reported that Jesus appointed twelve followers as apostles, that is, as persons empowered to represent him. They were to "be with him" and were eventually to be sent out to preach and to exorcize demons. In the meantime they have been with him. Now the time has come for their mission of preaching and exorcizing.

There is little doubt that such an event took place, but the tradition reported by Mark is very sketchy about details. Did the apostles travel as far as Judea? How long did the mission last? Why were they sent out only once? The tradition shows no interest in such questions. Indeed, more attention is given to what can and what cannot be taken along than to the mission itself. What comes through clearly in these travel instructions is that Jesus' representatives must be visibly self-forgetful. If they stay more than one night in a village, they must not move to better accommodations. Even a beggar's bag is denied them, so that no one may think that they hope to benefit materially from their preaching and healing.

A different version of the travel instructions appears in Luke's account of the mission of the seventy (Luke 10:2–12). Matthew 10:5–15 combines elements of the two versions. There is a striking disagreement. Whereas Matthew 10:10 forbids a staff and sandals, Mark explicitly requires them. Since it was normal for travelers to wear sandals and carry a staff (for protection against wild dogs as well as for assistance in walking), Mark's insistence on these items is astonishing. One suspects that Mark strongly opposes the more rigorous self-denial of the tradition represented by Matthew 10:10 and Luke 10:4. The tension between these two perspectives persists in modern missions. Some Christians believe that visible self-denial is necessary in order to authenticate the missionary's sincerity, while others insist that excessive self-denial arouses contempt rather than admiration. Both perspectives, however, can agree on the central point of the two Gospel traditions: Jesus' representatives must not allow the profit motive to obscure the gospel.

In view of the preceding narrative about the negative response to Jesus in Nazareth, it is not surprising that instructions are given concerning how to react in a nonaccepting community. The gesture of publicly removing the dust that represented contact with a village was a dramatic renunciation of any further responsibility. This is made explicit in Luke 10:11: "Even the dust of your town that clings to our feet, we wipe off in protest against you. Yet know this: the kingdom of God has come near." The gesture is attributed to Paul and Barnabas in Acts 13:51. In Acts 18:6 Paul shakes the dust from his clothes and declares, "Your blood be on your own heads! I am innocent."

Significant is the fact that emphasis is placed in verses 7 and 13 on exorcisms. This conforms with Mark's presentation of Jesus' own ministry, which began with an exorcism in the Capernaum synagogue (1:21–28). Just as Jesus' messianic authority is exhibited in his subjugation of evil spirits, so now that victorious authority is extended by means of his followers. In Luke's parallel narrative about the seventy, Jesus responds to the successful campaign with a cry of jubilation: "I watched Satan fall from heaven like a flash of lightning (Luke 10:18). This emphasis reminds us that being Christ's representatives today means opposing the powers of evil in his name. It is not enough to accentuate the positive; we must also negate the negative!

The mission of the twelve, like Jesus' own ministry, combined preaching with healing. Kingdom words had to be combined with kingdom deeds. Today's gospel must likewise be clothed with concern for the physical and emotional needs of those to whom it is addressed.

5. Jesus' Immense Popularity Prompts Antagonism
Mark 6:14–8:26

JOHN'S EXECUTION
FORESHADOWS THE CROSS
Mark 6:14–29

6:14 **King Herod heard of it, for Jesus' name had become known. Some were saying, "John the baptizer has been raised from the dead; and for this reason these powers are at work in him."** [15] **But others said, "It is Elijah." And others said, "It is a prophet, like one of the prophets of old."** [16] **But when Herod heard of it, he said, "John, whom I beheaded, has been raised."**
[17] **For Herod himself had sent men who arrested John, bound him, and put him in prison on account of Herodias, his brother Philip's wife, because Herod had married her.** [18] **For John had been telling Herod, "It is not lawful for you to have your brother's wife."** [19] **And Herodias had a grudge against him, and wanted to kill him. But she could not,** [20] **for Herod feared John, knowing that he was a righteous and holy man, and he protected him. When he heard him, he was greatly perplexed; and yet he liked to listen to him.** [21] **But an opportunity came when Herod on his birthday gave a banquet for his courtiers and officers and for the leaders of Galilee.** [22] **When his daughter Herodias came in and danced, she pleased Herod and his guests; and the king said to the girl, "Ask me for whatever you wish, and I will give it."** [23] **And he solemnly swore to her, "Whatever you ask me, I will give you, even half of my kingdom."** [24] **She went out and said to her mother, "What should I ask for?" She replied, "The head of John the baptizer."** [25] **Immediately she rushed back to the king and requested, "I want you to give me at once the head of John the Baptist on a platter."** [26] **The king was deeply grieved; yet out of regard for his oaths and for the guests, he did not want to refuse her.** [27] **Immediately the king sent a soldier of the guard with orders to bring John's head. He went and beheaded him in the prison,** [28] **brought his head on a platter, and gave it to the girl. Then the girl gave it to her mother.** [29] **When his disciples heard about it, they came and took his body, and laid it in a tomb.**

Mark's Gospel began with a narrative about John the Baptist, which culminated with Jesus' baptism by John. Then in 1:14 we were informed that Jesus' public ministry began after John was imprisoned. Now, by means of a flashback, we are told about the outcome of his imprisonment.

According to the first-century historian Josephus, Herod Antipas, tetrarch of Galilee, had John executed for political reasons. John's immense popularity, he felt, might lead to a revolt against the status quo. Josephus says nothing about John's criticism of Herod's marriage, but his report of the Baptist's death is preceded directly by a reference to the problem Herod created for himself by divorcing his first wife, the daughter of King Aretas of Nabatea. To avenge the insult, Aretas provoked a war with his former son-in-law and soundly defeated him. Josephus reports that some Jews felt that Herod's defeat represented divine punishment for his execution of John.

Mark's version of the execution is very different, but not necessarily in contradiction to that of Josephus. Because it was in order to marry Herodias that Herod repudiated the Nabatean princess, it is probable that any criticism of his second marriage will have been perceived as a political and not just a religious challenge. Herod doubly violated the laws of Leviticus 18 regarding marrying near relatives: Herodias was his niece as well as the wife of a living brother. If John protested against the marriage, it would not be surprising that Herodias nourished hatred toward him. Her role in the matter may have been either unknown or uninteresting to Josephus.

Neither here nor in the parallel in Matthew 14:1–12 is the daughter of Herodias named. (The manuscripts that read "his daughter Herodias" in v. 22 are clearly mistaken; the dancer is not Herod's daughter but his stepdaughter, and she would not have been given her mother's name.) From Josephus we learn that her name was Salome. She was probably a teenager at the time. Some have objected that no princess would have danced before a company of strange men, most of whom were probably drinking heavily; prostitutes were employed for such entertainment. The morals of the Herodian court, however, would not preclude such an exception, and it is unlikely that an ordinary prostitute would have captivated the king and his guests as much as the princess does in this story.

Less probable historically is Mark's portrayal of Herod's great respect for John, to whom he listened gladly (v. 20). It is possible, of course, that Herod was more ready than his wife to procrastinate over John's execution. One suspects that for Mark Herod's reluctance foreshadows Pilate's hesitation regarding the execution of Jesus.

Why does Mark include this grisly story? Undoubtedly because it anticipates Jesus' crucifixion. John is Jesus' forerunner in death as well as in life (see 1:2–8; 9:13).

The flashback is occasioned by the note that Herod (loosely designated "king"; the Romans denied him this title) has become aware of Jesus' activity. It is possible that Mark is intimating that the mission of the twelve has significantly increased Jesus' fame. Popular opinions about Jesus are reported. Some people think he is a manifestation of Elijah, who is expected to return at the end of the age (Mal. 4:5). Others regard him as a prophet comparable to the ancient prophets but not the reincarnation of any of them. Most remarkable, however, is the opinion, shared also by Herod, that Jesus is the resurrected John the Baptist. This is surprising, for John has not been dead long and Jesus was his contemporary. We are apparently not supposed to take this opinion literally. What is meant is simply that the spirit of John now rests on Jesus, just as Elijah's spirit rested on Elisha (2 Kings 2:15). Mark's readers, of course, know that all three opinions are mistaken. The issue of Jesus' identity, announced in 1:1 and reaffirmed by the voice from heaven in 1:11, will be taken up again in 8:27–30.

In the last verse (v. 29) there may be an implied criticism of Jesus' disciples. Whereas John's followers dutifully bury their master, the apostles of Jesus flee, leaving his corpse to be buried by a stranger (15:42–47).

JESUS FEEDS FIVE THOUSAND MEN
Mark 6:30–44

6:30 **The apostles gathered around Jesus, and told him all that they had done and taught.** [31] **He said to them, "Come away to a deserted place all by yourselves and rest a while." For many were coming and going, and they had no leisure even to eat.** [32] **And they went away in the boat to a deserted place by themselves.** [33] **Now many saw them going and recognized them, and they hurried there on foot from all the towns and arrived ahead of them.** [34] **As he went ashore, he saw a great crowd; and he had compassion for them, because they were like sheep without a shepherd; and he began to teach them many things.** [35] **When it grew late, his disciples came to him and said, "This is a deserted place, and the hour is now very late;** [36] **send them away so that they may go into the surrounding country and villages and buy something for themselves to eat."** [37] **But he answered them, " You give them something to eat." They said to him, "Are we to go and buy two hundred denarii worth of bread, and give it to them to eat?"** [38] **And he said to them,**

"How many loaves have you? Go and see." When they had found out, they
said, "Five, and two fish." [39] Then he ordered them to get all the people to
sit down in groups on the green grass. [40] So they sat down in groups of hundreds and of fifties. [41] Taking the five loaves and the two fish, he looked up
to heaven, and blessed and broke the loaves, and gave them to his disciples
to set before the people; and he divided the two fish among them all. [42] And
all ate and were filled; [43] and they took up twelve baskets full of broken
pieces and of the fish. [44] Those who had eaten the loaves numbered five
thousand men.

The fact that this miracle is reported in all four Gospels suggests that early
Christians found it especially meaningful. Modern readers are sometimes
less receptive, because the multiplication of loaves and fishes is so incomprehensible. Some interpreters have attempted to rescue the story by ex-
plaining it in naturalistic terms. According to one proposal, the meal was
symbolic only; each person received a small fragment of bread and was
spiritually, not physically, satisfied. A second suggestion is that the crowd
was so moved by the generosity of the boy who shared his lunch (John 6:9)
that they produced their own hidden resources and shared with any who
had none, so that all were filled. Although these are both edifying interpretations, neither does justice to the story. It is better simply to acknowledge that we cannot understand the miracle. An Old Testament an-
tecedent is provided in 2 Kings 4:42–44.

A remarkable feature of the story is that it concerns men only (*andres* in
v. 44 designates male human beings). Mark's report that the men were
arranged in groups of hundreds and fifties is reminiscent of military orga-
nization (similar to that described in the Dead Sea Scrolls). A military interpretation is also encouraged by the fact that in John's version the men's
response is an attempt to take Jesus by force to make him king (John 6:15).
In Mark, however, this revolutionary theme does not appear. Instead, the
men are made to lie down ("sit" in v. 39 is an inaccurate translation) on
the green grass in *symposia*, that is, groups gathered for table fellowship.
Reclining indicates that this is a festive occasion.

A messianic flavoring is provided by the note that Jesus was filled with
compassion because the men were like sheep without a shepherd. Although this image is used of Israel in a number of Old Testament passages,
it is most fully developed in Ezekiel 34. After excoriating Israel's shep-
herds (political leaders) for dereliction of duty, God declares: "I myself
will be the shepherd of my sheep" (Ezek. 34:15), and promises that this
will occur by means of a son of David: "I will set up over them one shepherd, my servant David, and he shall feed them" (Ezek. 34:23). Jesus' com-

passion, mirroring God's compassion for Israel, is expressed in *teaching* (v. 34). Presumably the primary subject of the teaching is the kingdom of God (see 1:14–15).

Although the miraculous meal might be seen as an anticipation of the messianic banquet at the end of the age, this possibility must not be exaggerated. There is no wine, fruit, or other delicacy appropriate to a banquet. The food provided is the simplest fare of poor Galileans—bread, with a small portion of fish as a condiment. Moreover, although all get enough to eat, the twelve basketfuls of leftovers constitute a very small amount in relation to the huge quantity of food consumed by five thousand men. Early Christians may have found in the story assurance that God would provide for their subsistence but with little extra to waste.

Mark relates this event to the mission of the twelve by giving the disciples special attention. In verse 33 he note that many saw *them* going and recognized *them*. Mark seems to be suggesting that men from the various villages the disciples have visited are able to recognize Jesus' group even though they have never seen Jesus himself. Mark may also be intimating that the disciples' mission has greatly intensified public interest in Jesus.

The RSV is less misleading than the NRSV in verse 41 by placing a comma after "blessed" ("he looked up to heaven, and blessed, and broke the loaves"). Jesus blesses not the loaves but God, the provider of all food. Jewish table prayers regularly began with the phrase "Blessed art thou, O God . . . " Jesus is represented not as imploring God for power to perform the miracle but as giving thanks to God for his goodness in supplying food.

This story reminds us that Jesus is able to do great things with the meager resources we place at his disposal. An excellent illustration of this is the great success of Habitat for Humanity. Thousands of poor folk have been provided with good housing through the dedicated efforts of volunteers, most of whom had minimal skills at the outset.

JESUS WALKS ON THE SEA
Mark 6:45–52

> 6:45 Immediately he made his disciples get into the boat and go on ahead to the other side, to Bethsaida, while he dismissed the crowd. ⁴⁶ After saying farewell to them, he went up on the mountain to pray.
>
> ⁴⁷ When evening came, the boat was out on the sea, and he was alone on the land. ⁴⁸ When he saw that they were straining at the oars against an adverse wind, he came towards them early in the morning, walking on the sea. He intended to pass them by. ⁴⁹ But when they saw him walking on the

sea, they thought it was a ghost and cried out; 50 for they all saw him and were terrified. But immediately he spoke to them and said, "Take heart, it is I; do not be afraid." 51 Then he got into the boat with them and the wind ceased. And they were utterly astounded, 52 for they did not understand about the loaves, but their hearts were hardened.

Like the preceding narrative, this story is hard for us to appropriate. First-century Christians had little difficulty believing that the God of creation would empower Jesus to transcend the laws of nature, but our modern worldview prompts skepticism. Naturalistic interpretations have been proposed, according to which Jesus was walking not on the waves but in shallow water at the north end of the lake or on the shore itself; an optical illusion created the impression reported in this story (Mark locates the incident in "the fourth watch"; that is, between 3:00 and 6:00 A.M.). Because the illusion would have been overcome as soon as the boat came near to Jesus, however, this is not a credible explanation.

Of a different order is the suggestion that this story evolved from a resurrection appearance similar to that reported in John 21. Although this possibility must be admitted, it cannot be substantiated. It is best to set aside the question of the historical basis of the story and concentrate instead on its meaning to Mark.

The most puzzling statement in Mark's version of the story (contrast Matt. 14:22–33; John 6:15–21) occurs in verse 48: "He intended to pass them by." Since Jesus' journey on the sea appears at first sight to be motivated by the disciples' distress, why does he want to go beyond them? The NIV softens the impression of callousness on Jesus' part by translating "He was about to pass by them" (similarly NEB, REB, TEV), but the problem remains: Why would Jesus pass them by if his intention was to aid them? The most satisfactory explanation is that Jesus' primary intention is not to rescue his disciples (they are not in mortal danger, as in the parallel story about Jesus calming the storm, 4:35–41) but rather to display his messianic status.

Some scholars propose that the idea of passing by echoes Old Testament passages in which God reveals himself to Moses and Elijah by passing by (Exod. 33:19–23; 34:6; 1 Kings 19:11). They also suggest that *egō eimi* (literally, "I am," translated "It is I" in v. 50) serves in the Greek translation of the Old Testament as a means by which God reveals his divine nature (Exod. 3:14; Isa. 41:4; 43:10). Since the Old Testament also speaks of God trampling the waves of the sea (Job 9:8), it is argued, this event is presented as a revelation of God. It is probably a mistake to interpret Mark in this way, however. Here we have not a revelation of God but God's revelation of Jesus as the supernaturally empowered Messiah. Divine power is his not by nature but by conferrral (see 1:10). His genuine humanity is emphasized by the act of praying (v. 46).

Mark carefully forges a link between this narrative and the preceding one by means of the conclusion: "And they were utterly astounded, for they did not understand about the loaves, but their hearts were hardened" (vv. 51–52). The disciples' astonishment at the sudden calm is due to the fact that they have totally failed to appropriate the revelation of Jesus as Messiah. The miracle of the loaves ought to have prepared them for this revelation, because in that event Jesus had presented himself as God's ultimate representative, the royal shepherd who feeds the flock on God's behalf. They had missed the significance of the miracle because "their hearts were hardened."

The theme of the disciples' spiritual blindness is important to Mark. It was introduced in paradoxical fashion in the parables discourse; the disciples were presented as "insiders" to whom the secret of the kingdom of God had been given, yet were upbraided for failure to understand the parable of the Six Seeds (4:10, 13). In the first sea miracle Jesus reproached his followers with the question, "Have you still no faith?" (4:40). The theme will appear again at various points, especially in the passages in which Jesus announces his passion (8:31–33; 9:31–33; 10:33–37). Mark's theological point is clear. Only the passion, death, and resurrection of Jesus can remove the hardness of heart that prevents his followers from understanding who he really is.

MULTIPLE HEALINGS
IN GENNESARET
Mark 6:53–56

> 6:53 **When they had crossed over, they came to land at Gennesaret and moored the boat.** [54] **When they got out of the boat, people at once recognized him,** [55] **and rushed about that whole region and began to bring the sick on mats to wherever they heard he was.** [56] **And wherever he went, into villages or cities or farms, they laid the sick in the marketplaces, and begged him that they might touch even the fringe of his cloak; and all who touched it were healed.**

Gennesaret was not a town, as readers are apt to assume, but a very fertile and densely populated plain on the west side of the Sea of Galilee. Jesus' fame is so great that he is immediately recognized, and wherever he goes he is anticipated by sick persons eager to be healed. As in the story of the hemorrhaging woman (5:25–34), many are healed simply by touching his clothing, so great is the divine power manifested in him.

The report in verse 56 that there were "marketplaces" on "farms" seems unlikely, but both translations are probably misleading. The "farms" must allude not to open acreage but to clusters of buildings constituting hamlets too small to be called villages, many of which were probably inhabited by a single extended family. The Greek word translated "marketplaces" originally referred to places of assembly; in this instance it is probably used loosely with reference to the open space in the middle of the cluster of homes and barns.

This report of Jesus' immense popularity with ordinary people serves as a foil to the immediately following story about the opposition to him on the part of scribes from Jerusalem and local Pharisees.

WHAT REALLY DEFILES
Mark 7:1–23

7:1 Now when the Pharisees and some of the scribes who had come from Jerusalem gathered around him, ² they noticed that some of his disciples were eating with defiled hands, that is, without washing them. ³ (For the Pharisees, and all the Jews, do not eat unless they thoroughly wash their hands, thus observing the tradition of the elders; ⁴ and they do not eat anything from the market unless they wash it; and there are also many other traditions that they observe, the washing of cups, pots, and bronze kettles.) ⁵ So the Pharisees and the scribes asked him, "Why do your disciples not live according to the tradition of the elders, but eat with defiled hands?" ⁶ He said to them, "Isaiah prophesied rightly about you hypocrites, as it is written,

'This people honors me with their lips,
   but their hearts are far from me;
⁷ in vain do they worship me,
   teaching human precepts as doctrines.'
⁸ You abandon the commandment of God and hold to human tradition."

⁹ Then he said to them, "You have a fine way of rejecting the commandment of God in order to keep your tradition! ¹⁰ For Moses said, 'Honor your father and your mother'; and 'Whoever speaks evil of father or mother must surely die.' ¹¹ But you say that if anyone tells father or mother, 'Whatever support you might have had from me is Corban' (that is, an offering to God)—¹² then you no longer permit doing anything for a father or mother,

13 thus making void the word of God through your tradition that you have handed on. And you do many things like this."

14 Then he called the crowd again and said to them, "Listen to me, all of you, and understand: 15 there is nothing outside a person that by going in can defile, but the things that come out are what defile."

[Please note that other ancient authorities include verse 16.]

17 When he had left the crowd and entered the house, his disciples asked him about the parable. 18 He said to them, "Then do you also fail to understand? Do you not see that whatever goes into a person from outside cannot defile, 19 since it enters, not the heart but the stomach, and goes out into the sewer?" (Thus he declared all foods clean.) 20 And he said, "It is what comes out of a person that defiles. 21 For it is from within, from the human heart, that evil intentions come: fornication, theft, murder, 22 adultery, avarice, wickedness, deceit, licentiousness, envy, slander, pride, folly. 23 All these evil things come from within, and they defile a person."

This important passage speaks to us concerning the ever present danger of separating religion from life. From the dawn of time it has been assumed that it is right and proper to honor the gods (or God) by the performance of various acts of piety, including prayers, sacrifices, and the observance of specified taboos. It was also assumed, of course, that such piety could win the favor of the gods and secure desired blessings. Religion that focuses on piety, however, is apt to treat ethics as a subordinate or extraneous concern.

The prophets of Israel vigorously attacked this view of religion, insisting that God was above all else a moral God and that the proper worship of God requires ethical living (Isa. 1:10–17; Amos 5:21–24; Mic. 6:6–8). In Mark 7 Jesus strongly affirms this prophetic perspective.

At issue is the ritual of rinsing the hands before eating. Nothing in the Old Testament requires this of lay people, as acknowledged by the opponents in verse 5, when they attribute the practice to "the tradition of the elders"; that is, to the Pharisees' oral tradition rather than to the written law. Because ritual washing was required of priests, pious Jews had begun to adopt the habit, on the principle of Exodus 19:6, "You shall be to me a kingdom of priests and a holy nation" (RSV). Mark probably exaggerates when he reports that "all the Jews" engage in the practice, however; it is unlikely that there was general conformity with the rule at this early date.

Jesus responds to the criticism of his disciples' piety by attacking the piety of the opponents with the words of Isaiah 29:13. Mark's rendering of the quotation depends in part on the Septuagint, the Greek translation of the Old Testament, but the point is the same as in the Hebrew text;

people are worshiping God with their lips, not their hearts, because they are more interested in human traditions about piety than in God's moral will.

This charge is illustrated by reference to a specific practice. According to Numbers 30:2, a valid vow cannot be annulled, on the assumption that failure to keep a vow constitutes a serious affront to God's holiness. In Judges 11, Jephthah must keep his vow, even though it means sacrificing his beloved daughter. The law of oaths was subject to serious abuse, however. An angry son could make a vow prohibiting his parents from benefiting from any of his possessions, using the Corban formula (v. 11). This involved a legal fiction; if all his possessions had truly been offered to God, he himself could not benefit from them. Even if he later repented, however, the vow could not be annulled; like Jephthah and his daughter, he and his parents had to suffer the consequences. The result, of course, is that God's will that children care for their parents, as enunciated in the Fifth Commandment (Exod. 20:12; Deut. 5:16), is treated as if it were null and void.

The law of oaths was biblically based, but the Corban practice was a matter of human tradition. It was the responsibility of scribal tradition to subordinate one biblical law to another when they were in conflict, as in the case of performing the work of circumcision on the sabbath (see John 7:22). Apparently the scribes taught that the law of vows took precedence over the Fifth Commandment, on the assumption that the former concerned an affront to God whereas the latter involved humans only. Jesus insists that this constitutes a terrible misunderstanding of their religion. To refuse to support one's parents is a far more serious affront to God's holiness than the nonobservance of an immoral vow that should never have been made in the first place. (In this connection it should be remembered that Jesus vigorously opposed the making of vows; see Matt. 5:33–37.) Eventually the rabbis, the successors of the scribes, agreed with Jesus' view and permitted the annulment of vows of nonsupport.

In verse 14 we return to the issue of defilement. The laws of purity constituted an essential feature of Israel's piety. At the end of a chapter in Leviticus specifying which animals, birds, fish, and "creeping things" are taboo, we read this explanation: "You shall not make yourselves detestable with any creature that swarms; you shall not defile yourselves with them, and so become unclean. For I am the LORD your God; sanctify yourselves therefore, and be holy, for I am holy" (Lev. 11:43–44). For example, to eat pork, meat from an unclean animal, rendered Jews "unclean" or "defiled" and thus made them unfit to worship the holy God.

Jesus' response to the purity issue is once again consonant with the prophetic tradition in which ritual is subordinated to ethics. The statement in verse 15, with its explication in verses 18–23, appears radical and is so understood by Mark's parenthetical comment in verse 19 ("Thus he declared all foods clean"). The inference is undoubtedly correct, just as it is fair to say that Paul's declaration in Galatians 3:28, "There is no longer slave or free," implies the abolition of slavery. It would be incorrect, however, to say that Paul *taught* that all slaves should be emancipated. In the same way it would be a serious mistake to assert that Jesus proclaimed the abolition of the food and purity laws of the Torah. There is not the slightest evidence that Jesus encouraged his followers to eat pork. The early church would not have struggled so painfully over eating with Gentiles if Jesus had unambiguously "declared all foods clean" (see Gal. 2:11–14). The statement in verse 15 is to be understood in conformity with the pattern found in Hosea 6:6, "For I desire steadfast love and not sacrifice, the knowledge of God rather than burnt offerings." The prophet by no means intends that the sacrificial system be abolished; he insists only that ritual be subordinated to ethics. Jesus' meaning is: "What *really* defiles people is not what they eat but what they do."

This passage is cited by some Christian scholars as evidence that Jesus attacked the law of Moses (and was subsequently crucified for this crime). Jewish scholars, however, generally disagree with this view. They point out that Rabbi Jochanan ben Zakkai, one of the most important rabbis of the first century, declared with respect to another cause of defilement, contact with a corpse: "It is not the dead that defiles nor the water that purifies! The Holy One, blessed be he, merely says: 'I have laid down a statute, I have issued a decree. You are not allowed to transgress my decree,' as it is written, 'This is the statute of the law' (Num. 19:2)" (see Davies, *The Setting of the Sermon on the Mount*, 171). By denying that unclean foods actually defile, Jesus does not annul the laws of purity; he merely subordinates piety to ethics. It is true that he was not concerned about keeping himself constantly in a state of ritual purity; he ate with sinners who were probably unclean (2:15), touched a leper (1:41), and did not object when a hemorrhaging woman communicated uncleanness to him. There is no evidence, however, that he taught his followers systematically to disobey all the purity rules.

Like us, Mark's Gentile readers were not concerned about Jewish food and purity regulations (as indicated by the fact that Mark must provide elementary information in vv. 3–4). Why, then, is so much space given to this controversy? Perhaps Mark feared that Gentile Christians would fall into the same trap of subordinating ethics to piety. That danger faces us day by day as we strive to work out our answer to the question "What does it mean to be truly religious?"

A GENTILE WOMAN PERSUADES JESUS
TO HEAL HER DAUGHTER
Mark 7:24–30

> 7:24 **From there he set out and went away to the region of Tyre. He entered a house and did not want anyone to know he was there. Yet he could not escape notice, 25 but a woman whose little daughter had an unclean spirit immediately heard about him, and she came and bowed down at this feet. 26 Now the woman was a Gentile, of Syrophoenician origin. She begged him to cast the demon out of her daughter. 27 He said to her, "Let the children be fed first, for it is not fair to take the children's food and throw it to the dogs." 28 But she answered him, "Sir, even the dogs under the table eat the children's crumbs." 29 Then he said to her, "For saying that, you may go— the demon has left your daughter." 30 So she went home, found the child lying on the bed, and the demon gone.**

No motive is provided for Jesus' trip into pagan territory. Some have speculated that he was fleeing either from the Jerusalem authorities of verse 1 or from Herod Antipas (see Luke 13:31). Nothing in the Gospels supports this conjecture. The story itself makes it clear that his purpose was not to preach the gospel to Gentiles. The house in which he stayed (v. 24) undoubtedly belonged to Jews. "The region of Tyre," which extended from the Mediterranean to Lake Huleh, and thus bordered on Galilee, contained a significant Jewish population. Jesus' intention may therefore have been to bring his message to Jews beyond the political borders of Jewish Palestine. Another proposal is that he took his disciples to a remote settlement so that he could teach them without the distraction of the Galilean crowds. Against this suggestion is the claim of 3:8 that Jesus' fame had spread to the territories of Tyre and Sidon. The story itself supports this: Jesus cannot remain incognito, and a Gentile woman finds him immediately.

The exorcism itself is remarkable in two respects: (1) it is accomplished at a distance, without any word of rebuke being addressed to the demon; and (2) Jesus exhibits supernatural knowledge concerning the success of the exorcism. The first feature is paralleled in Matthew 8:5–13 by the healing of the centurion's servant, who is presumably also a Gentile. The second feature appears more commonly in the Fourth Gospel (for example, John 4:46–54). The miracle itself, however, is unemphasized; attention is focused rather on the dialogue involving Jesus and the woman.

Many readers are distressed by the harshness of Jesus' refusal of the desperate woman's request (v. 27). The contrast between "children" and "dogs" suggests that she and other Gentiles are not worthy of Jesus' consideration. Three different attempts have been made by commentators to deal with this difficult saying.

One proposal is that the saying, which appears to us to be so out of character for Jesus, is inauthentic. It was created and attributed to Jesus by a conservative Jewish Christian who vigorously opposed the admission of Gentiles to the church (see Acts 11:2–3). The story, with its happy ending, was subsequently created by moderate Jewish Christians in order to take the sting out of the saying.

A second suggestion is that the saying was not nearly as harsh in its original setting. It was probably (it is proposed) a well-known proverb, roughly equivalent to our saying, "Charity begins at home." The reference to dogs is thus not abusive but simply a feature of the proverb. Jesus' statement may not have been intended as an outright refusal but rather as a stimulus to further conversation and as a test of the woman's faith.

More satisfactory is the third approach, which acknowledges the harshness of the saying and attempts to understand it in terms of Jesus' view of his mission. In Matthew's version of this story Jesus declares to his disciples, "I was sent only to the lost sheep of the house of Israel" (Matt. 15:24). The same restriction is placed on the disciples in Matthew 10:5–6, "Go nowhere among the Gentiles, and enter no town of the Samaritans, but go rather to the lost sheep of the house of Israel." This seems to be a matter of fact. The four Gospels, all of which were written for primarily Gentile audiences, indicate that Jesus' contacts with Gentiles were few and exceptional. It is not that he cared nothing about the fate of the Gentiles. Like other Jews, he was undoubtedly convinced that God would include at least a portion of the Gentiles in the Age to Come, as prophesied in Isaiah 2:2–4. He apparently felt absolutely certain that his mission was restricted to Israel. Paul, the apostle to the Gentiles, acknowledges this in Romans 15:8, "Christ has become a servant of the circumcised . . . in order that he might confirm the promises given to the patriarchs."

It must be noted that Jesus uttered "harsh" words to Jews also. One of the harshest is his response to a would-be follower who begs time to bury his father: "Follow me, and let the dead bury their own dead" (Matt. 8:22). Another is reported in Luke 10:4, "Greet no one on the road."

Jesus prohibits a normal and expected courtesy! Both sayings emphasize the extreme urgency of his mission. Time is of the essence. His statement to the Syrophoenician woman must be read in this light.

The woman's spirited and humble response causes Jesus to make an exception to his rule. Her use of the same symbols, "children" and "dogs" for Jews and Gentiles, acknowledges the priority of Israel in God's plan of salvation, as enunciated by Paul: "to the Jew first and also to the Greek" (Rom. 1:16). By responding positively to her expression of faith, Jesus acknowledges her as the vanguard of the Gentiles whom God will include in the kingdom.

JESUS HEALS A DEAF MAN
Mark 7:31–37

> 7:31 **Then he returned from the region of Tyre, and went by way of Sidon towards the Sea of Galilee, in the region of the Decapolis. 32 They brought to him a deaf man who had an impediment in his speech; and they begged him to lay his hand on him. 33 He took him aside in private, away from the crowd, and put his fingers into his ears, and he spat and touched his tongue. 34 Then looking up to heaven, he sighed and said to him, "Ephphatha," that is, "Be opened." 35 And immediately his ears were opened, his tongue was released, and he spoke plainly. 36 Then Jesus ordered them to tell no one; but the more he ordered them, the more zealously they proclaimed it. 37 They were astounded beyond measure, saying, "He has done everything well; he even makes the deaf to hear and the mute to speak."**

Scholars have sometimes accused Mark of ignorance concerning Palestinian geography, for he has Jesus return to the Sea of Galilee "by way of Sidon," a very circuitous route indeed. The city of Sidon was twenty miles north of Tyre. In Mark's defense, it must be remembered that he probably means the territory of Sidon, not the city itself. Accordingly, he suggests that Jesus made a large arc, northeast in the direction of Damascus and then southward on the east side of the Jordan valley, through the area belonging to the Decapolis, ending up on the east shore of the Sea of Galilee. His point seems to be that Jesus remains in pagan territory during the entirety of this extensive trip.

This does not mean, however, that the man who is healed in this story is a Gentile. In view of the fact that Jesus' healing of a Gentile was presented in the preceding story as truly exceptional, we must assume that the deaf man, if he were a non-Jew, would be identified as such. Presumably the people who bring him are also Jewish. A significant Jewish population was to be found in the area controlled by the Decapolis (see my comments on 5:1–20). For Mark and his Gentile readers, of course, the location of this story in Gentile territory may have been symbolic of the future mission in which Gentile ears would be opened to hear the gospel and tongues loosed to praise God for the salvation wrought in Jesus.

It is generally believed by scholars that both Matthew and Luke developed their Gospels on the basis of the structure and contents of Mark. It is interesting that this and the parallel narrative in 8:22–26 are the only Markan miracle stories that appear in neither Matthew nor Luke. One explanation is that only in these stories does Jesus employ saliva in order to effect a cure, instead of healing with a word of command or a touch; perhaps the later Gospel writers thought that the use of saliva reduced Jesus to the status of a run-of-the-mill magical healer. The Fourth Evangelist, however, who presents Jesus as nothing less than the Word of God incarnate, is not averse to attributing to Jesus the application to a blind man's eyes of mud made with saliva (John 9:6). In the ancient world it was widely believed that saliva had curative powers, especially the saliva of a powerful or holy person.

The deaf man is not presented as mute from birth but as able to speak with difficulty, that is, with some impediment that makes his words hard to understand. Presumably his ability to speak clearly deteriorated when he lost his hearing.

Privacy is required by Jesus both here and in the parallel story in 8:22–26. No reason is given. The explanation that this reflects the desire of the Hellenistic magician to keep his methods secret is very improbable, in view of the openness attributed to Jesus in most of the miracle stories. Similarly, the use in verse 36 of *ephphatha* (probably Aramaic, possibly Hebrew), a foreign word to most Gentiles, does not constitute a parallel to the magicians' use of incomprehensible foreign phrases as part of their hocus pocus. *Ephphatha* was comprehensible to Jesus' audience and is translated for the benefit of Mark's. Its closest parallel is offered instead by the Aramaic phrase spoken by Jesus to Jairus's daughter, which is also translated (5:41). The gestures of looking up to heaven and groaning (v. 34) are also not to be associated with magical practice. In Mark 6:41 Jesus looks up to heaven in prayerful expectation of divine help in feeding the multitude. Groaning or sighing is elsewhere attributed to Jesus only at Mark 8:12. There it reflects Jesus' anger at sin. Here it is his angry response to disease and physical handicaps that afflict God's children.

As in 1:40–45, Jesus' stern insistence on silence is immediately disobeyed. Those in the crowd nearest to the healed man pass the joyful news to those further back until the whole multitude, in the style of the chorus in a Greek drama, can proclaim, "He has done everything well; he even makes the deaf to hear and the mute to speak" (v. 37). Because they refer to deaf and mute people in the plural (which is hidden in most English translations), they are making a statement about Jesus' ministry as a whole. Many scholars see in this verse an echo of Isaiah 35:5–6, a passage generally regarded by Jesus' contemporaries as a prophecy concerning the messianic age. By fulfilling the prophecy that the deaf will hear and the mute speak, Jesus reveals himself as God's Messiah. Although the crowd does not unambiguously confess Jesus as the Messiah, in Mark's view their utterance foreshadows Peter's confession in 8:29.

Like early interpreters, modern Christians can appropriate the narrative symbolically. We too have had our ears opened to hear the gospel; we too have had our tongues loosed to speak God's praise. If not, we should pray for a miracle!

JESUS FEEDS FOUR THOUSAND
Mark 8:1–10

8:1 In those days when there was again a great crowd without anything to eat, he called his disciples and said to them, 2 "I have compassion for the crowd, because they have been with me now for three days and have nothing to eat. 3 If I send them away hungry to their homes, they will faint on the way—and some of them have come from a great distance." 4 His disciples replied, "How can one feed these people with bread here in the desert?" 5 He asked them, "How many loaves do you have?" They said, "Seven." 6 Then he ordered the crowd to sit down on the ground; and he took the seven loaves, and after giving thanks he broke them and gave them to his disciples to distribute; and they distributed them to the crowd. 7 They had also a few small fish; and after blessing them, he ordered that these too should be distributed. 8 They ate and were filled; and they took up the broken pieces left over, seven baskets full. 9 Now there were about four thousand people. And he sent them away. 10 And immediately he got into the boat with his disciples and went to the district of Dalmanutha.

Like the earlier feeding of five thousand, this story is difficult for many modern readers. We find it easier to believe in Jesus' healings than in the satisfaction of so many appetites with seven loaves and a few small fish. (For various approaches to the feeding miracles, see my comments on 6:30–44.)

Scholars are inclined to regard this story as a "doublet" of the earlier one. They reason that, despite differences in detail, the stories are so similar that they are probably divergent reports of the same event (similar differences in detail distinguish the version in John 6:1–14 from those found in the other Gospels).

Early interpreters, however, asked not why there were two reports but why there were two events. It was frequently proposed that the first feeding involved Jews, the second Gentiles. Support for this understanding was found in the numbers; the number five in five thousand stood for the Five Books of Moses, and the twelve baskets of leftovers represented the twelve tribes of Israel. In the feeding of the four thousand, four stands for the four corners of the earth or the four points of the compass, thus designating the pagan world, and the seven baskets point to the seventy nations, into which the human race was thought to be divided.

Although modern scholars are not nearly so impressed with this numerical typology, some are convinced on other grounds that Mark presents the second event as involving Gentiles. The setting is clearly in pagan territory on the east side of the lake (see my comments on 7:31–37). The phrase "from afar" ("from a great distance" in the NRSV) echoes, it is suggested, the Jewish way of referring to Gentiles (see Eph. 2:13). The reference in verse 7 to blessing the fish reflects Gentile practice; Jews blessed not food but God, the giver of food. None of these features conclusively point to a Gentile feeding, however. Although the story is set in Gentile territory, many Jews were to be found there. In view of the fact that Mark writes for a predominantly Gentile church, it is exceedingly improbable that he would have failed to make it explicit that Jesus here ministers to Gentiles. This would be truer yet if, as some propose, Jesus here initiates table fellowship of Jews with Gentiles. The story of the Syrophoenician woman makes it absolutely clear that Jesus' ministering to Gentiles was limited to a few exceptional cases (see my comments on 7:24–30). Moreover, "those from afar" constitute only a part of the crowd, and it is implied that they are in the gravest danger of weakness from hunger. The words, therefore, should be taken in their normal sense. The fact that some have come from a great distance emphasizes Jesus' fame and popularity (compare 3:7–8).

Because he reports two feedings, the disciples' skeptical question in verse 4 must have theological significance for Mark. After having experienced the first feeding, have the disciples still no faith in Jesus' ability to provide? This theme will be developed more explicitly in 8:14–21.

Some find eucharistic overtones in this story, especially in view of the fact that the fish course has been separated from the eating of the bread

(v. 7). Such a possibility cannot be ruled out, but very little suggests that Mark intended his readers to be reminded of the Lord's Supper.

The story concludes with the report that Jesus and his disciples crossed the sea to Dalmanutha. There is no other reference to this place in the Bible or outside it. Scholars conjecture that it was on the west side of the lake, perhaps in the vicinity of Magdala (Magdala is substituted in some manuscripts, probably because it was better known; other manuscripts, have Magadan, as in the parallel at Matt. 15:39, but Magadan is also unknown). It is probable that Mark assumed that Dalmanutha was in Galilee, because the Pharisees appear immediately (they are never mentioned when Jesus is in pagan territory).

TWO KINDS OF UNFAITH
Mark 8:11–21

8:11 The Pharisees came and began to argue with him, asking him for a sign from heaven, to test him. [12] And he sighed deeply in his spirit and said, "Why does this generation ask for a sign? Truly I tell you, no sign will be given to this generation." [13] And he left them, and getting into the boat again, he went across to the other side.

[14] Now the disciples had forgotten to bring any bread; and they had only one loaf with them in the boat. [15] And he cautioned them, saying, "Watch out—beware of the yeast of the Pharisees and the yeast of Herod." [16] They said to one another, "It is because we have no bread," [17] And becoming aware of it, Jesus said to them, "Why are you talking about having no bread? Do you still not perceive or understand? Are your hearts hardened? [18] Do you have eyes, and fail to see? Do you have ears, and fail to hear? And do you not remember? [19] When I broke the five loaves for the five thousand, how many baskets full of broken pieces did you collect?" They said to him, "Twelve." [20] "And the seven for the four thousand, how many baskets full of broken pieces did you collect?" And they said to him, "Seven," [21] Then he said to them, "Do you not yet understand?"

Although two different incidents are reported in this passage, they are linked by a common motif—lack of faith. The first scene involves the Pharisees, the second the disciples. There is thus a parallel with the parables discourse, which is also concerned with spiritual insight, and which has regard, first, to the "outsiders" who see but do not perceive (4:11–12), and then to the disciples, who also do not understand until Jesus explains everything to them (4:13, 34).

The Pharisees come to "test" Jesus (as they will again with respect to other matters in 10:2; 12:15). The underlying Greek verb can also mean "tempt" (as in 1:13, "tempted by Satan"). It is possible that both of these overlapping meanings are present here. By demanding a sign the Pharisees may, in Mark's view, be trying to seduce Jesus into sin, for Deuteronomy 6:16 (quoted by Jesus in response to Satan in Matthew 4:7; Luke 4:12) prohibits putting God to the test. For Jesus to implore God to provide a sign from heaven merely in order to satisfy his opponents would indeed be sinful.

Jesus' miraculous healings have been signs of God's power, but for those without faith such evidence is meaningless; indeed, in a previous passage the Pharisees ascribe Jesus' exorcisms to collusion with the powers of evil (3:22). Jesus' miracles are in fact ambiguous; they may *elicit* faith but they do not *demand* faith, because faith that is based on demonstrable fact is not faith. By testing Jesus, the Pharisees seem to be saying, "If you can produce incontrovertible evidence by means of a cosmic sign, then we will acknowledge you as God's authorized representative." They refuse faith and demand knowledge! Cosmic signs are promised in 13:24–25, but then it will be too late for faith; at that time the victorious Jesus will return from heaven to gather the elect (13:26–27).

Jesus' immediate response is to sigh or groan deeply in his spirit. This strange phrase may reflect the prophet's excitement before delivering a strong oracle of judgment. More probably it is intended to indicate Jesus' angry sorrow at the failure of many to respond in faith to what God has been doing through him. Although it is the Pharisees who bring the demand, Jesus regards them as representative of "this generation." In some contexts "generation" has a theologically negative connotation with respect to a specific generation that is lacking in faith and/or disobedient to God (Deut. 1:35; Psalm 95:10; Mark 9:19).

The negative promise of verse 12 is more emphatic in the original than in our English translation. "Truly" is a very weak rendering of "Amen," a word used by Jews and Christians at the end of a prayer or hymn with the meaning "So be it." Jesus alone used "Amen" at the beginning of statements, thereby investing them with special emphasis and authority. "Amen" was also used by Jesus in 3:28, in another dispute with the Pharisees.

The next scene is set on a boat during a trip that will apparently terminate at Bethsaida (8:22). Mark tells us that the disciples have neglected to obtain a sufficient number of loaves of bread for the journey. In the warning of verse 15, "Watch out—beware of the yeast of the Pharisees and the yeast of Herod," yeast is used as a negative metaphor (as in 1 Cor. 5:6; Gal. 5:9). It speaks of the way poisonous attitudes and behavior can spread in groups and communities (and churches!). The metaphor is used positively in Matthew 13:33; the kingdom spreads secretly like leaven in dough.

The saying about yeast falls on deaf ears, because the disciples are arguing with one another about the forgotten loaves (a literal rendering of the best manuscripts is: "And they argued with one another, because they did not have loaves"). Without reiterating his warning, Jesus responds to the disciples' concern with a series of questions challenging their lack of faith. Although the saying about leaven seems to be ignored in the rest of the narrative, it is implicitly present: Jesus warns his disciples of the danger of falling into the kind of unfaith exhibited by both the religious Pharisees and the worldly but superstitious Herod (see 6:14–16; Luke 23:8).

The second half of the Gospel, which begins at 8:27, emphasizes Jesus' teaching of the twelve in anticipation of his passion and resurrection. In this penultimate narrative of the first half of the book, Mark brings to a head a theme that he has been developing since 4:11–13. The disciples, in contrast to the outsiders, have been given the secret of the kingdom of God and yet they seriously lack faith and understanding. At the end of the tandem miracles of feeding the five thousand and walking on the sea, Mark comments on the disciples' unjustified astonishment: "They did not understand about the loaves, but their hearts were hardened" (6:52). If they had responded with faith, they would not have been so surprised.

In this passage Jesus does not condemn the disciples for their lack of faith. Instead of using declarative sentences—"You have eyes, and fail to see!"—he uses probing questions that are meant to encourage, not extinguish, the little faith the disciples already have, while at the same time pointing to the danger of falling back into unfaith.

One tool of this encouragement is remembering; Jesus reminds them of the amazing things God has done through him. The theme of remembering was and is an indispensable ingredient of Israel's faith. The great festivals commemorate the exodus, the giving of the Torah, and other deeds of God's grace. "One generation shall laud your works to another, and shall declare your mighty acts" (Psalm 145:4). Mark warns his readers that instead of worrying about their daily bread they should renew their trust in God by remembering all that God has done.

This insight concerning the nourishment of faith by remembering was captured in an old gospel hymn: "Count your many blessings, name them one by one, and it will surprise you what the Lord hath done."

JESUS HEALS A BLIND MAN
NEAR BETHSAIDA
Mark 8:22–26

8:22 **They came to Bethsaida. Some people brought a blind man to him and begged him to touch him.** [23] **He took the blind man by the hand and led him out of the village; and when he had put saliva on his eyes and laid his hands on him, he asked him, "Can you see anything?"** [24] **And the man looked up and said, "I can see people, but they look like trees, walking."** [25] **Then Jesus laid his hands on his eyes again; and he looked intently and his sight was restored, and he saw everything clearly.** [26] **Then he sent him away to his home, saying, "Do not even go into the village."**

According to John 1:44, Bethsaida was the *city* of Peter, Andrew, and Philip. Mark (8:23, 26) refers to it as a *village*. The confusion is understandable. Bethsaida was a fishing village on the northeastern shore of the Sea of Galilee, just east of the point where the Jordan empties into the lake. Herod Philip, tetrarch of Gaulanitis, greatly enlarged Bethsaida by building a new city just north of it, which he called Julias (in honor of the daughter of Augustus Caesar). In terms of population, the complex of Bethsaida and Julias constituted a city, but Bethsaida proper seems to have retained the political status of a village. Although located in Gaulanitis, a predominantly Gentile territory, Bethsaida seems to have been largely Jewish. Indeed, it is referred to loosely as Galilean in John 12:21, and in Matthew 11:21 it is mentioned as the site of extensive healing activity on Jesus' part.

Like the parallel miracle story in 7:31–37, this one is found only in Mark. As in the earlier narrative, Jesus first removes the patient from public attention and then uses saliva and touch to accomplish the healing. In both cases Jesus demands silence. In the first instance that demand is totally ignored. Here Jesus insists that the man whose sight has been restored must go home without returning to the village. This assumes either that the man lives elsewhere or that his home is on the outskirts rather than at the center of the village. As in previous instances, the insistence on silence is meant to show that Jesus did not perform healings in order to gain publicity or earn a fortune like other itinerant healers. He performs healings as God's Son (1:1, 11), herald of the kingdom of God (1:14–15).

This is the only miracle story in the four Gospels in which Jesus heals in two stages. From our perspective this feature appears to diminish Jesus' power, but from the standpoint of first-century readers it probably enhanced his status. The question "Can you see anything?" indicates that this is a particularly difficult case. The fact that he is able to restore the man's vision completely demonstrates that Jesus is successful even in such cases.

Many scholars believe that Mark found this story paired with the healing of the deaf man (7:31–37) and that he placed them in different places in his Gospel for theological reasons. Be that as it may, it is safe to assume that the story was undated, that is, that Mark felt free to place it at any point in Jesus' Galilean ministry. It appears that he placed the cure of the blind man precisely here because of the blindness of the disciples, which was hinted at in 8:18 and which will be exhibited by Peter in 8:32. Although the disciples come to see Jesus as the Messiah, their sight is very imperfect; they cannot accept the fact that the Messiah must suffer, die, and be raised. This blindness will be cured only by the miracle of the resurrection.

3. Preparing the Disciples for the Passion

Mark 8:27–10:52

6. The First Passion Announcement and the Transfiguration
Mark 8:27–9:29

PETER'S CONFESSION PROMPTS THE FIRST PASSION ANNOUNCEMENT
Mark 8:27–9:1

8:27 Jesus went on with his disciples to the villages of Caesarea Philippi; and on the way he asked his disciples, "Who do people say that I am?" 28 And they answered him, "John the Baptist; and others, Elijah; and still others, one of the prophets." 29 He asked them, "But who do you say that I am?" Peter answered him, "You are the Messiah." 30 And he sternly ordered them not to tell anyone about him.

31 Then he began to teach them that the Son of Man must undergo great suffering, and be rejected by the elders, the chief priests, and the scribes, and be killed, and after three days rise again. 32 He said all this quite openly. And Peter took him aside and began to rebuke him. 33 But turning and looking at his disciples, he rebuked Peter and said, "Get behind me, Satan! For you are setting your mind not on divine things but on human things."

34 He called the crowd with his disciples, and said to them, "If any want to become my followers, let them deny themselves and take up their cross and follow me. 35 For those who want to save their life will lose it, and those who lose their life for my sake, and for the sake of the gospel, will save it. 36 For what will it profit them to gain the whole world and forfeit their life? 37 Indeed, what can they give in return for their life? 38 Those who are ashamed of me and of my words in this adulterous and sinful generation, of them the Son of Man will also be ashamed when he comes in the glory of his Father with the holy angels."

9:1 And he said to them, "Truly I tell you, there are some standing here who will not taste death until they see that the kingdom of God has come with power."

With this passage we reach the watershed of Mark's Gospel. As "a passion narrative with an extended introduction" (see the Introduction), the

Gospel has from the very beginning implicitly presented Jesus as the Messiah who must die. Now the implicit will be rendered explicit.

The scene is set near "the villages of Caesarea Philippi." Philip's Caesarea (thus distinguished from the Caesarea that his father, Herod the Great, built on the Mediterranean coast; see Acts 10:1) had been recently expanded by Philip to serve as the capital of his tetrarchy. Situated almost twenty-five miles north of the Sea of Galilee on the lower slopes of Mount Hermon, it was primarily a pagan city and featured a magnificent temple in honor of the emperor. Jesus is represented as visiting not the city itself but the surrounding villages, where a Jewish population was to be found. Mark gives no motive for the trip; we are probably to assume that this is another missionary tour. This possibility is enhanced by Mark's introduction of a crowd in verse 34.

The question of Jesus' identity was raised in 6:14–15. Herod claimed that John the Baptist had been resurrected and had empowered Jesus to perform miracles (perhaps on the analogy of Elijah's spirit resting on Elisha; 2 Kings 2:9, 15). Some conjectured that Jesus was the reincarnation of Elijah, who had performed astonishing miracles (1 Kings 17–18), or as the eschatological Elijah of Malachi 4:5–6, because of Jesus' role in the spiritual renewal movement. Others regarded him as a prophet like one of Israel's ancient prophets. These opinions are now rehearsed in order to provide a foil for the disciples' estimate of Jesus' role.

Because of Matthew's emphasis on the revelatory significance of Peter's utterance (Matt. 16:16–19), this passage is usually referred to as "Peter's Confession." This may not be fair to Mark's perspective, however. Here Peter seems to speak on behalf of all the disciples, and there is no suggestion that they have only at this moment come to regard Jesus as the Messiah. Indeed, there is here no conflict with John 1:41, according to which Andrew announced even before Peter met Jesus, "We have found the Messiah."

"Christ" is the English rendering of *christos*, the nearest equivalent in Greek to the Hebrew word *mashiach*, "anointed." In ancient Israel, kings were anointed with oil during the coronation ceremony. In the books of Samuel, the king is frequently referred to as "the Lord's anointed" (1 Sam. 24:6, 10; 26:9, 16; 2 Sam. 1:14; 19:21). Similarly, in the royal psalms the king is identified as God's anointed ("his anointed," Psalm 2:2; 18:50; "my anointed one," 132:17; "your anointed," 89:38, 51; 132:10). Although the technical term "the Anointed," that is, the Messiah, does not occur in the Old Testament and is rare in Jewish literature prior to the time of Jesus, there is no doubt that the idea was widespread among first-century Jews.

The Messiah was usually conceived of as David's successor, who would be supernaturally empowered to punish wicked exploiters and exalt the poor, and thus establish a golden age of peace and prosperity. Because of Roman power, the Messiah was often thought of as a military general capable of leading his people to victory over the hated Gentiles. Just a century after Jesus' death, the leader of the Second Jewish Revolt was hailed as the Messiah by the most famous rabbi of the time.

When the disciples identify Jesus as the Messiah, they do not mean that he is a military leader who will conduct a successful war against the Romans. Rather, they believe that he is the man destined by God to put down the oppressors by means of supernatural power, as prophesied in Isaiah 11:4, "He shall strike the earth with the rod of his mouth, and with the breath of his lips he shall kill the wicked."

Jesus' stern command that the disciples keep silent about his role as Messiah is historically comprehensible. If word of this got around, his life would be in jeopardy before his work was done. More important, Jesus probably believed that only God could proclaim him Messiah, or that he could publicly claim this role only at a moment ordained by God. (In the early 1990s, members of the ultraorthodox Jewish Lubavitcher sect strongly hinted that their leader, Rabbi Menachem Schneerson, was the Messiah, but they stopped short of an open identification.)

The disciples' confession provides the occasion for the first passion announcement: The Son of man must suffer, be rejected, die, and be resurrected ("must" implies divine necessity). In referring to himself indirectly as "the Son of Man" Jesus is not suggesting that he prefers the title "the Son of Man" to "the Messiah." Nowhere in the Gospel does "the Son of Man" serve as a title; it conveys nothing concerning Jesus' role to any audience (see my comments on 2:1–12). It is a peculiar self-designation, used normally in statements about Jesus' vocation and destiny, where the use of first-person language ("I") might appear immodest. Here as always it is clear that "the Son of Man" refers to Jesus, not to someone else.

What is shockingly new in the passion announcement is that the Messiah must suffer and die. As far as we know, such a notion had never occurred in earlier Jewish thinking. The Messiah was supposed to inflict suffering, not experience it himself. Of what possible good could a dead Messiah be?

This first passion announcement, like the second (9:31) and third (10:33–34), includes the promise that Jesus will not remain a dead Messiah because he will be resurrected "after three days." To modern readers this prediction seems to be in conflict with the details of the story (Jesus died on Friday and arose on Sunday; see 15:42; 16:2; that is, "on the third day," as in the parallels in Matt. 16:21; Luke 9:22). According to the Semitic reckoning of time, parts of days counted as whole days (see Gen. 42:17–18; 2 Chron. 10:5, 12). "After three days" may have been used by Jesus as a vague reference to a short period of time, as in our colloquial expression "a couple of days." Perhaps he intended an allusion to Hosea 6:2 "After two days he will revive us; on the third day he will raise us up, that we may live before him." An early Aramaic paraphrase of Hosea interpreted this verse as referring to the general resurrection. Despite the fact that Jesus "said all this quite openly," the disciples are apparently unable to comprehend and believe the promise of his resurrection. Peter responds only to that part of the announcement that deals with suffering and death. The same will be true of the response to the second announcement (9:31–32).

Mark emphasizes that Jesus spoke "openly," in order to stress that Peter's response is not due to misunderstanding of the words but resistance to the idea. Although Peter's rebuke prompts a harsh counter-rebuke, we are not to think of Peter as more resistant than the other disciples. Following each of the other passion announcements, there is also a narrative in which the disciples demonstrate how closed they are to the theology of the cross (see 9:33–37; 10:35–40).

The words "Get behind me, Satan!" do not mean that Peter is at this moment the incarnation of the devil, but rather that the disciple is functioning as a tempter, trying to seduce Jesus from the way God has ordained for him. Peter is not accused of satanic thoughts but of human thoughts, and thus of failing to perceive that God can make positive use of suffering. "Get behind me" does not banish Peter but commands him to resume his proper stance as a follower; he must follow after Jesus on the road to suffering. Mark probably intends that his readers experience the same rebuke. We must be guided not by natural human instincts of self-survival but by God's thoughts as manifested in the cross of Christ, a stumbling block and folly to human thought, but nonetheless the power and wisdom of God (1 Cor. 1:23–25).

Earlier in the Gospel Jesus' opponents have been the Pharisees and their scribes. Now for the first time we learn that his mortal foes will be the chief priests, scribes, and elders. The term "chief priests" designates a group consisting of the current high priest and his living predecessors and of priests exercising important administrative functions, such as the Captain of the Temple, who supervised the temple police (Acts 4:1; 5:24–26). Scribes were experts on the law who advised the priests and laymen of the high court, the Sanhedrin, on legal issues. Some, perhaps most of them, adhered to the party of the Pharisees, but this is not certain. "Elders" refers to laymen who belonged to the court by virtue of their aristocratic status, wealth, or power. Because the chief priests and elders functioned in Jerusalem, the first passion announcement implicitly identifies Jerusalem as the location of Jesus' death. At this point Mark gives us no hint about *why* the Messiah must suffer, die, and be resurrected. We must wait until after the third passion announcement to learn that the Son of Man's death will serve as a ransom for many (10:45).

The section of the passage following Jesus' rebuke of Peter consists of sayings concerning discipleship supplemented by two sayings about judgment and the coming of God's rule. In verse 34 Mark introduces "the crowd" (omitted in the parallels at Matthew 16:24; Luke 9:23), probably as a reminder to the readers that these sayings are directed to all, not just to Jesus' first disciples. There is no need to assume that the sayings were all uttered by Jesus on one occasion; parallels are scattered in Luke (12:9; 14:27; 17:33). It appears that Mark has brought them together in order to underscore his conviction that it is not enough to confess faith in Jesus as Messiah, the Son of God; one must put one's faith in the *suffering* Messiah and exhibit that faith in daily living that incarnates the principle of self-denial.

Scholars sometimes object that the saying of verse 34 cannot be authentic, since Hebrew and Aramaic did not have any verb corresponding to the Greek verb meaning "deny oneself." The Greek verb, however, is probably a loose translation for a Greek-speaking audience of the difficult Hebrew or Aramaic idiom used in Luke 14:26, "Whoever comes to me and does not hate father and mother, wife and children, brothers and sisters, yes, and even life itself, cannot be my disciple." "Hate," of course, is not meant literally; it is an emphatic way of pointing to the necessity of setting priorities. Loyalty to Jesus and his program must come first. Self must be subordinated.

Because the passion announcement in verse 31 does not specify that Jesus will die by crucifixion, the allusion to carrying one's cross to the execution site may seem premature, but this is a mistaken impression. Jesus' audience knew full well that many who had dared to challenge Roman power had paid for their dream by being crucified (see my comments on 15:27). Those engaged in anti-Roman activity knew that they risked crucifixion. In this saying Jesus tells his followers that they must be as daring as the freedom fighters; they must be as fiercely loyal to him as revolutionaries are to the dream of driving the Romans from their homeland. Because crucifixion was the most shameful form of execution, the saying also demands of Jesus' followers the willingness to be shamed publicly because of their loyalty to him.

It is unlikely that Jesus intended that this saying be taken in its most literal sense. Because he was not a guerrilla captain, there was no reason to anticipate that his followers would be crucified, and, as it turned out, none were (the crucifixion of Peter in Rome is probably legendary). Cross bearing serves rather as a powerful metaphor in reinforcement of the demand for subordination of the self out of loyalty to Jesus. Followers of a king who will suffer and die before he reigns must imitate his readiness to accept hardship and shame. Luke is thus justified in adding the word "daily" (Luke 9:23, "take up their cross daily").

It is a mistake, however, to trivialize Jesus' demand by referring to personal problems as crosses we must bear. Cross bearing means being willing to be shamed in front of others because of stubborn loyalty to Jesus and his teaching. An illustration of this was provided by a small-town surgeon, who discovered that the prisoners in the county jail had Gideon Bibles, but no one was interested in providing them with Bible study. When he offered to do this his medical colleagues and friends were greatly amused, but he persisted in his teaching ministry for fifteen years. No ridicule could divert him from his calling.

Jesus' call for self-denial and cross bearing can be misunderstood as a demand for ascetic practices, such as denying oneself the pleasure of marital relations and limiting oneself to a bare subsistence diet. To engage in self-denial for the sake of self-denial is to miss Jesus' point entirely. To use a modern analogy, anorexia is not a denial of the self but a desperate attempt to put the self in control. And enforced self-denial, such as is experienced by many women because of male dominance, is certainly not what Jesus had in mind. This saying asks women to subordinate themselves only to Jesus and his way. Implicit, of course, is the requirement of mutual subordination of men and women called for in Ephesians 5:21.

The paradoxical saying of verse 35 depends upon a wordplay; *psychē*, here translated "life," can refer both to physical life and to the soul, and thus to life after death. A parallel in John 12:25, employing the same wordplay, uses different verbs: "Those who love their life lose it, and those who hate their life in this world will keep it for eternal life." In both versions Jesus' followers are warned that they must repress the natural impulses concerned with security and self-preservation when these conflict with loyalty to him and his gospel.

The rhetorical questions of verses 36–37 again employ *psychē* with reference to life after death. What point is there in increasing one's material wealth to an incredible level ("the whole world") if in the end life eternal is forfeited (see the parable of the Rich Fool; Luke 12:16–21)? And who can bargain with God and obtain life after death by means of a bribe?

In verse 38 we have the first indication of Jesus' post-Resurrection role. The one who was confessed as Messiah in verse 29 now announces that followers who are ashamed of him and his words will discover that he is ashamed of them when he returns in heavenly glory to exercise his messianic rule. Jesus here refers to his future role by means of the phrase "the Son of Man." Mark's readers already know on the basis of 2:10 and 2:28 that this is Jesus' peculiar self-designation, not the title of a heavenly figure distinct from himself. A fuller parallel is found in Luke 12:8–9 and Matthew 10:32–33. There is no reason to doubt that some form of the saying was uttered by Jesus. If he did in fact believe that he was the Messiah (which is probable, in view of the titulus on the cross; see my comments on 15:26) and, anticipating his violent death, regarded it as part of God's plan, he must also have believed that God would raise him from the dead and empower him to rule as Messiah.

Jesus here refers to God as his Father. The Messiah was known as the Son of God, on the basis of the prophecy concerning David's successor in 2 Samuel 7:14, "I will be a father to him, and he shall be a son to me" (see also Psalm 2:2, 7). The allusion to "his father" corresponds to 1:11: "You are my Son, the Beloved," and anticipates the heavenly declaration in the next passage, "This is my Son, the Beloved" (9:7).

The last verse of the passage, 9:1, has created difficulties for interpreters. If it is both authentic and literal, Jesus appears to be guilty of false prophecy, for he has not yet returned in glory to establish the kingdom of God. Interpreters have attempted to circumvent the problem by suggesting that the kingdom of God appeared in power at the transfiguration (which Mark places in the immediately following passage), the resurrection, or Pentecost. Others propose that the saying is inauthentic; it was created by someone in the early church who, like Paul, thought that Jesus' return was near at hand (see Rom. 13:11–12: 1 Cor. 7:29–31). There is no theological error, however, in regarding this Amen saying ("Truly" is a very weak rendering of *Amēn*) as both authentic and inaccurate. Sound doctrine concerning the meaning of Christ insists that Jesus' divinity did not at all compromise his full humanity, which means that Jesus could be inaccurate. In 13:32, moreover, Jesus asserts that not even the Son knows when the end will come. In any event, it is probable that when Mark wrote his Gospel, just before or after A.D. 70, some of Jesus' first followers were still alive, and consequently the prophecy had not yet been falsified. The intention of the saying, however, is not to give a precise date for the arrival of God's rule but to provide assurance that God is in control and will establish the kingdom in his own time.

THE TRANSFIGURATION OF JESUS
Mark 9:2–13

9:2 **Six days later, Jesus took with him Peter and James and John, and led them up a high mountain apart, by themselves. And he was transfigured before them, ³ and his clothes became dazzling white, such as no one on earth could bleach them. ⁴ And there appeared to them Elijah with Moses, who were talking with Jesus. ⁵ Then Peter said to Jesus, "Rabbi, it is good for us to be here; let us make three dwellings, one for you, one for Moses, and one for Elijah." ⁶ He did not know what to say, for they were terrified. ⁷ Then a cloud overshadowed them, and from the cloud there came a voice, "This is my Son, the Beloved; listen to him!" ⁸ Suddenly when they looked around, they saw no one with them any more, but only Jesus.**

⁹ As they were coming down the mountain, he ordered them to tell no one about what they had seen, until after the Son of Man had risen from the dead. ¹⁰ So they kept the matter to themselves, questioning what this rising from the dead could mean. ¹¹ Then they asked him, "Why do the scribes say that Elijah must come first?" ¹² He said to them, "Elijah is indeed coming first to restore all things. How then is it written about the Son of Man, that he is to go through many sufferings and be treated with contempt? ¹³ But I tell you that Elijah has come, and they did to him whatever they pleased, as it is written about him."

The event narrated here is usually called "the transfiguration," from a Latin verb meaning to change in shape or appearance or transform, because of the use in verse 2 of the Greek verb *metamorphoō*, from which we derive "metamorphosis." Implied is not simply a momentary, superficial alteration in outward appearance but a permanent, profound change. (The same verb is found in Romans 12:2, "Do not be conformed to this world, but be *transformed* by the renewing of your minds.") In this passage the inner circle of the twelve—Peter, James, and John (see also 5:37; 14:33; at 13:3 Andrew is included)—have a vision of Jesus' future heavenly glory. In earthly terms the change is not permanent; after the event Jesus will appear as before. The transfiguration is in this sense an anticipation only; it is a "sneak preview" of the metamorphosis Jesus will undergo when he is exalted by resurrection to the right hand of God (Psalm 110:1; Mark 12:36).

We must be careful not to read too much into the story. A careless pagan reader might assume that Jesus is here presented *as a god*. Mark's monotheism would not tolerate such nonsense (see 12:29). The Second Evangelist does not possess the sophisticated theology of incarnation found in John's Gospel ("And the Word became flesh," John 1:14). When the heavenly voice (that is, God) declares in verse 7, "This is my Son, the Beloved," this may remind us of the later trinitarianism that elaborated the idea of God the Son, but Mark is innocent of such theology. For most early Jewish Christians (apart from John, Paul, and the author of Hebrews), the phrase "the Son of God" served as an alternate title for the Messiah, on the basis of 2 Samuel 7 (see also Psalm 89:26–27, and my comments on Mark 8:29). Despite the "heavenly" setting on a very high mountain (the geographical location is of no interest to Mark; its height is primarily symbolic), the association with Jesus of Elijah and Moses, two heavenly residents who are humans, emphasizes Jesus' humanity. It is, however, a humanity that has been transformed by God's glory, so that Jesus now ranks above great Moses, through whom the law had been given to Israel, and Elijah, whose greatness was certified by his removal to heaven in a chariot of fire (2 Kings 2:11). For Mark—and all subsequent Christians—Jesus is the unique man through whom God effected his purposes in a climactic and unrepeatable way. Trinitarian theology has helped us to express this conviction more satisfactorily; in Jesus the creative Word of God became incarnate, so that we honor him as both human and divine.

Whereas both Matthew 17:3 and Luke 9:30 list Moses and Elijah in their chronological order (which is also their order of importance), Mark names Elijah first. It is likely the emphasis is laid on Elijah because of his significance in Jewish thought about the End. The second half of the passage will deal with this expectation. Luke 9:31 reports that the heavenly conversation was focused on "his departure [*exodos*], which he was about to accomplish at Jerusalem." Mark, however, gives no hint of the topic; he is interested only in the association of these ancient worthies with the Messiah. This association serves to validate the shocking assertion of 8:31, namely, that Jesus is and remains the Messiah despite the fact that he must suffer a shameful execution.

The presence of Elijah and Moses ought to have been sufficient to assure the disciples of this truth, but they are represented as totally nonplussed. Peter, their spokesman, proposes the erection of three tabernacles to commemorate the summit conference of these three spiritual leaders. He cannot conceive of the astonishing fact the this teacher ranks above Moses, Elijah, and all others in God's redemptive history. Peter addresses Jesus as "Rabbi." The word, meaning literally, "My great one," was a way of addressing honored religious teachers. Only after A.D. 70 did it gradually become a technical term designating ordained legal experts of the Pharisaic tradition.

Most of the stories in Mark carry no indication of when the reported event took place. This passage is an exception. Puzzled by the reference to six days, interpreters have proposed a variety of symbolic meanings, many of which are farfetched, and there is no consensus. It seems more probable that the temporal reference was firmly affixed to the story as Mark received it. Whatever its origin, its function in Mark's context is to tie the event closely to the preceding one, in order to provide heavenly confirmation both of Peter's declaration that Jesus is the Messiah and of Jesus' announcement that the Messiah must suffer and die.

As they descend the mountain, the disciples are again commanded to maintain silence about Jesus (see 8:30). In this case, however, a terminus is named; they are to keep the secret until Jesus has been raised from the dead. His resurrection, already promised in the passion announcement of 8:31, is beyond their comprehension. Contemporary Jews believed in the general resurrection of the dead at the last day, as promised in Daniel 12:2–3, but the idea of a singular resurrection (as distinct from the elevation to heaven of a living person, as in Elijah's case; 2 Kings 2:11) was totally foreign to them. Nothing in Jewish religious thought prepared the disciples for Easter. It had to be experienced to be believed. In verse 10 the disciples ask one another, quite naturally, what can possibly be meant by *this* rising from the dead (the NRSV word "this" does not correspond to anything in the Greek, but constitutes a good interpretive addition; the disciples are not wondering about the general resurrection of the dead).

Instead of bringing their puzzle directly to Jesus, the disciples ask him a very different question, which is nonetheless indirectly related to the prior issue concerning the dying and rising Messiah. According to Malachi 4:5–6, God has promised to send Elijah just prior to the end "to turn the hearts of parents to their children and the hearts of children to their parents." The effect of their question in verse 11, accordingly, is to contrast the traditional understanding of this passage, namely, that Elijah will remove all strife from Israel and thus prepare the people to meet their God, with Jesus' announcement that the Messiah must die. If Elijah comes first and prepares the way for the Messiah by removing all contention, there can be no explanation for the Messiah's violent death.

The first half of verse 12 is so puzzling that some scholars argue that it should be read as a question: "Does Elijah indeed come first to restore all things?" According to this reading, Jesus calls into question the traditional understanding of Malachi 4:5–6. If we take the sentence as a statement instead of as a question, little is changed, however. Jesus affirms the scriptural truth of Malachi but proposes a radically different interpretation: Elijah's prophesied coming is not future but past. He did indeed attempt to renew Israel with his baptism of repentance for the forgiveness of sins (1:4), but human sinfulness resisted his ministry and rendered it finally ineffectual: "they did to him whatever they pleased, as it is written about him" (v. 13; see 6:14–29).

Because nowhere in the Old Testament or in Jewish intertestamental literature is it predicted that the returning Elijah will be persecuted and martyred, the reference of the clause "as it is written about him" is unclear. It may be an allusion to the common motif of the abuse of God's messengers (2 Chron. 36:15–16; Jer. 2:30; see Matt. 23:29–31; Luke 13:33–34; Acts 7:52). On the other hand, the reference to scriptural fulfillment may refer in a general way to "Elijah" (John the Baptist) as the Messiah's forerunner. That is, verse 13 can be understood only in relation to verse 12b, "How then is it written about the Son of Man, that he is to go through many sufferings and be treated with contempt?" Again, we can only guess at the scriptural reference of this statement. Some scholars find here an allusion to Isaiah 53:3, "He was despised and rejected," whereas others prefer Psalm 118:22, "The stone that the builders rejected has become the chief cornerstone." In favor of the second proposal is the fact that Mark later quotes this verse (12:10). In any event, this passage intimates that it is in accordance with God's plan revealed in scripture that the suffering Messiah be preceded by a suffering Elijah. The fate of John the Baptist anticipates and confirms the meaningfulness of Jesus' violent fate.

The idea of a suffering end-time Elijah was just as scandalous to religious Jews as that of a suffering Messiah. Only the resurrection of Jesus could overcome the scandal and enable Jesus' followers to acknowledge the redemptive power of suffering. In Colossians 1:24 Paul boldly writes, "I am now rejoicing in my sufferings for your sake, and in my flesh I am completing what is lacking in Christ's afflictions for the sake of his body, that is, the church." He by no means suggests that Jesus' atoning death was inadequate and must be supplemented, but rather that all vicarious suffering on the part of Jesus' followers has medicinal value for the continued health of the church.

During the first centuries of the church's existence, pagans were utterly amazed at the way Christians nursed their sick during fearful epidemics that killed 25 percent or more of the population. While pagans fled from their own flesh and blood in a desperate attempt to save their lives, Christians bravely faced the threat in order to care for one another, often themselves succumbing to the disease. Through their suffering, however, as many as two thirds of the Christian sick were saved, and the church grew from strength to strength.

JESUS' LAST EXORCISM
Mark 9:14–29

> 9:14 When they came to the disciples, they saw a great crowd around them, and some scribes arguing with them. ¹⁵ When the whole crowd saw him, they were immediately overcome with awe, and they ran forward to greet him. ¹⁶ He asked them, "What are you arguing about with them?" ¹⁷ Someone from the crowd answered him, "Teacher, I brought you my son; he has a spirit that makes him unable to speak; ¹⁸ and whenever it seizes him, it dashes him down; and he foams and grinds his teeth and becomes rigid; and I asked your disciples to cast it out, but they could not do so." ¹⁹ He answered them, "You faithless generation, how much longer must I be among you? How much longer must I put up with you? Bring him to me." ²⁰ And they brought the boy to him. When the spirit saw him, immediately it convulsed the boy, and he fell on the ground and rolled about, foaming at the mouth. ²¹ Jesus asked the father, "How long has this been happening to him?" And he said, "From childhood. ²² It has often cast him into the fire and into the water, to destroy him; but if you are able to do anything, have pity on us and help us." ²³ Jesus said to him, "If you are able!—All things can be done for the one who believes." ²⁴ Immediately the father of the child cried out, "I believe; help my unbelief!" ²⁵ When Jesus saw that a crowd came running together, he rebuked the unclean spirit, saying to it, "You spirit that keeps this boy from speaking and hearing, I command you, come out of him, and never enter him again!" ²⁶ After crying out and convulsing him terribly, it came out, and the boy was like a corpse, so that most of them said, "He is dead." ²⁷ But Jesus took him by the hand and lifted him up, and he was able to stand. ²⁸ When he had entered the house, his disciples asked him privately, "Why could we not cast it out?" ²⁹ He said to them, "This kind can come out only through prayer."

Epilepsy is indicated in both descriptions of the illness (vv. 18, 20). Since the cause of epilepsy was unknown, it is understandable that the abnormal behavior that characterizes this disease was seen as the result of demon possession.

This exorcism story is especially noteworthy because of its location in the Gospel. Mark's healing and exorcism narratives are set almost exclusively in the first half of the Gospel, prior to Peter's confession and the first announcement of the passion (8:29–31). None occur in the extended passion narrative that begins with Jesus' triumphal entry into Jerusalem at 11:1. In the intervening section (8:27–10:52), which focuses on the disciples and what it means to follow Jesus, there are only two such stories, this one and the cure of blind Bartimaeus, which concludes the section (10:46–52). Both are presented by Mark as relevant to discipleship.

Whereas the disciples play only a minor role or are not mentioned at all in most of the exorcism narratives, here their presence at the beginning and end gives the story its special significance. In the opening verses we learn that the nine disciples who did not accompany Jesus to the mount of transfiguration were presented with a particularly difficult case of demon possession. Although they had performed successful exorcisms during their mission (6:13), they have now experienced utter failure. When Jesus and the "inner three" find them, a great crowd, which includes some scribes, is arguing with them ("arguing" can go with "crowd" as well as "scribes"). Although Mark does not tell us what the argument was about either in verse 14 or verse 16, we may assume that it concerned the disciples' claim to exorcistic power, which had been publicly refuted by their failure (v. 18). Because this section on discipleship has Mark's readers especially in mind, the disciples' embarrassment may represent the experience of later followers (ancient and modern) who claim the power to overcome evil and are ridiculed for their failure.

This theme is picked up again at the end of the story, when the disciples are alone with Jesus in a house (v. 28). Their failure is explained by Jesus as due to the fact that such severe cases require concentrated prayer. The addition "and fasting" found in many ancient manuscripts and in the KJV is not original; it erroneously suggests that successful exorcisms depend on ascetic techniques rather than on prayerful dependence on the power of God. Mark and his early readers will have seen no inconsistency in the omission of any reference to Jesus' praying in this instance; Jesus the Messiah was revered as a more direct channel of divine power than was possible for his followers. Instead of imitating Jesus, the nine disciples ought to have humbly exhibited their dependence on God's power by resort to prayer. The same, of course, holds true for modern followers. For example, those who want to "exorcize" the spirit of strife from a congregation that has become dysfunctional through constant quarreling must pray fervently for all concerned, remembering that "all things can be done for the one who believes" (v. 23).

In the middle of the story another theme is developed. Here not the failure of the disciples but the crowd's failure is the focus of attention. Jesus' angry outburst in verse 19 is directed not against the disciples (who do not constitute or represent a "faithless" or "unbelieving generation") but against those who have exhibited their lack of faith in God by arguing with the disciples. The rebuke is reminiscent of a number of passages in the Old Testament in which God expresses exasperation at Israel's lack of faith, such as Numbers 14:11, "How long will this people despise me? And how long will they refuse to believe in me, in spite of all the signs that I have done among them?" Occurring as it does in Mark's last exorcism story, the rebuke "How much longer must I be among you? How much longer must I put up with you?" anticipates Jesus' departure through death and resurrection.

Although in verse 17 the demoniac's father represents the unbelieving crowd, in his dialogue with Jesus he stands for many later believers, who would like to believe in the power of God as revealed in Jesus ("*If* you are able to do anything," v. 22) but find their will-to-believe inhibited by skepticism based on everyday experience. The tension between faith and doubt is powerfully expressed in the father's anguished cry, "I believe; help my unbelief!" (v. 24). Here we are reminded that even faith itself is not a human achievement but the gift of God's grace.

7. The Second Passion Announcement
Mark 9:30–10:31

JESUS AGAIN ANNOUNCES HIS PASSION
Mark 9:30–32

> 9:30 **They went on from there and passed through Galilee. He did not want anyone to know it;** [31] **for he was teaching his disciples, saying to them, "The Son of Man is to be betrayed into human hands, and they will kill him, and three days after being killed, he will rise again."** [32] **But they did not understand what he was saying and were afraid to ask him.**

The setting of the second passion announcement is a journey that begins at the site of the exorcism of 9:14–29 and ends in Capernaum. Although this is territory in which Jesus and his disciples have become well known, Mark stresses that Jesus is seeking to avoid public attention because this is a time for the private instruction of his closest followers. As elsewhere in Mark, Jesus refers to his vocation and destiny in indirect (third-person) language, using his preferred self-designation, "the Son of Man" (see my comments on 2:10).

The second passion announcement is the shortest of the three (compare 8:31; 10:33–34). Whereas the first stresses divine necessity ("the Son of Man *must* suffer"), the second hints that God is the supreme actor in the drama of the passion. The verb translated "is to be betrayed" literally means "is being handed over" or "is being delivered up." Many scholars regard the passive voice of this verb as pointing to activity on God's part ("divine passive") and see here an allusion to the Greek translation of Isaiah 53:6, "and the Lord delivered him up for our sins" (see also Isa. 53:12, Rom. 4:25; 8:32, where the same verb is used). This second passion announcement thus reminds the reader that the Messiah's death is not a meaningless example of injustice but the focal point of God's plan for the redemption of the world (see 10:45). Such an interpretation is supported by the fact that in a number of Old Testament passages God is said to deliver Israel "into the hand of" their enemies on account of their sin (2 Kings 21:14; Neh. 9:27; Jer. 12:7; Ezek. 39:23).

Mark portrays the disciples' response to this second announcement of the passion as incomprehension and awe (they "were afraid to ask him"). Even though we live on the Easter side of the passion, this remains an appropriate response. Although we gladly and confidently affirm "Christ died for our sins in accordance with the scriptures" (1 Cor. 15:3), the atonement remains an impenetrable mystery hidden in the heart of God.

THE DISCIPLES QUARREL
OVER RANK
Mark 9:33–37

> 9:33 They they came to Capernaum; and when he was in the house he asked them, "What were you arguing about on the way?" 34 But they were silent, for on the way they had argued with one another who was the greatest. 35 He sat down, called the twelve, and said to them, "Whoever wants to be first must be last of all and servant of all." 36 Then he took a little child and put it among them; and taking it in his arms, he said to them, 37 "Whoever welcomes one such child in my name welcomes me, and whoever welcomes me welcomes not me but the one who sent me."

Following each of the three passion announcements (8:31; 9:31; 10:33–34) is a passage that demonstrates how completely the disciples misunderstand and resist the theology of the cross. In response to Peter's rebuke Jesus declares, "You are setting your mind not on divine things but on human things" (8:33). The same reprimand would be just as appropriate here and in 10:35–45.

Instead of pondering among themselves why God would allow the Messiah to suffer and die, the disciples quarrel about rank and status. Mark is not interested in giving any details of this dispute, but the narrative of the transfiguration provides a possible cause: Will Peter, James, and John be more important in the Messiah's kingdom because Jesus selected them for this event? Even though Jesus' announcement that he will be killed clearly implies that the messianic kingdom will be very different from the kingdoms of this world, the disciples continue to think in traditional ways about how important they will be.

Jesus challenges his followers with a question. In response to their embarrassed silence, he sits (assuming the posture of a teacher), summons the twelve (the verb used here suggests a louder voice than normal), and utters a basic principle of the topsy-turvy kingdom of God: "Whoever wants to be first must be last of all and servant of all" (v. 35). In Jesus' own case becoming the servant of all will involve giving his life as a ransom (10:45). His followers need not imitate him by becoming martyrs, but they must submit to a drastic reorientation of their priorities. The quest for rank and status is fired by the desire for power over others and by the deep-seated human need to be somebody special. Jesus announces that in God's kingdom there will be no place for domination over other people, and the desire to be somebody special will be fully satisfied when all treat others as special.

Jesus dramatizes this principle by placing in their midst a child, a powerless person who ranks little above a slave (see Gal. 4:1). This child of unspecified gender and age (the same word is used for Jairus's daughter; 5:39–40) belongs among this followers because Jesus himself has welcomed it with an embrace ("embracing it" is a more accurate translation than "taking it in his arms"; see my comments on 10:16). By implication, if a lowly child belongs in the Messiah's entourage, so also do women and slaves, and all are to be treated with special respect because the Messiah has welcomed them. The attached saying displays the other side of the coin: "Whoever welcomes one such child in my name welcomes me." This utterance is reminiscent of the missionary instructions of 6:11 ("If any place will not welcome you . . ."), but here the reference is not to the hospitality shown to missionaries but to the reception of new members into the fellowship of Jesus' followers. To welcome a new believer "in my name" is to act under Jesus' authority: Jesus has empowered his followers to include people of low status in their fellowship. They are not to show partiality toward the rich and the powerful, because Jesus himself has received even a child. (James 2:1–7 strongly condemns discrimination against the poor in church gatherings.) Moreover, to welcome a child or another person of low status is to welcome Jesus himself. Here we are reminded of the "parable" of the Sheep and the Goats, in which Jesus declares that those who have shown compassion to the "least" of his brothers and sisters have in fact shown compassion to him (Matt. 25:31–46).

The final clause of verse 37 is startling: To "welcome" Jesus is to "welcome" God. Lying behind this line is the principle of Jewish law that "a man's representative is as the man himself." According to this rule, a duly authorized representative could negotiate a contract, even a marriage, on behalf of the one who sent him. This is the first utterance in Mark's Gospel in which Jesus clearly identifies himself as God's authorized representative (the idea, of course, has been implicit from 1:1, where Jesus is identified as the Son of God). Whoever despises Jesus rejects God who sent him. Contrariwise, those who welcome Jesus, that is, receive him into their hearts and homes, "receive" God; they acknowledge his rightful sovereignty as proclaimed by Jesus.

It is possible to see in verse 37 an anticipation of Jesus' elevation of love for God and love for neighbor as the greatest commandments (12:29–31). These two commands are one; to love the neighbor, especially the poor and powerless neighbor, is to love God.

ANOTHER EXORCIST
INVOKES JESUS' NAME
Mark 9:38–41

> 9:38 John said to him, "Teacher, we saw someone casting out demons in your name, and we tried to stop him, because he was not following us." [39] But Jesus said, "Do not stop him; for no one who does a deed of power in my name will be able soon afterward to speak evil of me. [40] Whoever is not against us is for us. [41] For truly I tell you, whoever gives you a cup of water to drink because you bear the name of Christ will by no means lose the reward."

It was widely believed in the ancient world that many illnesses, as well as mental disorders, were due to demon possession. Exorcists were consequently in great demand. From various sources we learn that Jewish exorcists were regarded as particularly effective by many pagans. Early Christians who practiced exorcism by appealing to the authority of Jesus found themselves in competition with non-Christian Jews. Acts 19:11–16, after reporting Paul's success in driving out demons in Ephesus, relates that some Jewish exorcists attempted to adjure demons "by the Jesus whom Paul proclaims," but with dire results. In Mark's story, John, speaking on behalf of the other disciples, tells Jesus that they attempted to stop an unauthorized use of his name. What is remarkable in this story is the fact that the exorcist has apparently been successful, and there is no indication that he has desisted as a result of the disciples' objection that he is an outsider.

Some scholars regard it as unlikely that Jesus' name would have been used in this way during his lifetime and consequently treat the story as arising later. It is clear, however, that he was regarded as an extraordinary exorcist even by his enemies (see 3:22). There is nothing improbable in the report that another exorcist attempted to draw on his power. In view of the negative attitude toward the use of Jesus' name by outsiders evidenced both here and in Acts 19, it is more likely that the story is authentic than that it was created by someone in the early church. Here Jesus manifests the kind of generosity toward outsiders that is reflected in his eating with tax collectors and other "sinners" (see 2:15) and his teaching about nonretaliation and love for enemies (Matt. 5:38–48). Whereas John wants to draw a narrow circle around Jesus and his immediate followers, Jesus extends the circle to include all who are not against him.

Matthew 12:30 seems at first glance to present a contradictory image of Jesus: "Whoever is not with me is against me, and whoever does not gather with me scatters." In Matthew's context, however, the saying constitutes a response to enemies who foolishly claim that Jesus casts out demons by calling on the power of Satan; here Jesus places outside the circle those who do not join him in opposing Satan's power. In the Markan saying, he includes any who join him in this battle, even if they do not follow him.

In Mark's setting, the story serves to reinforce the point of the preceding narrative; the disciples are unable to understand that a kingdom that is inaugurated by the suffering and death of the king calls into question the thinking of this world. The exclusivism manifested in their response to the outsider, although normal behavior in societies ancient and modern, shows how little they understand their master and his kingdom.

The attached saying concerning a cup of water (v. 41) seems at first to bear little relation to the story. The connection is probably as follows. Although those who extend such minimal hospitality toward Jesus' wandering missionaries are in one sense outsiders, they must be regarded as belonging within the wider circle. (The phrase "because you bear the name of Christ" is likely the result of post-Easter editing; an earlier version may have read something like "on my account" as in Matthew 5:11. Sayings similar to Mark 9:41 are found in Matthew 10:40–42.)

Although Christians must themselves resist the seduction of "lowest common denominator" religion, this passage instructs us to be generous to all outsiders, whatever their religious affiliation, who join battle with us against the forces of evil in our world.

WARNINGS ABOUT HELLFIRE
Mark 9:42–50

9:42 "If any of you put a stumbling block before one of these little ones who believe in me, it would be better for you if a great millstone were hung around your neck and you were thrown into the sea. ⁴³ If your hand causes you to stumble, cut it off; it is better for you to enter life maimed than to have two hands and to go to hell, to the unquenchable fire. ⁴⁵ And if your foot causes you to stumble, cut if off; it is better for you to enter life lame than to have two feet and to be thrown into hell. ⁴⁷ And if your eye causes you to stumble, tear it out; it is better for you to enter the kingdom of God with one eye than to have two eyes and to be thrown into hell, ⁴⁸ where their worm never dies, and the fire is never quenched.

⁴⁹ "For everyone will be salted with fire. ⁵⁰ Salt is good; but if salt has lost its saltiness, how can you season it? Have salt in yourselves, and be at peace with one another."

[Please note that verses 44 and 46, which are identical to verse 48, are not included in the ancient authorities.]

In contrast to Matthew's Gospel, in which we read often about hell and the "outer darkness" where there will be "weeping and gnashing of teeth" (for example, Matt. 22:13), Mark contains no reference to hell and its torments outside of this passage. Some such punishment may be implied in certain sayings such as 8:38, which promises that, when he returns in glory, Jesus will be ashamed of those who have been ashamed of him, but no attempt is made there or elsewhere in Mark to describe what will happen to those who are not admitted to the kingdom of God. It may be significant, therefore, that Mark places these sayings about hellfire precisely in this passage, in which the focus is on the *disciples* and their failure to understand the ways of God's kingdom. Not unbelievers, but Jesus' own followers are threatened with hellfire!

The passage divides naturally into three segments: a saying about causing little ones to stumble, three warnings about self-induced sin, and three sayings about salt. The three segments are tied together by a common emphasis on divine judgment.

The reference in verse 42 to "these little ones" binds the sayings to the unit that began in verse 33 with the disciples' quarrel and climaxed in the saying of verse 37: "Whoever welcomes one such child in my name welcomes me." What was stated positively in verse 37 is now given a negative formulation (the two sayings are side by side in Matthew 18:5–6). Because the lowly status of the child is presented by Jesus as a judgment upon the disciples' thirst for prominence, the child also becomes a symbol for ordinary, unsophisticated believers who claim no leadership role. Verse 42 issues a stern warning to the disciples, who for Mark represent church leaders; they will forfeit their participation in the kingdom of God if they are guilty of causing one of the ordinary believers to stumble.

The verb translated "put a stumbling block before" in verse 42 and "causes to stumble" in verses 43–47 is ambiguous. It may mean either "causes to sin"—that is, causes to behave immorally (it is so understood by RSV, NIV—or "causes to lose faith" (as in TEV; see also 4:17). Like the NRSV, the REB attempts to maintain the ambiguity with the rendering "causes the downfall of." It is possible that Mark intends the ambiguity. The church leaders will bear their guilt whether their example encourages ordinary believers to sin or their striving for power and prestige shakes the faith of the little ones and drives them from the church.

The severity of the punishment such leaders will face is indicated by means of a comparison; it will be far worse than if a person were drowned with a donkey millstone (one so large that it must be turned by donkey power) around his neck to ensure that his corpse could not be retrieved for burial (a fate dreaded by Jesus' compatriots).

The three sayings in verses 43, 45, and 47–48 are all concerned with sins "caused" by a part of one's own body. Interpreters are inclined to see all three as referring to sexual sins, because of the parallel in Matthew 5:27–30. It is possible, however, that the sayings originally had a wider application, referring to any transgressions involving the use of one's body, such as theft and physical violence.

It is disputed whether or not Jesus meant these sayings to be taken literally; but most interpreters, both ancient and modern, insist that Jesus would not have intended that his followers maim themselves as a way of controlling sinful desires and habits. The sayings use hyperbole as a means of shocking sinners into taking drastic steps to avoid practices that are hateful to God. Some ancient commentators allegorized hand, foot, and eye as sinful members of one's family from whom one must separate. Although this is probably not what Jesus had in mind, it reminds us that the drastic steps required of a modern follower of Jesus may include firmly divorcing oneself from a dysfunctional family or from friends who encourage evil habits.

Troubling to many Christians is the reference in these verses to eternal hellfire. Verse 48 (which was employed as a recurring "chorus" in verses 44 and 46 in many ancient manuscripts) is a quotation of Isaiah 66:24. It is clear in the Isaiah passage that the apostates whose worm and fire are unending are "dead bodies." There is no suggestion that these evil persons will *suffer* eternally; their carcasses will remain indefinitely as a reminder of their rebellion against God. By the first century, however, the idea of eternal suffering for the wicked was widespread, as witnessed by Matthew 25:46 and Luke 16:23. It is remarkable, however, how little attention this idea receives in the New Testament. Even Revelation 20:10, which speaks of a torment that will be "day and night forever and ever," refers explicitly only to the devil, the beast, and the false prophet, not to the wicked in general. A few verses later it is stated that those whose names are not written in the book of life will be thrown into the lake of fire, which is identified as "the second death" (Rev. 20:14–15). This can be taken as implying extinction rather than a continued "life" of torment. In most passages in the New Testament where hell is mentioned, there is no *explicit* suggestion of eternal suffering. These sayings in Mark may or may not imply that the damned will experience torment for ever; what is *explicit* is merely that the fires of Gehenna burn eternally. ("Gehenna" is derived from the Hebrew name "Valley of Hinnom," Jerusalem's garbage dump, where maggots and fire were continually at work.)

Although many find the New Testament pictures of a fiery hell repulsive, we should not abandon the idea merely because the imaginative language with which it is clothed is not attractive to us. The basic notion of divine judgment is of central importance, because it reminds us that God is by nature holy and just. It is the biblical way of saying that we live in a moral universe, where violence, injustice, and degradation are of lasting significance. Mafia bosses may die quietly in their beds, but that is not the end of the story. Although Christians need not subscribe to every picturesque detail in the Bible concerning the last judgment and its sequel, we must not lose hold of the morality of God to which the idea of hell witnesses.

The three concluding sayings concerning salt are connected to what precedes by the reference to judgment in the first: "For everyone will be salted with fire." This is a puzzling verse, but "fire" suggests either punishment (as in the preceding verses) or, more probably, "testing," as in 1 Corinthians 3:13–15. The verb "will be salted" conveys the idea that the testing will be like sprinkled salt that falls in an apparently indiscriminate fashion but nevertheless achieves its goal.

The point of the second saying depends upon the fact that salt from the Dead Sea was impure; the sodium chloride could be leached out, leaving behind other chemicals that did not taste salty (compare Matt. 5:13). This simple analogy also implies judgment: Christians who give up their distinctiveness by blending in with their environment will fail the "quality control" test.

In the final saying a transition is made from salt as a distinctive flavoring to salt as a preservative and a symbol of hospitable fellowship (see Ezra 4:14). "In yourselves" is probably to be taken corporately instead of individually: "Have salt among yourselves," that is, in your common life. Because this verse concludes the larger unit that began with the disciples' dispute over greatness, Mark may understand it as referring to the "rottenness" or "decomposition" that occurs in a Christian group when the salt of the gospel is leached out. Peace requires subordination of egos and respect for others, as dramatized by the child in the midst (vv. 36–37).

JESUS TEACHES ABOUT DIVORCE
Mark 10:1–12

> 10:1 **He left that place and went to the region of Judea and beyond the Jordan. And crowds again gathered around him; and, as was his custom, he again taught them.**
> ² **Some Pharisees came, and to test him they asked, "Is it lawful for a man to divorce his wife?"** ³ **He answered them, "What did Moses command you?"** ⁴ **They said, "Moses allowed a man to write a certificate of dismissal and to divorce her."** ⁵ **But Jesus said to them, "Because of your hardness of heart he wrote this commandment for you.** ⁶ **But from the beginning of creation, 'God made them male and female.'** ⁷ **'For this reason a man shall leave his father and mother and be joined to his wife,** ⁸ **and the two shall become one flesh.' So they are no longer two, but one flesh.** ⁹ **Therefore what God has joined together, let no one separate."**
> ¹⁰ **Then in the house the disciples asked him again about this matter.** ¹¹ **He said to them, "Whoever divorces his wife and marries another commits adultery against her;** ¹² **and if she divorces her husband and marries another, she commits adultery."**

In the preceding passage (9:33–50) Jesus and his disciples were in Capernaum on the shore of the Sea of Galilee. Now the scene shifts abruptly to "the region of Judea and beyond the Jordan." No reason is given by Mark for Jesus' first southern trip since his baptism (in John's Gospel Jesus makes many trips to Judea and Jerusalem), but Christian readers, aware that Jesus will die in Jerusalem, perceive that the Messiah has now begun his journey to the cross. This will be made explicit later in the chapter in connection with the third passion announcement (vv. 32–34). Although Jesus is now in unfamiliar territory, he is surrounded by crowds as formerly in Galilee, and he continues to teach.

The first topic is prompted by a question about divorce posed by some

Pharisees. Because the Pharisees have already been portrayed as hostile to Jesus (3:6), their question is presented by Mark as one intended to "test" or "tempt" him (in 12:13 they will attempt to "trap" him with a question about taxes). Perhaps they have already heard about Jesus' position on divorce, and hope to bring him into disfavor with the crowds by compelling him to voice an unpopular view. Jesus' counter question allows them to affirm that the current divorce practice is permitted by the law of Moses. Jesus then challenges the practice, not by proposing that Deuteronomy 24:1–4 derives from Moses, not God (all Jews, including Jesus and Paul, regarded the law in its entirety as delivered to Moses by God), but rather by insisting that this legislation was created because of the hardheartedness of the people, that is, as a concession to human sinfulness. God's original intention, Jesus argues, is indicated in Genesis 1:27 and 2:24. In making human beings male and female God intended that a young man leave his parental home and become "one flesh" with his wife. Although "one flesh" alludes at the most literal level to the sexual union, Jesus interprets it as referring to the marriage relationship as a whole. Although marriages are often regarded as private contracts, Jesus insists that marital unions are brought about by God and are therefore indissoluble.

Once again Jesus' public teaching has its sequel in private instruction to the disciples "in the house" (compare 7:17). Now the focus is not so much on divorce as on remarriage. Jesus explains that, because the first marriage is indissoluble in God's intention, a second marriage is not authentic but simply a long-term adulterous affair.

The wording of the statement is of special interest on two counts. First, Jesus declares that the divorcing husband who remarries commits adultery *against her*, that is, against his first wife. In this phrase Jesus challenges the definition of adultery that is assumed in the Old Testament, namely, that adultery is a crime against a married man, whose exclusive rights to his wife have been violated (whether the male offender is married or not is irrelevant); if a married man has intercourse with an unmarried woman, this does not count as adultery. By insisting that the second marriage is a crime against the first wife, Jesus takes a significant step toward the abolition of the double standard. Second, because the law of Moses treated polygamy as legal (Deut. 21:15–17), a second marriage was always permissible. By declaring the second marriage adulterous, Jesus abrogates polygamy.

Verse 12 may not derive directly from Jesus, for it was not possible for Jewish women to divorce their husbands. It may have been added for the benefit of Gentile women who were entitled to initiate divorce proceedings (see 1 Cor. 7:13). Even if not original, the verse correctly expounds Jesus' intention.

In Mark's presentation of Jesus' teaching on divorce and remarriage, no mention is made of an exception (see also Luke 16:18). Twice in Matthew, however, we are informed that the prohibition of divorce does not hold when the marriage has been fractured by unchastity (5:32; 19:9). In Matthew 1:19 Joseph resolves to divorce Mary, his betrothed, when he discovers that she is pregnant (betrothal could be terminated only by divorce). Although Mark's version of the divorce rule seems more rigorous than Matthew's, this is not necessarily true. Jesus and his Jewish audience may have assumed that infidelity ended the marriage. Under a strict interpretation of the law, the adulteress was to be stoned (Deut. 22:22–24). Even though capital punishment was no longer enforced in adultery cases, the unfaithful wife may have been regarded as "dead" by those who took the law seriously, and thus prohibited to her husband. A similar situation prevailed in Roman society. Under an adultery law introduced by Augustus, husbands were forbidden to pardon adulterous wives and could be punished for persisting in the marriage.

Until well into the twentieth century, many states and nations prohibited divorce except for adultery, in accordance with Matthew's version of Jesus' teaching. Now that this prohibition has been relaxed for society in general, Christians wonder whether they are still required to observe Jesus' rule. It is important to remember that Jesus is here speaking of God's intention for marriage, not proposing the excommunication of any of his followers who divorce. Marriage, Jesus teaches, is a sacred covenant to which God also is partner; it is not a temporary arrangement that can be discontinued whenever either partner finds a more attractive mate. Divorce, however, is not on that account to be regarded by Christians as an unforgivable sin. Many marriages deteriorate to such an extent that what is left is mere form without substance. There is little point in speaking of such unions as indissoluble—they have dissolved! In addition, there are marital relationships that are downright destructive, and in such cases divorce is not merely the lesser of two evils but a positive step. Marriages of this kind are sinful, and Christians ought not to persist in sin. If this reasoning is sound, Christians are surely justified in inferring that divorced persons ought to be granted another chance at achieving a marriage that is in accord with God's original intention.

CHILDREN ARE WELCOMED BY JESUS
Mark 10:13–16

10:13 **People were bringing little children to him in order that he might touch them; and the disciples spoke sternly to them.** [14] **But when Jesus saw this, he was indignant and said to them, "Let the little children come to me; do not stop them; for it is to such as these that the kingdom of God belongs.** [15] **Truly I tell you, whoever does not receive the kingdom of God as a little child will never enter it."** [16] **And he took them up in his arms, laid his hands on them, and blessed them.**

The habit of reading this passage at the celebration of infant baptism has encouraged the assumption that the children who are brought to Jesus are infants or toddlers whom Jesus takes "up" in his arms. The word for children used here occurs also in 5:39–41 with reference to a twelve-year-old girl, however, and the verb translated "took up in his arms" simply means "embraced." The passage may very well refer to children of various ages; possibly younger children are brought to Jesus by older ones (we are not told who brought the children or whom the disciples rebuked).

Also unspecified are the reasons for the disciples' rebuke and Jesus' indignation. Probably we are supposed to interpret this passage in the light of 9:33–37, where the same words for "child" and "embrace" are used. There the disciples' argument about being important is countered by Jesus' placing a child in the midst and declaring, "Whoever welcomes one such child in my name welcomes me." Here the disciples demonstrate that they have not taken Jesus' teaching seriously. They refuse to welcome the children, presumably because children are not important (in terms of social status, a child ranked not much better than a slave; see Gal. 4:1). Little wonder that Jesus is indignant! To these men who want to exclude children as unimportant Jesus declares, "To such [children] the kingdom of God belongs" (v. 14). As Robert Gundry points out (*Mark*, 544, 547), it is not to children in general that Jesus refers in this saying but to those who have demonstrated faith by coming to him (see also 9:42). Although this saying speaks of "possessing" the kingdom (similarly, v. 17 refers to "inheriting" eternal life), this must be taken as a metaphor for participation in God's rule. As in 9:36, Jesus demonstrates how important children are to him, and to the One who sent him, by hugging them.

This little story was treasured by the early church as authorization for including children in the church. Whereas pagan mystery religions tended to segregate men and women and exclude children, the Christian faith brought people together as families. This was undoubtedly one of the factors that encouraged the rapid growth of Christianity in the Roman world. It is therefore entirely appropriate to read this passage when children are baptized, for baptism constitutes the sign that God includes them in the fellowship of the church.

Because of the attached saying in verse 15, the passage is also important as a statement about participation in the kingdom of God. Now the children become symbols or models for adults who want to be associated with God's rule: "Truly I tell you: whoever does not accept the kingdom of God like a child will never enter it" (REB). In this paradoxical saying the kingdom of God is spoken of as a present reality that can be "accepted," "received," or "welcomed" now, and also as a future reality that can be "entered" later. To receive God's rule is to acknowledge God's sovereign authority and submit to it. To enter it means to participate in the Age to Come, when God's rule is fully established (compare 9:1, 47; 14:25; 15:43).

What does it mean to receive the kingdom of God *like a child?* Several possibilities have been considered. One proposal is that a person must receive the kingdom in the same way that one should receive a child (compare 9:37). Another is that we should receive the kingdom in the way children receive it, that is with an unquestioning, trusting faith. More common is the view that takes its cue from the parallel in Matthew 18:3, "Truly I tell you, unless you change and become like children, you will never enter the kingdom of heaven" (compare John 3:3). Accordingly, to receive the kingdom as a child means to be or become childlike in some way or other (suggestions include: innocent, humble, dependent, ready to learn). A fourth proposal is that in this saying Jesus is referring not to any subjective quality of children or their responsiveness but simply to their objective status as persons of low rank (as in 9:33–37). On this interpretation the lowly child, who has not yet done anything that could count as a claim for a reward from God, receives the right to participate in the kingdom as a pure gift, that is, on the basis of God's grace alone. Adults who want to enter the kingdom must relinquish any claim they think they have and submit themselves humbly to God's sovereign grace.

What is clear from this multiplicity of proposals is that the saying is ambiguous and thus open-ended. Like the parables of the kingdom (see 4:1–34), it is intended to tease our minds into thinking new thoughts about what it means for us to become grasped by God's rule.

A RICH MAN REFUSES
JESUS' INVITATION
Mark 10:17–31

10:17 As he was setting out on a journey, a man ran up and knelt before him, and asked him, "Good Teacher, what must I do to inherit eternal life?" [18] Jesus said to him, "Why do you call me good? No one is good but God alone. [19] You know the commandments: 'You shall not murder; You shall not commit adultery; You shall not steal; You shall not bear false witness; You shall not defraud; Honor your father and mother.'" [20] He said to him, "Teacher, I have kept all these since my youth." [21] Jesus, looking at him, loved him and said, "You lack one thing; go, sell what you own, and give the money to the poor, and you will have treasure in heaven; then come, follow me." [22] When he heard this, he was shocked and went away grieving, for he had many possessions.

[23] Then Jesus looked around and said to his disciples, "How hard it will be for those who have wealth to enter the kingdom of God!" [24] And the disciples were perplexed at these words. But Jesus said to them again, "Children, how hard it is to enter the kingdom of God! [25] It is easier for a camel to go through the eye of a needle than for someone who is rich to enter the kingdom of God." [26] They were greatly astounded and said to one another, "Then who can be saved?" [27] Jesus looked at them and said, "For mortals it is impossible, but not for God; for God all things are possible."

[28] Peter began to say to him, "Look, we have left everything and followed you." [29] Jesus said, "Truly I tell you, there is no one who has left house or brothers or sisters or mother or father or children or fields, for my sake and for the sake of the good news, [30] who will not receive a hundredfold now in this age—houses, brothers and sisters, mothers and children, and fields with persecutions—and in the age to come eternal life. [31] But many who are first will be last, and the last will be first."

Early Christians who heard or read this story must have found it very shocking, on a number of counts. First, Jesus rebuffs the man's salutation, "Good teacher," with the question, "Why do you call me good?" Because Christians believed that Jesus was sinless, it was difficult to understand why Jesus would reject the epithet. Matthew avoided possible misunderstanding by altering the dialogue (Matt. 19:16–17). In the following centuries some interpreters attempted to resolve the problem by taking Jesus' question as a test of the man's theology: "You rightly call me good only if you acknowledge that I am God the Son, for only God is good." This, of course, is to read Mark in the light of later theology. More satisfactory is the proposal that, because Mark undoubtedly assumed that Jesus was sinless, he did not regard Jesus' question as denying this fact but rather as witnessing to Jesus' humility in relationship to God (compare 14:36). Instead of accepting a superficial compliment, Jesus attempts to turn the man's attention to the goodness of God.

Second, Christians must have been shocked by what appears to be a pre-Christian answer to the question "What must I do to inherit eternal life?" Instead of challenging the man to repent and believe in the gospel (1:14–15), Jesus seems simply to be reminding him of the Old Testament axiom that life is promised to those who keep God's commandments. It is helpful to compare this story with the similar one in Luke 10:25–37, in which a lawyer asks the same question, "Teacher, what must I do to inherit eternal life?" When Jesus replies, "What is written in the law?" the lawyer quotes the two great commandments concerning loving God and one's neighbor. To this Jesus responds, "You have given the right answer; do this, and you will live" (Luke 10:28). In Mark's story, however, Jesus does not say, "Do these and you will live." His statement "You know the commandments" (followed by items from the Ten Commandments: Exodus 20:12–16; Deuteronomy 5:16–20; and from Leviticus 19:13) neither affirms nor denies that commandment keeping is all that is required. It merely implies that obeying the commandments is an important way of acknowledging the sovereignty of God. Submission to the commandments is submission to God. But does such obedience guarantee total submission?

When the man declares that he has kept the commandments, Jesus looks steadily at him and loves him. By this phrase Mark may mean either that Jesus gives the man a loving look or that he looks intently and then makes a loving gesture, such as putting his arm around him. It is clear that Mark presents Jesus as warmly approving the fact that the man has led a decent, moral life in accordance with God's law. Nevertheless, decent living does not in itself constitute full submission to God's sovereignty. Like a doctor who has just diagnosed a fatal disease, Jesus prescribes a radical treatment: "Get rid of what you own, and follow me!" The patient, however, is willing neither to accept the diagnosis nor to submit to the cure. He goes away grieving, because he has many possessions. Even though he is a religious man, interested in the age to come and sufficiently motivated to seek out the famous teacher from Nazareth in order to ask what he must do, the cost is more than he is willing to pay. His present possessions mean more to him than his future life. We should probably not accuse him of rank materialism, however. It is not possessions as such that are so precious to him as what they mean socially. Wealth confers status and power. Jesus is not asking him simply to dispose of superfluous wealth but to give up his world and enter, like a child, into a new world in which status and power are unimportant. It is surely not accidental that this incident is placed directly after the story about Jesus and the children, in which Jesus declares, "Truly I tell you, whoever does not receive the kingdom of God as a little child will never enter it" (v. 15).

Third, early hearers and readers of this story will have been shocked by Jesus' declaration, "It is easier for a camel to go through the eye of a needle than for someone who is rich to enter the kingdom of God" (another of Jesus' striking hyperboles is found in Matthew 7:3). Although the wicked rich are roundly condemned in many Old Testament passages, there was also a widespread assumption that wealth was a sign of God's favor (Abraham and Job are two illustrious examples). It is not surprising, therefore, that the disciples are represented as expressing their utter astonishment with the question "Then who can be saved?" This strikes us as odd at first glance, for none of them was rich. The point seems to be: If this rich man, who is not only decent, moral, and religious but also the object of God's favor (as evidenced by his wealth), cannot gain entrance to the kingdom, what hope is there for the rest of us? Jesus reminds his disciples that the rich man is only an extreme instance of what is true for all. Even the poor cling to their old world when confronted by Jesus' new world. For rich and poor alike it is not a simple possibility to abandon the familiar and comfortable for something new and untried. Only by God's grace can one start afresh as a child.

In the final verse the focus shifts abruptly from grace to rewards. In contrast to the sorrowful rich man, the disciples have left everything (with certain reservations: Peter seems to have maintained his home in Capernaum; 1:29). Jesus assures his itinerant band that those who have left houses, fields, and relatives in order to be missionaries of the gospel will find that they have houses, fields, and relatives everywhere in the new, extended family of believers (see 3:31–35). The reference to persecutions is an ominous reminder that there will be a collision of worlds wherever Jesus' followers go. The concluding verse speaks of the "grand reversal." In the Age to Come those who have been rich and important will be reduced in size, and the poor, whom they considered insignificant, will be recognized as "special."

Francis of Assisi responded to the challenge of this passage by renouncing his family's wealth. The New Testament as a whole, however, does not require this of all. Wealthy people such as Lydia (Acts 16:14), Phoebe (Rom. 16:1–2), Priscilla and Aquilla (Rom. 16:3–5), and Gaius (Rom. 16:23) played a very important role in the spread of the gospel by making their spacious homes available for Christian gatherings. More important than the renunciation of wealth itself, Mark's story teaches, is the renunciation of the attitudes characteristic of the world of the wealthy.

8. The Third
Passion Announcement
Mark 10:32–52

JESUS PREDICTS
HIS PASSION IN DETAIL
Mark 10:32–34

10:32 **They were on the road, going up to Jerusalem, and Jesus was walking ahead of them; they were amazed, and those who followed were afraid.
He took the twelve aside again and began to tell them what was to happen
to him, [33] saying, "See, we are going up to Jerusalem, and the Son of Man
will be handed over to the chief priests and the scribes, and they will condemn him to death; then they will hand him over to the Gentiles; [34] they will
mock him, and spit upon him, and flog him, and kill him; and after three
days he will rise again."**

In this book I have proceeded on the assumption that a Gospel is a passion narrative with an extended introduction (see the Introduction).
Christian readers know the end of the story, however, before they even
begin; they know that Jesus will be crucified and resurrected in Jerusalem.
There is consequently a literary tension between what the readers expect
and what they are told. In the first half of the Gospel, there are only veiled
hints of the passion (such as 2:20; 3:6). Following Peter's confession in
8:29 we have a series of passion announcements by which the disciples
(and readers) are informed that Jesus will soon die. We have now reached
the third and final member of the series.

Historically speaking, it is not at all improbable that Jesus predicted his
violent death. He knew what happened to John the Baptist. For Mark,
however, the passion announcements are important primarily because of
the theological point they make; they testify to the fact that Jesus' death
was not a meaningless accident of history. As Messiah, Jesus foresaw his
fate as part of God's mysterious plan and went willingly to meet it.

No mention is made in the first two passion announcements (8:31; 9:31) of the place where Jesus is to die, but the reference to the chief priests strongly implies Jerusalem, the center of priestly power. Similarly, although 10:1 speaks of a journey that takes Jesus out of Galilee into Judea, no hint is given that the journey will terminate with Jesus' death in Jerusalem. Here in verse 32 we finally learn that Jesus and his disciples are on their way to the holy city. The ominous nature of the trip is under-scored by Mark's language: "and Jesus was walking ahead of them; they were amazed, and those who followed were afraid." Because the twelve are specifically mentioned in the next verse, it seems likely that those who are amazed and those who follow in fear constitute two different groups, pos-sibly fellow pilgrims (the amazed) and a larger body of Jesus' followers (Acts 1:15 reports that one hundred and twenty followers were together in Jerusalem soon after his resurrection). Mark does not identify the rea-sons for the amazement and fear, but we should probably assume that it is Jesus' behavior that prompts these responses. Jesus is walking ahead of them, silent and determined, striding alone toward his fate. Luke's phrase is apt: "When the days drew near for him to be taken up, *he set his face* to go to Jerusalem" (Luke 9:51, italics added).

The third passion announcement is much more detailed than the first two. Indeed, some scholars propose that Mark here presents a "table of contents" for the forthcoming passion narrative. Here for the first time we are informed that Gentiles will put Jesus to death and that a significant as-pect of his suffering will be the humiliating treatment he will receive from non-Jews. In this connection we should remember that Mark was writing for a primarily Gentile audience.

Like the first two passion announcements, the third concludes with a prediction of the resurrection "after three days" (for an explanation of this phrase, see my comments on 8:31). As in the previous instances, there is no response to this astonishing prediction. Mark implies again that the resurrection must be experienced to be believed.

JAMES AND JOHN'S
INAPPROPRIATE REQUEST
Mark 10:35–45

10:35 James and John, the sons of Zebedee, came forward to him and said to him, "Teacher, we want you to do for us whatever we ask of you." 36 And he said to them, "What is it you want me to do for you?" 37 And they said to him, "Grant us to sit, one at your right hand and one at your left, in your glory." [38] But Jesus said to them, "You do not know what you are asking. Are you able to drink the cup that I drink, or be baptized with the baptism that I am baptized with?" [39] They replied, "We are able." Then Jesus said to them, "The cup that I drink you will drink; and with the baptism with which I am baptized, you will be baptized; [40] but to sit at my right hand or at my left is not mine to grant, but it is for those for whom it has been prepared."

[41] When the ten heard this, they began to be angry with James and John. [42] So Jesus called them and said to them, "You know that among the Gentiles those whom they recognize as their rulers lord it over them, and their great ones are tyrants over them. [43] But it is not so among you; but whoever wishes to become great among you must be your servant, [44] and whoever wishes to be first among you must be slave of all. [45] For the Son of Man came not to be served but to serve, and to give his life a ransom for many."

Each of the three passion announcements (8:31; 9:31; 10:33–34) is followed by a passage that demonstrates how little the disciples comprehend what Jesus is talking about. Here James and John play the role. Instead of asking Jesus what he means or showing their loyalty by promising to die with him, they approach him with the request that they be given the second and third highest positions in the messianic kingdom (subordinate only to Jesus himself). "In your glory" can of course refer to Jesus' post-Resurrection glory (8:38), but it can just as well allude to the supernatural power with which the Messiah would be endowed at the inauguration of a this-worldly rule (see Isa. 11:4). That is, the brothers' request may assume that Jesus will be installed as glorious king without having to die, despite what he has said. In any event, the notion that the suffering of the Messiah renders obsolete all striving for rank and status (see 8:34–37; 9:33–37) has completely eluded them.

In his first response Jesus challenges Zebedee's sons with a question: Can you qualify for such exalted positions by sharing the Messiah's trials? Two powerful metaphors are employed in the question. In the Old Testament, "cup" can refer to blessings (Psalm 23:5) or judgment (Psalm 75:8; Jer. 25:15, 17, 28). In Jewish apocryphal literature, the cup metaphor is used occasionally with reference to the natural death of an individual. Here it seems to refer not simply to death but to an untimely, painful death. A similar use of the metaphor recurs in 14:36, where Jesus prays, "Remove this cup from me" (see also John 18:11). "Baptism" is likewise used figuratively of Jesus' coming passion, perhaps on the basis of Old Testament texts that compare disaster to drowning (see, for example, Psalm 42:7; Lam. 3:54; Jonah 2:3–5). A similar saying is found in Luke 12:50, "I have a baptism with which to be baptized, and what stress I am under until it is completed!"

The brothers' glib answer, "We are able," is weighted with irony; James and John will desert Jesus and flee for their lives in the garden of Gethsemane (14:50). Mark's earliest readers, many of whom had faced persecution, may have winced at the brothers' *self*-confidence, having learned that only by God's grace can one remain faithful in the midst of fiery trials (see 1 Pet. 4:12–19).

In his second response, Jesus assures James and John that they will indeed undergo suffering. It is not necessary to take verse 39 as implying that they will experience exactly the same sufferings as Jesus. Neither brother was crucified. According to Acts 12:2, James was executed with a sword (probably by beheading). Tradition claims that John lived to a ripe old age in Ephesus, but he undoubtedly experienced various forms of persecution (see Acts 4:1–3). Nevertheless, even willingness to share Jesus' sufferings will not guarantee them the special honors they are seeking. Jesus again humbly subordinates himself to God (see my comments on 10:18; 13:32; 14:36); not the Messiah but God alone will determine who will be given the places of greatest honor in the messianic kingdom. There is here a subtle rebuff to the self-seeking apostles (and any church leaders who follow in their train). Those who are impressed with their own importance may be greatly surprised to discover what humble people God has selected for special honor!

Mark does not explain the anger of the other disciples. Perhaps they resent the "pushiness" of Zebedee's sons. Possibly they are annoyed that they have allowed James and John to get ahead of them in the quest for future favors. In any event, Mark presents it as an inappropriate anger prompted by this-worldly thinking about rank and status. The kingdoms of this world are ruled by might, and the highest honors go to those who can seize and hold power. God's kingdom, Jesus explains, is of a very different order. Those who want to be great must make themselves small by serving others like humble slaves.

The climax of the passage, indeed of the entire section that began with Peter's confession (8:27–30), is reached in verse 45. The three passion announcements have prepared the readers for the forthcoming passion (also 9:9–12), but nowhere has it been stated *why* Jesus must suffer. Each was followed by misunderstanding on the part of the disciples and teaching that discipleship involves self-sacrifice and service. Now the entire complex is brought to its culmination with the statement that Jesus the Messiah came not to be served (as other kings are) but to serve and to give his life as a ransom for many.

Paul asserts that those who were Christians before him told him that "Christ died for our sins in accordance with the scriptures" (1 Cor. 15:3).

This idea—so precious to Paul, John, and others—was not, however, the only interpretation of the death of Jesus. In the great Christ hymn quoted by Paul in Philippians 2:6–11 there is no suggestion that Jesus' suffering atoned for sin. Some early Christians apparently understood the crucifixion rather as a testing of Jesus' readiness to obey God to the uttermost; passing the test qualified him to be inaugurated as God's Messiah. Clearly, Mark stands nearer to 1 Corinthians 15:3 than to Philippians 2:6–11. Neither here in 10:45 nor in the cup saying at the Last Supper (14:24)—the only two passages in Mark that interpret Jesus' death—is there any explicit mention of sin; but in both passages it is stated that Jesus' death is *for many*. Mark surely implies that the Messiah's undeserved suffering will be beneficial to many *in their relationship to God;* that is, his death will overcome the obstacle created by sin.

The practice of animal sacrifice is often used by New Testament writers as a metaphor for the meaning of Jesus' death. Jesus is identified in John 1:29 as "the Lamb of God who takes away the sin of the world!" In Mark 10:45 we have a different metaphor. The word "ransom" refers to a payment made to a captor for the release of a prisoner or to a slaveowner for the emancipation of a slave (Lev. 25:47–55). Exodus 13:11–16 declares that every firstborn male of livestock and of human beings belongs to God and must either be killed or ransomed. In Mark 10:45 this metaphor suggests that Jesus' death ransoms those who otherwise must remain captives (to sin) or die (in punishment for sin). Early interpreters disputed whether the ransom was paid to God or to the devil, but this was to press the metaphor too far. The verse merely asserts that Jesus' death had a liberating effect. "For many" should not be taken restrictively. In the Dead Sea Scrolls, "the many" is frequently used with reference to the community as a whole.

With the utterance of this saying, Mark's "extended introduction" to the passion narrative (see the Introduction) is essentially completed. All that remains is the transitional narrative of the healing of a blind man on the last part of Jesus' journey to the city where he will die.

BARTIMAEUS GAINS HIS SIGHT
AND FOLLOWS JESUS
Mark 10:46–52

10:46 **They came to Jericho. As he and his disciples and a large crowd were leaving Jericho, Bartimaeus son of Timaeus, a blind beggar, was sitting by**

the roadside. ⁴⁷ When he heard that it was Jesus of Nazareth, he began to shout out and say, "Jesus, Son of David, have mercy on me!" ⁴⁸ Many sternly ordered him to be quiet, but he cried out even more loudly, "Son of David, have mercy on me!" ⁴⁹ Jesus stood still and said, "Call him here." And they called the blind man, saying to him, "Take heart; get up, he is calling you." ⁵⁰ So throwing off his cloak, he sprang up and came to Jesus. ⁵¹ Then Jesus said to him, "What do you want me to do for you?" The blind man said to him, "My teacher, let me see again." ⁵² Jesus said to him, "Go; your faith has made you well." Immediately he regained his sight and followed him on the way.

This last healing narrative has special importance because of its location and its symbolic power. Mark reports, "They came to Jericho," without indicating what occurred there. Since this city was less than thirteen miles from Jerusalem, it may well have been the site of an overnight stop. On the basis of later references to Jesus' days in Jerusalem, it has been inferred that he arrived in Jericho on Friday afternoon, rested there on the sabbath, and departed for Jerusalem on Sunday morning. Luke 19:1–10 has Jesus visit the home of Zacchaeus during this time.

Jesus and his company find the blind son of Timaeus (*Bar* is the Aramaic word for "son") sitting beside the road leading out of Jericho, begging coins from the passing pilgrims. When the blind man learns that the famous teacher is coming by, he confidently shouts, "Jesus, Son of David, have mercy on me!" Attempts to silence him only increase the intensity of his cry for help.

Although "Son of David" could be used nontechnically of any male descendant of David (Joseph is so addressed by an angel in Matt. 1:20), it more commonly served as a synonym for "the Messiah." This is the only instance of the phrase in Mark. Its use here prepares us for the shout of the crowd accompanying Jesus into Jerusalem: "Blessed is the coming kingdom of our ancestor David!" (11:10) and for Jesus' enigmatic question about David's relationship to the Messiah (12:35–37).

In view of Jesus' firm insistence that his disciples tell no one that he is the Messiah (8:30), Bartimaeus's use of "Son of David" is startling. Readers are apt to ask, "How did the blind man learn the secret?" According to Matthew 12:23 and John 6:14–15; 7:26, 41, however, there was widespread speculation concerning whether or not Jesus was the Messiah. When facing Jesus directly, Bartimaeus addresses him as "Rabbouni." This reverential Aramaic form of address, meaning "My master," a heightened form of "Rabbi," is found elsewhere in the New Testament only in John 20:16. Whereas John translates the word for his Greek-speaking audience, Mark leaves it untranslated, perhaps to enhance its deferential tone (see NSRV footnote).

The miracle itself is related with remarkable brevity, in contrast to the fullness of detail provided for the healings in chapter 5. All emphasis is placed on the blind man's faith: "Go; your faith has made you well" (literally, "has saved you"; does Mark intend a double meaning?).

The narrative—and the entire section that began at 8:27—concludes with the notice that the man's sight was instantly restored and he "followed him on the way." It is possible that the last phrase has no special significance apart from demonstrating new sight and gratitude. Because of the location of the story, however, some interpreters maintain that Mark has endowed these words with symbolic power. Although many healings are reported in this Gospel, only two concern blind people. The first is placed just prior to Peter's confession and the succeeding complex consisting of three passion announcements and their sequels, in which the disciples appear blind to the significance of Jesus' forthcoming passion. At the conclusion of this complex, just before the beginning of the passion narrative, the reader is confronted by this second report of Jesus' opening the eyes of a blind person. Because "the way" along which Bartimaeus follows Jesus is the way to the cross, it seems likely that his restored sight serves as a foil to the continuing blindness of the disciples. They will be able truly to "see" and "follow" on the way of humble self-sacrifice only when their eyes have been opened by a miracle—the miracle of the resurrection.

4. The Passion and Resurrection of Jesus

Mark 11:1–16:8

9. The Messiah's Royal Arrival in Jerusalem
Mark 11:1–25

THE TRIUMPHAL ENTRY
Mark 11:1–11

11:1 **When they were approaching Jerusalem, at Bethphage and Bethany, near the Mount of Olives, he sent two of his disciples** 2 **and said to them, "Go into the village ahead of you, and immediately as you enter it, you will find tied there a colt that has never been ridden; untie it and bring it.** 3 **If anyone says to you, 'Why are you doing this?' just say this, 'The Lord needs it and will send it back here immediately.'"** 4 **They went away and found a colt tied near a door, outside in the street. As they were untying it,** 5 **some of the bystanders said to them, "What are you doing, untying the colt?"** 6 **They told them what Jesus had said; and they allowed them to take it.** 7 **Then they brought the colt to Jesus and threw their cloaks on it; and he sat on it.** 8 **Many people spread their cloaks on the road, and others spread leafy branches that they had cut in the fields.** 9 **Then those who went ahead and those who followed were shouting,**

"Hosanna!
Blessed is the one who comes in the name of the Lord!
10 **Blessed is the coming kingdom of our ancestor David!**
Hosanna in the highest heaven!"

11 **Then he entered Jerusalem and went into the temple; and when he had looked around at everything, as it was already late, he went out to Bethany with the twelve.**

The word *passion* is used by Christians with reference to the sufferings and death of Jesus. Scholars employ the term *passion narrative* broadly to include the events of Jesus' final days in Jerusalem, beginning with his royal procession into the city. The significance of the passion is underscored by the fact that Mark devotes over a third of his book to this last week.

The story of the triumphal entry is told in all four Gospels. Because the event is reenacted each Palm Sunday in the imagination of worshipers, there is a natural tendency to superimpose elements from the other Gospels on the Markan narrative. We may remember palm branches (John 12:13), the donkey and the quotation from Zechariah 9:9 (Matt. 21:2, 5; John 12:14–15), and Jesus weeping over the city (Luke 19:41–44). None of this is in Mark. Although it is historically probable that the animal on which Jesus rode was a donkey, the Greek word Mark uses, correctly translated "colt," more often referred to a young horse; readers of this Gospel in the Greek and Roman world would not automatically assume that a young donkey bore Jesus. Apparently, Mark was not concerned about this ambiguity; the connection with Zechariah was not uppermost in his mind. And instead of waving palm branches, Mark's crowd spreads leaves, grass, straw, or rushes on the road in front of Jesus ("leafy branches" is an inaccurate translation).

The feature of Mark's version (followed by Matthew and Luke) that most sharply distinguishes it from John's is the emphasis placed on the finding of the animal. Whereas John simply states that Jesus found a young donkey and rode it (John 12:14), Mark relates with considerable detail how Jesus instructed two disciples to locate a colt in a certain village (we are not told which one), to untie it, and to respond to objectors with the statement "The Lord needs it and will send it back here immediately." Because Mark does not tell us why this part of the story is so important, we are left to conjecture. Perhaps Mark wants to bear testimony to Jesus' supernatural knowledge or clairvoyance; he knows in advance what will happen in the village. Possibly he wants to present Jesus as acting in royal fashion. Because a king has the right to impress a privately owned animal into his service as need arises, the statement "The Lord needs it" suggests that Jesus is asserting a royal prerogative. The effect of this subplot is clear at any rate; Jesus' decision to ride into Jerusalem is not a casual one. Because it was customary for pilgrims to walk into the holy city, this choice sets him apart. The royal significance of his mount is reinforced by the stipulation that the young animal must not have been previously ridden. The occasion requires not just any animal but one that has not been defiled by common use. A later rabbinic document, which may reflect first-century custom, claims that no other person may ride on the king's horse.

A major point of dispute among interpreters is whether or not the demonstration is regarded by Mark as explicitly messianic, that is, whether the enthusiastic pilgrims accompanying Jesus regard him as the Messiah or simply as a prophet of the coming messianic kingdom. The fact that people lay their outer garments on the road as a "carpet" for him to ride on, in reminiscence of the treatment accorded the new king in 2 Kings 9:13, strongly supports the messianic interpretation. It is unlikely that a prophet would be honored in this way. Although their cry "Blessed is the coming kingdom of our ancestor David" is ambiguous, the public use of the title "Son of David" a few verses earlier (10:47–48) suggests that Jesus is being hailed as the Messiah. Other interpreters insist that Mark does not intend that the procession be openly messianic, for in that case he would have to explain why the Romans do not promptly intervene and arrest Jesus. Moreover, this would make incredible Mark's later claim that the authorities can find no evidence against Jesus (14:53–61). Why does the crowd simply disappear at the end of this narrative? If they truly regard Jesus as the Messiah, why do they not remain with him? Why do they not try to protect him from the authorities later in the week?

The fact is that the issue cannot be resolved by arguments of this kind, because we inevitably confuse two different matters: the historical incident and Mark's portrayal of that incident. Possibly the actual event was more ambiguous or on a smaller scale than is suggested by the four evangelists and thus eluded official attention. On the other hand, perhaps news of it reached Pilate and contributed to his decision to put "the King of the Jews" (15:26) to death. It seems probable, in any event, that Mark intends that the readers perceive Jesus' arrival as royal. Because Jesus' status as Messiah has supposedly remained a secret since Peter's confession (8:27–30), this procession, following Bartimaeus's public use of "Son of David," provides the only narrative explanation for the high priest's question in 14:61, "Are you the Messiah?" Nevertheless, in the procession Jesus' messianic claim remains implicit only. Not until the high priest raises the issue at the trial will Jesus publicly assert that he is indeed the Messiah (14:62). Mark is not concerned about such historical questions as why the Romans did not interrupt the procession and why the crowd abandoned their Messiah, because he correctly regards the procession as nonpolitical. The unarmed pilgrims are not planning a revolution with Jesus as their leader; they expect God to install Jesus as Messiah in God's own time.

The crowd shouts, "Hosanna! Blessed is the one who comes in the name of the Lord!" (v. 9). These words apparently come from Psalm 118, one of the psalms regularly used at the annual temple festivals. "Hosanna" represents the Hebrew phrase "Save us, we beseech you" (Psalm 118:25). The fact that the phrase is not translated suggests that "Hosanna," like "Hallelujah," had come to have a new function; it is no longer a prayer but an acclamation, a shout of praise, as indicated by its repetition in Mark

11:10, "Hosanna in the highest heaven!" (A similar phenomenon can be seen in Rev. 19:1, where "salvation" is used as a praise word.) The statement "Blessed is the one who comes in the name of the LORD" (Psalm 118:26) was normally understood as referring to arriving pilgrims, who were greeted by those already present with the words immediately following in the psalm, "We bless you from the house of the LORD." There is evidence, however, that the words came to be regarded as having messianic significance; "in the name of the LORD" suggested one who would come with full authority as God's end-time representative. Such an understanding is implied by the attached blessing in Mark 11:10, "Blessed is the coming kingdom of our ancestor David!"

The last verse of the passage seems anticlimactic. Unlike the other Gospel writers, Mark includes nothing about the objections raised by the Pharisees (Luke 19:39; John 12:19) or the response of Jerusalemites (Matt. 21:10). Instead, Jesus merely looks around at everything inside the temple area and then departs to find a place to sleep in Bethany. Although this may appear to us as if Jesus is behaving like a tourist, we must remember that as a loyal Jew he must have attended many temple festivals. Mark represents the Messiah as making a brief inspection tour of the temple in preparation for the next day's action.

The Palm Sunday narrative is heavy with irony. Christian readers know that the man who is here hailed as Messiah by a throng of joyful pilgrims will soon be condemned by his nation's leaders and suffer an excruciating and shameful execution. Explicit joy is thus overshadowed by implicit sorrow. Nevertheless, because the readers know also that the Messiah's death will constitute "a ransom for many" (10:45) and that its shame will be annulled by the glory of resurrection (16:1–8), the joy of the triumphal entry remains valid.

THE CURSING OF THE FIG TREE
Mark 11:12–14

> 11:12 On the following day, when they came from Bethany, he was hungry. [13] Seeing in the distance a fig tree in leaf, he went to see whether perhaps he would find anything on it. When he came to it, he found nothing but leaves, for it was not the season for figs. [14] He said to it, "May no one ever eat fruit from you again." And his disciples heard it.

This narrative is usually referred to as "The Cursing of the Fig Tree," even though the word *curse* does not occur. Jesus is represented as uttering a vehement wish, which subsequently has a destructive effect on the tree and is therefore interpreted by Peter as a curse (see v. 21).

Many readers find this story very upsetting, since it portrays Jesus as acting petulantly against an innocent tree, which is unable to satisfy his hunger simply because it is not the season for figs. Although the main fig harvest occurs in the fall, early fruit that develops on the old wood matures in June, six weeks or so after Passover. A few figs that failed to develop during the previous fall may ripen in the early spring, but such instances are rare. Jesus' anger seems so much out of character (he refuses to curse even his worst enemies) that many interpreters have attempted to explain Mark's story as due to misunderstanding. It has been suggested, for example, that a landmark skeleton of a tree along the Jericho-Jerusalem road later reminded his followers that Jesus had once been disappointed by a fruitless tree (in June or later, when fruit was to be expected), and the legend grew that his disappointment caused the death of this particular tree. Another proposal is that a parable about a sterile tree (perhaps similar to the one in Luke 13:6–9) was mistakenly transposed into a historical narrative. A third suggestion is that Jesus, using prophetic symbolism (see Jer. 8:13; Mic. 7:1), once drew attention to a fruitless fig tree as an object lesson about the punishment human unfaithfulness will incur, and the promise of punishment was later "historicized" into a story about the tree's destruction.

Although we cannot be certain what historical incident underlies this narrative, we can learn what it means to Mark by studying the sequel in verses 20–25.

THE CLEANSING OF THE TEMPLE
Mark 11:15–19

> 11:15 Then they came to Jerusalem. And he entered the temple and began to drive out those who were selling and those who were buying in the temple, and he overturned the tables of the money changers and the seats of those who sold doves; 16 and he would not allow anyone to carry anything through the temple. 17 He was teaching and saying, "Is it not written,
> 'My house shall be called a house of prayer for all the nations'?
> But you have made it a den of robbers."
> 18 And when the chief priests and the scribes heard it, they kept looking for a way to kill him; for they were afraid of him, because the whole crowd was spellbound by his teaching. 19 And when evening came, Jesus and his disciples went out of the city.

As rebuilt by Herod the Great, the Jerusalem temple was one of the wonders of the ancient world. Although the central shrine itself was comparatively small, in conformity with biblical specifications (see 1 Kings 6; 2 Chronicles 3), the temple precinct contained a number of impressive buildings and was immense in size. Approximately fifteen hundred feet from north to south and a thousand feet from east to west, it comprised over thirty-five acres. In front of the temple proper was the Court of the Priests, with the high altar where sacrifices were offered. Just east of this, facing the temple, was the Court of Israel, behind which was the Court of the Women. The remainder, perhaps two-thirds of the whole, was referred to as the Court of the Gentiles, for non-Jews were permitted to enter it. In this area, perhaps in the southeast corner, there was a market where worshipers could purchase unblemished animals and birds for sacrifice, and exchange everyday money for the special coins required for the payment of the temple tax (see Matt. 17:24–27).

With prophetic zeal Jesus singlehandedly expels both buyers and sellers, and overturns the tables of the money changers and the seats of the dove merchants. He forbids the use of the temple precinct as a shortcut for secular purposes (v. 16). He charges that the buyers, sellers, and carriers are secularizing holy space, quoting the Greek translation of Isaiah 56:7, "My house shall be called a house of prayer for all the Gentiles" (in the New Testament the Greek word in Mark 11:16 rendered "nations" by the NRSV usually refers to non-Jewish individuals, not to corporate entities such as "the nation of the Romans"). The passage in Isaiah from which this quotation comes looks forward to a golden age when foreigners will worship in the temple. In the parallels in Matthew 21:13 and Luke 19:46 the phrase "for all the Gentiles" is omitted, perhaps because by the time these Gospels were written the temple had been destroyed and it seemed unlikely that this rubble-strewn area would ever become a house of prayer for all the Gentiles.

Jesus insists that a holy place intended for prayer has been made instead into "a den of robbers" (Jer. 7:11). This phrase has led many interpreters to assume that Jesus is attacking unfair business practices and price gouging. There is no support for this interpretation in the text. Jesus expels buyers as well as sellers! Although there may well have been instances of overcharging, it is probable that competition from the four markets on the Mount of Olives kept such abuses in check. "A den of robbers" refers not to a place where robbery occurs but to the safe haven to which brigands return with their booty. Jeremiah condemns not unholy acts in the temple but people who steal, murder, and commit adultery elsewhere and then come into the temple and say, "We are safe!" (Jer. 7:9–10). Because such persons cannot offer up the genuine worship that springs from hearts responsive to God, "den of robbers" represents the secularizing of worship in "the house of prayer."

It is sometimes argued that Jesus' violent behavior in the temple was intended not to reform an abuse but to symbolize the forthcoming destruction of the temple. The false accusation presented at his trial, "We heard him say, 'I will destroy this temple . . .'" (14:58) is related, scholars suggest, to this incident. Closing down the temple market, however, should have had little effect on the sacrifices, for animals were obtainable elsewhere. If Jesus wanted to dramatize God's rejection of the sacrificial system as a whole, he should have attempted to interrupt the offering of sacrifices in the inner court. The fact that his followers continued to frequent the temple after his death and resurrection (Acts 2:46) constitutes sufficient evidence that Jesus did not teach them that God had abandoned the temple.

Another proposal is that Jesus' act was meant to dramatize the conviction that prayer should be substituted for animal sacrifices. The second-century Gospel of the Ebionites attributes to Jesus the saying, "I have come to annul sacrifice, and if you will not cease to sacrifice the wrath will not turn from you." In the New Testament, however, there is no hint that Jesus opposed the sacrifices, and therefore we ought not to read such a conviction into this passage.

Is the narrative historically credible? Could one person have interrupted business in the temple court? Some maintain that the temple police or Roman soldiers would have immediately put an end to the incident by arresting Jesus. Acts 21:27–36 reports the prompt response of the Roman detachment stationed just north of the temple when an angry crowd attempted to kill Paul. It is probable, however, that the Romans would not have reacted to the prophetic protest of a single individual. The temple police may have been overawed by Jesus; powerful, holy men were regarded with a reverence bordering on fear (compare the response of the police in John 7:46). Moreover, Mark is careful not to exaggerate the extent of Jesus' action; he claims only that Jesus *began* to drive out the merchants and their customers. The whole incident may have been over before the authorities heard about it.

Did Jesus intend that his protest be perceived as an attack on the chief priests, who were ultimately responsible for the temple market? The text does not tell us. We learn only that "the chief priests and scribes" (by which Mark means the temple establishment) wanted to destroy Jesus because they were afraid of his influence on the crowds. The note that the whole crowd "was spellbound by his teaching" repeats exactly the words used in 1:22 at the beginning of Jesus' ministry, "They were astounded at his teaching" (the same Greek verb is used in both verses). These verses bracket the public ministry and serve to contrast the popular response to Jesus with that of his people's leaders.

Although the overturning of tables and chairs can readily be understood as a prophetic gesture, Mark undoubtedly sees it also as a messianic act. The Psalms of Solomon, written shortly before Jesus' birth, promises that the Lord Messiah will purge Jerusalem so that Gentiles may come to see his glory (17:30–31). The purging effected by the Messiah from Nazareth is symbolic only, however. Before his glorious reign is inaugurated, the temple will be utterly destroyed (13:2).

THE LESSON FROM THE WITHERED FIG TREE
Mark 11:20–25

> 11:20 **In the morning as they passed by, they saw the fig tree withered away to its roots.** [21] **Then Peter remembered and said to him, "Rabbi, look! The fig tree that you cursed has withered."** [22] **Jesus answered them, "Have faith in God.** [23] **Truly I tell you, if you say to this mountain, 'Be taken up and thrown into the sea,' and if you do not doubt in your heart, but believe that what you say will come to pass, it will be done for you.** [24] **So I tell you, whatever you ask for in prayer, believe that you have received it, and it will be yours.**
>
> [25] **"Whenever you stand praying, forgive, if you have anything against anyone; so that your Father in heaven may also forgive you your trespasses."**
> *[Please note that some ancient authorities include verse 26.]*

Because Mark "sandwiches" the cleansing of the temple between the two halves of the fig tree story, it is frequently argued that each story interprets the other; the leafy tree that bears no fruit represents the temple, which, despite its magnificence, has become a den of robbers instead of a house of prayer for all. Jesus' cursing of the tree, it is proposed, enables us to see that the act in the temple constitutes not an attempted reform but an announcement of destruction. Some interpreters would take this line of thought even further. Because Israel is sometimes symbolized by a fig tree (Jer. 8:13), Jesus' denunciation in the temple, like his cursing of the tree, applies to the nation as a whole, in anticipation of God's rejection of Israel because of persistent unfruitfulness.

Such an interpretation would be more defensible if Mark did *not* include the sequel to the fig tree story! Because he does, we must interpret the tree incident on the basis of what is explicit, not what we suppose may be implicit. These verses indicate that Mark himself wants us to see the withering of the fig tree as an inspiring example of the power of God, to which Jesus had direct access, and which is available to his followers through faith and prayer. (If there is an explicit relationship with the temple story, it is through the word "prayer" in v. 17.)

Although Mark has twice portrayed Jesus as praying (1:35; 6:46), the only teaching about prayer included earlier in the Gospel is the brief suggestion about the importance of prayer for effective exorcism (9:29). On the other hand, the role of faith in healing has been repeatedly mentioned (2:5; 5:34, 36, 6:6; 10:52). Although the object of faith is not specified in any of these passages, presumably Mark is referring to faith that God's power is available through Jesus. Now the themes of faith and prayer are presented together.

The saying about faith that can move mountains may have been proverbial, based perhaps on Old Testament texts about God's ability to level mountains (Isa. 40:4), but it suits Jesus' love of hyperbole (see 10:25; Matt. 7:3). A similar saying about faith that can uproot a mulberry tree and plant it in the sea is found in Luke 17:6. Mark's version stresses that miracle-working faith must be undivided; there can be no mixture of faith and doubt. The verb here translated "doubt" normally means "separate," "distinguish," or "decide." Its use in the New Testament with the meaning "hesitate" (Acts 10:20), "waver" (Rom. 4:20; Jude 22), or "have doubts" (Rom. 14:23) probably arises from the basic meaning "separate": one who doubts is internally divided. Paul presents Abraham as a prime example of single-minded faith: "No distrust made him waver concerning the promise of God, but he grew strong in his faith as he gave glory to God, being fully convinced that God was able to do what he had promised" (Rom. 4:20–21). James 1:6–8 calls the doubter "double-minded" and compares him or her to "a wave of the sea, driven and tossed by the wind."

Whereas verse 23 speaks of an individual, verse 24 returns to the plural of verse 22. Although the saying could, of course, apply to individuals praying in isolation, the shift from singular to plural suggests group prayer. The corporate requests of gathered believers who single-mindedly envision God's response will be granted.

In presenting these sayings on faith and prayer, Mark does little to protect readers from misunderstanding and misuse. Both scripture and experience teach that petitions of even the most fervent believers are not always granted. Prayer is not a magical technique for achieving personal goals, as is occasionally suggested by radio evangelists ("Follow my prayer method, and you can earn a million dollars!"). Even prayers for healing, Paul discovered, are sometimes answered otherwise than one hopes: "Three times I appealed to the Lord about this, that it would leave me, but he said to me, 'My grace is sufficient for you, for power is made perfect in weakness'" (2 Cor. 12:8–9). Genuine prayer acknowledges divine sovereignty by subordinating every request to God's will: "Not what I want, but what you want" (14:36).

Two other misconceptions of these sayings must be avoided. Inability to work miracles does not mean that one's faith is not genuine. The authenticity of faith is demonstrated more truly by obedient living than by miracles. As Paul pointedly remarks, "If I have all faith, so as to remove mountains, but do not have love, I am nothing" (1 Cor. 13:2). Again, the Gospel saying about mountain moving should not be limited to miracles. Through faith and prayer many ordinary believers have been empowered to accomplish incredible things, such as holding a broken family together, effecting reconciliation between warring factions in a church, or creating a home for the homeless. Such miracles are no less significant than miracles of healing!

The collection of sayings on faith and prayer concludes with one that is more familiar to us in the version accompanying the Lord's Prayer in the Sermon on the Mount (Matt. 6:14). The notion occurs also in pre-Christian Judaism: "Forgive your neighbor the wrong he has done, and then your sins will be pardoned when you pray" (Sir. 28:2). The point is not that forgiving others earns God's forgiveness, but rather that an unforgiving spirit constitutes a form of impenitence that constricts the flow of divine forgiveness. In this context the forgiveness saying constitutes a reminder that effective prayer involves the horizontal as well as the vertical, because our relationship to God is inextricably interwoven with our relationships with others. Negative praying is thus excluded; we cannot pray *against* others. It is significant that this is the only place in Mark's Gospel where God is referred to as "your Father in heaven" ("your" is plural). Like all language about God, "Father" is a metaphor. Its function is not to argue for the masculinity of God but to remind us that the God we worship has made us brothers and sisters in one family.

10. Jesus Refutes His Opponents
Mark 11:27–12:44

In this section we are presented with a series of disputes in the temple involving Jesus and various opponents. The function of these narratives is to prepare us for the capital case against Jesus by demonstrating that he is opposed by all the influential groups in Israel. Although the crowds are spellbound by his teaching, the leaders resolutely refuse to believe that God has sent him. They interact with him not to learn from him but to embarrass him in front of the crowds and to secure evidence that can be used against him.

JESUS' AUTHORITY IS CHALLENGED
Mark 11:27–33

11:27 **Again they came to Jerusalem. As he was walking in the temple, the chief priests, the scribes, and the elders came to him** [28] **and said, "By what authority are you doing these things? Who gave you this authority to do them?"** [29] **Jesus said to them, "I will ask you one question; answer me, and I will tell you by what authority I do these things.** [30] **Did the baptism of John come from heaven, or was it of human origin? Answer me."** [31] **They argued with one another, "If we say, 'From heaven,' he will say, 'Why then did you not believe him?'** [32] **But shall we say, 'Of human origin'?"—they were afraid of the crowd, for all regarded John as truly a prophet.** [33] **So they answered Jesus, "We do not know." And Jesus said to them, "Neither will I tell you by what authority I am doing these things."**

The first group of opponents is the most dangerous, for the council that will condemn Jesus to death consists of chief priests, scribes, and elders (14:53–64; for a description of these three groups, see my comments on 8:31). Their role has already been predicted in the first passion announcement (8:31). The chief priests and scribes are mentioned without the elders in the third passion announcement (10:33–34), and in 11:18 we hear that the chief priests and scribes are looking for a way to kill Jesus (see also 14:1). These previous references make it clear that in this passage the leaders come not with genuine questions but with negative intent. Although Mark uses the definite article with all three categories, we should not assume that the entire council has assembled in the open air to interview Jesus. When they are ready as a judicial body to deal with him, he will be summoned before them, and their leader, the high priest, will preside.

The representatives of the council address two questions to Jesus concerning the *nature* and *source* of his authority. The first challenges Jesus to identify his role: Does he act as a holy man, teacher of the law, prophet, or Messiah? The second demands his credentials: Who has taught him, laid hands on him, or invested him with authority? They are not asking, "Has God sent you?" for an affirmative reply would be unverifiable. "These things" refers most naturally to the temple cleansing of 11:15–17, but it may in Mark's view include the triumphal entry and Jesus' ministry as a whole. The leaders' intent is to demonstrate in front of the crowd that Jesus has usurped a leadership role to which he is not entitled by birth or training.

In a fashion common among later rabbis, Jesus responds with a counterquestion. Interpreters disagree about whether Jesus' question is merely a rhetorical ploy, intended only to embarrass his questioners publicly, or a genuine response to their challenge. By placing his opponents on the horns of a dilemma that allows them no escape without losing face, Jesus successfully evades their challenge and proves himself a debating champion. On the other hand, his counterquestion is by no means irrelevant to the issue they have raised. He could have responded simply, "If you don't know, I won't tell you." From his first appearance in Galilee (1:14–15), Jesus has implicitly claimed that it is God alone who has authorized him to speak and act. In the synagogue his teaching authority was validated by a public display of God's power (1:21–28). His response to the Jerusalem leaders implies that they are incapable of acknowledging the source of his authority; they have already demonstrated this incapacity by refusing to accept John as God's prophet.

Ironically, Jesus exhibits his authority by his very refusal to answer the powerful representatives of Israel's highest court. He implicitly claims that his authority supersedes theirs! Later, when facing a formal session of the council, he will deny their authority over him by refusing to respond to the testimony brought against him (14:61).

Narratively speaking, the question about Jesus' authority is posed by opponents, but existentially it engages every reader of the Gospel. Is Jesus of Nazareth just another wandering Jewish exorcist, religious teacher, or deluded would-be Messiah, or is he God's supreme representative?

JESUS' OPPONENTS
ARE WARNED IN A PARABLE
Mark 12:1–12

12:1 **Then he began to speak to them in parables. "A man planted a vineyard, put a fence around it, dug a pit for the wine press, and built a watchtower; then he leased it to tenants and went to another country. ² When the season came, he sent a slave to the tenants to collect from them his share of the produce of the vineyard. ³ But they seized him, and beat him, and sent him away empty-handed. ⁴ And again he sent another slave to them; this one they beat over the head and insulted. ⁵ Then he sent another, and that one they killed. And so it was with many others; some they beat, and others they killed. ⁶ He had still one other, a beloved son. Finally he sent him to them, saying, 'They will respect my son.' ⁷ But those tenants said to one another, 'This is the heir; come, let us kill him, and the inheritance will be ours.' ⁸ So they seized him, killed him, and threw him out of the vineyard. ⁹ What then will the owner of the vineyard do? He will come and destroy the tenants and give the vineyard to others. ¹⁰ Have you not read this scripture:**

> **'The stone that the builders rejected**
> **has become the cornerstone;**
> **¹¹ this was the Lord's doing,**
> **and it is amazing in our eyes'?"**

¹² When they realized that he had told this parable against them, they wanted to arrest him, but they feared the crowd. So they left him and went away.

Had this story been told by a pagan philosopher in Athens, its point would undoubtedly have been taken to be that crime does not pay; those who indulge in less serious forms of lawlessness are likely to become guilty of progressively more vicious crimes until they bring destruction down upon their heads. Because it is a Jewish story, however, it was surely understood by its first hearers in terms of Jewish symbolism. In a number of Old Testament passages, Israel is compared to a vine or vineyard planted by God (Psalm 80:8–16; Isa. 5:1–7; Jer. 2:21). The importance of this symbolism was reinforced by an architectural detail in Herod's temple. The Jewish historian Josephus reported with pride that Herod adorned the space above the main entrance with a golden vine so large that its grape clusters were the size of a man. Later, during the Jewish revolt of A.D. 66–70, the rebels issued coins bearing the image of a vine. Even without elaboration, therefore, Jesus' statement "A man planted a vineyard" would be quickly taken to refer to the relationship between God and Israel. As the parable is reported by Mark, however, there are clear allusions to Isaiah 5:2, "he built a watchtower in the midst of it, and hewed out a wine vat in it."

A second element in the story that reflects Jewish tradition is the motif of the maltreated messengers. In accordance with 2 Chronicles 36:15–16 and Nehemiah 9:26, it was widely believed by Jews that their people had constantly rejected and abused God's prophets. A little first-century document called *The Lives of the Prophets* attributed martyrdom to a number of prophets who probably died of natural causes. The liveliness of this tradition is witnessed by other noncanonical Jewish writings, Josephus, and the New Testament (Matt. 5:12; 23:37; Acts 7:52). It is striking that, according to this tradition, the people bear the guilt even though it is often their leaders who are responsible for the crimes. On this basis it is urged by some interpreters that the parable of the Wicked Tenants in its original form denounced Israel as a whole for its rejection of the prophets and Jesus. This must remain a matter of conjecture. In its present form and setting, it clearly refers to Israel's leaders rather than the people. It functions as Jesus' judgment upon the chief priests, scribes, and elders who have just challenged his authority (11:27–33) and who will soon condemn him to death (14:53–64; see also 8:31). In his conclusion Mark notes that Jesus' adversaries realize that Jesus has applied this parable to them and would arrest him on the spot if it were not for the crowd's sympathy for him (12:12).

A number of scholars argue that this is not an authentic parable of Jesus but an allegory created by someone in the early church, because of the obvious reference to Jesus in verse 6 ("a beloved son"). For Mark this is surely an allusion to 1:11 and 9:7, where the voice from heaven identifies Jesus as God's beloved Son. The adjective "beloved" may well be Mark's embellishment. The reference to the owner's son, however, does not require that we treat the passage as an allegory. The murder of the son is an essential ingredient of the story as parable; the murder of a final servant would not provide the necessary climax because it would not exhibit the ultimate rebellion, namely, the attempted takeover of the vineyard. For a first-century audience this was a believable story because of the deep hostility with which many tenant farmers in Palestine viewed their foreign landlords. If a landlord died without an heir, Jewish law permitted current tenants to have the first claim to the land. In this story the tenants may assume that the owner has died and the son has come to claim his inheritance.

Although it is possible that this was originally a simple parable about rebelliousness (as in the shorter version found in the Gospel of Thomas), it seems more likely that it was created by Jesus as a response to the murderous intentions of his enemies. It is hard to conceive of any other occasion for the parable than the one attributed to it by Mark. Like the parable addressed by Nathan to David in 2 Samuel 12:1–4, this is a judgment parable directed against people whose behavior God condemns. Just as it is not David's sins in general that are in question but his adultery with Bathsheba and his plot to destroy her husband, so here it is specifically the Jerusalem leaders' intention to destroy Jesus that is the main point of the parable. The tradition of Israel's persecution of the prophets is alluded to only in order to give greater emphasis to the climactic instance, the murder of God's ultimate messenger, the Messiah. Because the Messiah could be referred to as God's Son on the basis of 2 Samuel 7:14 (as confirmed by the Dead Sea Scrolls), the parable was implicitly messianic. Scholars who are convinced on other grounds that Jesus did not regard himself as the Messiah must, of course, treat the parable as inauthentic. There is, however, a good case for the view taken in this study that Jesus did believe that he was the Messiah. The parable, in conjunction with Jesus' royal procession from the Mount of Olives (11:7–10), may in fact have contributed to Pilate's decision to execute "the King of the Jews" (15:26). In terms of Mark's literary presentation, the christological parable prepares for the high priest's question in 14:61, "Are you the Messiah, the Son of the Blessed One?"

The original parable may or may not have stressed the transfer of the vineyard to others. This is an appropriate ingredient of the story as story. We should probably assume, however, that this final detail was understood by Mark as referring to the transfer of spiritual responsibility for Israel from the Jerusalem Sanhedrin to the followers of Jesus. In Matthew's version this understanding is made even more explicit (see Matt. 21:43).

The function of the attached proof text from Psalm 118:22–23 is to counter the pessimism of the passion parable with an optimistic conclusion; the murder of the Messiah is not the end of the story. Because the verb "reject" has been anticipated in the first passion announcement, where Jesus predicts that he will be rejected by the elders and chief priests and scribes (8:31), the quotation corresponds to the prediction of the resurrection with which the passion announcement concludes. This and other "stone" texts were treasured by early Christians, apparently in part because of a play on words (the Hebrew words for "son" and "stone" are similar). First Peter 2:4–8, for example, alludes not only to Psalm 118:22–23 but also to Isaiah 8:14 and 28:16 (see also Rom. 9:32–33). Many interpreters, consequently, are inclined to regard verses 10–11 as added by Mark or an earlier Christian. There is no good reason, however, why Jesus cannot have supplemented the parable in this way, especially in view of the fact that the psalm was interpreted as referring to God's future triumph over his enemies (see my comments on 11:1–11 concerning the use of the same psalm in the story of the triumphal entry). Jesus must have been sure that God would vindicate him following the apparent victory of his enemies. It is uncertain whether the phrase literally rendered by KJV as "head of the corner" means chief cornerstone (NRSV) or capstone (NIV), but the significance is the same in either case, as correctly paraphrased in TEV: "The stone which the builders rejected as worthless turned out to be the most important of all."

Because this parable lays all blame for Jesus' death on Jews (the Roman role is not mentioned), there is always a danger that it will be misused by the few who perpetuate the age-old anti-Semitism that rallied around the cry "Christ-killers!" We must emphasize that the parable is directed against the Jerusalem council, not against the Jewish people as a whole. It has many antecedents in the Old Testament, where prophets announce God's vengeance against Israel's leaders (Jer. 23:11–12; Ezek. 34:1–10).

RENDER TO GOD WHAT IS GOD'S
Mark 12:13–17

> 12:13 Then they sent to him some Pharisees and some Herodians to trap him in what he said. [14] And they came and said to him, "Teacher, we know that you are sincere, and show deference to no one; for you do not regard people with partiality, but teach the way of God in accordance with truth. Is it lawful to pay taxes to the emperor, or not? [15] Should we pay them, or should we not?" But knowing their hypocrisy, he said to them, "Why are you putting me to the test? Bring me a denarius and let me see it." [16] And they brought one. Then he said to them, "Whose head is this, and whose title?" They answered, "The emperor's." [17] Jesus said to them, "Give to the emperor the things that are the emperor's, and to God the things that are God's." And they were utterly amazed at him.

For Mark's readers—as for us—the question about whether or not taxes should be paid to Caesar was irrelevant. Although there was probably as much grumbling about taxes then as now, it was an accepted axiom that the state has the right to collect taxes. The point of the question arises from the special situation of Jewish Palestine. Because scripture taught that the land promised to Abraham and his posterity belonged to God (Lev. 25:23), it could be asked whether it was lawful, that is, in accordance with Torah, to acknowledge the emperor's claim to the Holy Land by paying taxes. Should true believers protest against the Romans' theft of the land from God by refusing to pay?

The question is not posed by true believers, however, but by "some Pharisees and some Herodians," the same unlikely combination of opponents that was presented as plotting Jesus' death early in the Gospel (3:6). They come not of their own volition, but are sent. From the context we infer that the senders are "the chief priests, the scribes, and the elders" of 11:27, against whom Jesus has told the parable of the Wicked Tenants (12:1–12). The intention of the question is to "trap" Jesus; the questioners assume that he will lose, however he answers. If he responds negatively, "No, God's Torah teaches us that we must not pay taxes to Caesar," they will have sound evidence on which to turn him over to Pilate as a revolutionary. On the other hand, if he answers positively, he will lose much of his popularity with the crowd, for whom the Roman tax was a hated symbol of Israel's subjection to a foreign power. Just under the surface of Mark's narrative is the issue of Jesus' messiahship, as intimated in the royal procession from the Mount of Olives (11:1–11). Will Jesus affirm his claim to the throne of David by denying Caesar's sovereignty, or will he disavow his royal status by bowing to imperial power?

The long preamble, which flatters Jesus as a courageous teacher who disregards the consequences of speaking the truth, is meant to lure Jesus into the trap. For Mark there is a delicious irony in the flattery; despite their evil intention, the opponents publicly acknowledge Jesus' true character!

In two earlier passages, the Pharisees have been presented by Mark as "testing" Jesus (8:11; 10:2). Here it is not the narrator but Jesus who points out that the opponents are trying to "test" or "tempt" him (the same verb is used with reference to Satan's "tempting" Jesus in 1:13). Instead of merely noting the fact, Jesus challenges it: "*Why* are you putting me to the test?" This counterquestion has the force of drawing attention not only to the questioners' malicious game but also to the futility of their strategy ("What makes you think that you can trip me up with trick questions?").

Jesus evades both horns of the dilemma posed him by diverting attention from the theoretical religious issue to the practical religion of his antagonists. The Roman tax had to be paid in Roman coins, such as the silver denarius. This coin, the normal day's wage of a common laborer (see Matt. 20:2) bore the image of Tiberius, the reigning emperor, and an inscription that identified him as "the son of divine Augustus" and as "Pontifex Maximus," that is, chief priest of the Roman civic religion. Although images were strictly forbidden by the Second Commandment (Exod. 20:4), Jesus' enemies have no difficulty in producing a denarius bearing the image of a pagan priest, even here in the temple, the most holy sanctuary of the Lord God! Because the questioners do not hesitate to use Caesar's coins in daily business and even bring them into the temple, they have no right to raise a question about whether or not paying taxes to Caesar accords with the law of Moses.

Jesus' famous epigram, "Give to the emperor the things that are the emperor's, and to God the things that are God's," was a rhetorical triumph (as underlined by the narrative response, "And they were utterly amazed at him"), but very ambiguous. Taken in isolation, the saying seems to teach a "two realms" theology; there is a secular world in which the state is supreme and a spiritual sphere in which God is supreme. The rest of the Bible, however, clearly teaches that this is a false understanding of reality. There can be no neat separation between the religious and the secular, because God claims sovereignty over all of life, including the workaday world of earning money and paying taxes. In another famous epigram, "You cannot serve God and wealth" (Matt. 6:24), Jesus insists that every other allegiance must be strictly subordinate to allegiance to God.

Consequently, we must visualize what is referred to in the saying of verse 17 not as two independent circles that never touch, but as one small circle, representing duty to the state, within an all-encompassing circle, representing our duty to God. If Caesar has the right to collect taxes in the land of Israel, it is only because God's mysterious plan has temporarily granted him this right. Paul makes the same point in Romans 13:1, "Let every person be subject to the governing authorities; for there is no authority except from God, and those authorities that exist have been instituted by God."

Neither Jesus nor Paul intended to suggest that God expects unquestioning obedience to the state when the state makes immoral demands, however. Christian sensitivity on this issue was quickened by Nazism. An evil state must be resisted. When it is not a matter of conscientious objection, however, the state must be obeyed, because God wills order, not chaos, in the life of people and nations.

Christians are sometimes disappointed by this passage, because it fails to provide specific guidance on matters of controversy involving the church and the state. Its importance, however, lies precisely in its generality. Jesus' epigram does not tell us when to resist the state, but it keeps us mindful of the fact that our loyalty to the state is always conditional, because our conscience is subject to God alone.

BELIEVE IN THE GOD OF RESURRECTION!
Mark 12:18–27

> 12:18 Some Sadducees, who say there is no resurrection, came to him and asked him a question, saying, [19] "Teacher, Moses wrote for us that 'if a man's brother dies, leaving a wife but no child, the man shall marry the widow and raise up children for his brother.' [20] There were seven brothers; the first married and, when he died, left no children; [21] and the second married her and died, leaving no children; and the third likewise; [22] none of the seven left children. Last of all the woman herself died. [23] In the resurrection whose wife will she be? For the seven had married her."
>
> [24] Jesus said to them, "Is not this the reason you are wrong, that you know neither the scriptures nor the power of God? [25] For when they rise from the dead, they neither marry nor are given in marriage, but are like angels in heaven. [26] And as for the dead being raised, have you not read in the book of Moses, in the story about the bush, how God said to him, 'I am the God of Abraham, the God of Isaac, and the God of Jacob'? [27] He is God not of the dead, but of the living; you are quite wrong."

Little is known about the Sadducees except that they were a party of religious conservatives who vigorously opposed the Pharisees' changes in the way the law was observed. They regarded only the Torah (the first five books of the Bible) as authoritative scripture. Because the resurrection of the dead is nowhere clearly taught in the Torah, they rejected it as an unscriptural innovation.

Mark does not tell us why the Sadducees were antagonistic to Jesus, but presumably they had more than one objection, not just the issue discussed in this passage. The anecdote suggests that, like the Pharisees and Herodians of the preceding scene, they intend to embarrass Jesus in front of his admiring public. Knowing that he, like the Pharisees, believes that God will raise the dead at the end of the age, they pose an extreme case that they think will demonstrate how foolish the belief is.

According to the Levirate law of Deuteronomy 25:5–10, the brother of a man who dies childless is obligated to marry the widow so that she may bear a son to perpetuate the name of her dead husband (see also Gen. 38:8; Ruth 3:12–13; 4:1–10). Although there is little evidence that this law was observed in Jesus' day, such hypothetical cases were often debated by experts in the law. The Sadducees propose that, because the woman was married to seven brothers in this life, it will be lawful for her to sleep with all of them after the resurrection. They imply that this preposterous situation proves how foolish is the belief in the resurrection.

Jesus agrees that the situation they describe is ridiculous. He rejects the view found in certain first-century Jewish writings that in the Age to Come after the resurrection men will beget children in large numbers, the chief difference being that their wives will give birth painlessly. Jesus insists that resurrection life will be very different from life now; men and women will not engage in marriage as we know it but will be "like angels in heaven" (v. 25), that is, related to one another in an unearthly way. The comparison will have meant little to the Sadducees, who, according to Acts 23:8, denied the existence of angels.

Jesus' counterattack focuses on the ignorance of the Sadducees; they know neither the scriptures nor the power of God. He does not attempt to convince them of the resurrection by quoting Daniel 12:2, the clearest articulation of the belief in the Hebrew scriptures ("Many of those who sleep in the dust of the earth shall awake, some to everlasting life, and some to shame and everlasting contempt"), because they did not acknowledge Daniel as authoritative scripture. Instead he turns to their authority, the books of Moses, and asks them whether they have ever seriously considered what is implied in God's statement to Moses in Exodus 3:6, "I am the God of your father, the God of Abraham, the God of Isaac, and the God of Jacob." At first glance Jesus' response appears totally irrelevant as an argument in support of the resurrection. He seems to be suggesting that Exodus 3:6 implies that the patriarchs are still alive, for God would not claim to be merely the God of dead persons. Such an argument, even if accepted by his audience, would not justify belief in the resurrection, however, for Abraham, Isaac, and Jacob have not been raised from their graves. We must therefore seek a profounder meaning. The Exodus statement, which prefaces the great story of God's rescue of Israel from Egyptian slavery, recalls the covenant that God made with Abraham and renewed with Isaac and Jacob. It implies that God has the power to maintain covenant relationships, including those that seem to have been broken by death. By denying the resurrection, the Sadducees are denying God's power. Their God is too small!

Our yearning for life after death is incurable. To be human is to dream dreams of immortality. Most forms of the dream identify the self with a "soul" that is by nature immortal, which leaves the human body at death and goes on to some other life. The skeptics among us insist that there is no empirical evidence in support of this distinction; when the body dies, the self dies too. Although it may seem strange to many modern readers, this correctly represents the view of first-century Jews and Christians. They conceived of the human being as a unity of body and soul. For them life after death had to involve a body, because a disembodied self would be a horribly incomplete person (see 2 Cor. 5:2–4). Thus their expectation of a future life was framed in terms of resurrection, not of the immortality of the soul. Restoration to life was accordingly conceived of not as a *natural* event ("It is the soul's *nature* to persist") but a *supernatural* one; only God can raise the dead.

Belief in the resurrection of decayed bodies seemed like a foolish superstition to many then as now. The New Testament writers make it clear, however, that when they speak of resurrection they are not thinking of the restoration of physical bodies to their predeath state. In this passage Jesus suggests that we will be "like angels." Paul proposes that we will be transformed from physical to "spiritual" bodies (1 Cor. 15:35–54). The point of such scriptural statements about the resurrection of the dead is that God has the power to give us new life *as recognizable individuals* who are capable of joining once again in the relationships of God's covenant people. Some pagan mystics thought of the soul as a drop of the divine that was destined at death to return to the ocean from which it came. Jews and Christians had a much more activistic expectation. They conceived of heaven as a busy community in which all were actively engaged in praising God (Revelation 7). When reciting the Apostles' Creed, Christians declare, "I believe . . . in the resurrection of the body." With these words we affirm our faith that God has promised us *community* in the life hereafter. This faith is based not on speculation about the soul but on the resurrection of Jesus by the power of God (1 Cor. 15:12–23).

THE GREATEST COMMANDMENTS
Mark 12:28–34

12:28 **One of the scribes came near and heard them disputing with one another, and seeing that he answered them well, he asked him, "Which commandment is the first of all?"** 29 **Jesus answered, "The first is, 'Hear, O**

> Israel: the Lord our God, the Lord is one; [30] you shall love the Lord your God
> with all your heart, and with all your soul, and with all your mind, and with
> all your strength.' [31] The second is this, 'You shall love your neighbor as
> yourself.' There is no other commandment greater than these." [32] Then the
> scribe said to him, "You are right, Teacher; you have truly said that 'he is
> one, and besides him there is no other'; [33] and 'to love him with all the heart,
> and with all the understanding, and with all the strength,' and 'to love one's
> neighbor as oneself,'—this is much more important than all whole burnt of-
> ferings and sacrifices." [34] When Jesus saw that he answered wisely, he said
> to him, "You are not far from the kingdom of God." After that no one dared
> to ask him any question.

Although the questions brought by the three previous groups (the chief
priests, scribes, and elders, 11:27–28; the Pharisees and Herodians, 12:13–
15; the Sadducees, 12:18–23) were all hostile in intent, the question of the
scribe (legal expert) is presented by Mark as neutral (in contrast to the parallels in Matt. 22:34–35 and Luke 10:25–28). There is no polite address
("Sir" or "Teacher"), but neither is there any indication of malevolence.
The request is posed only after the scribe has observed that Jesus has answered the Sadducees well. Because he agrees with Jesus on the resurrection issue, he is ready to pursue another matter with him. What kind of
commandment does Jesus consider most important? (The Greek word in
v. 28 translated "which" often means "of what kind".)

Although all the commandments in the law were regarded as equally
binding, because all had been delivered to Moses by God, the rabbis sometimes debated which were the "heaviest." In one such discussion it was
proposed that the Fourth Commandment, "Honor your father and your
mother," was "the weightiest of the weighty." In another debate during a
time of persecution, it was argued that all the commandments could be
broken under threat of death except those concerning sexual immorality,
murder, and idolatry.

Jesus declares that the most important commandment is neither a
moral law nor one prohibiting idolatry, but a still more basic law that is
aimed primarily at *attitude* and only secondarily at *behavior*. The command
that we love God (Deut. 6:4–5) does not require us to *do* anything, and yet,
if taken seriously, it affects everything we do.

Scholars believe that in Jesus' time, as today, synagogue services gave
special prominence to the recitation of Deuteronomy 6:4–5, known as the
Shema ("Hear!"). The passage was also included in the *phylacteries* worn
by pious Jews (see Matt. 23:5). (Phylacteries were leather boxes containing slips inscribed with scriptural passages. They were traditionally worn

on the left arm and on the head by Jewish men during morning weekday prayers.) The commandment that Jesus names as first of all was thus one of the most familiar. He is suggesting in effect: Let this commandment that is primary in your worship be primary in your life as well.

In Hebrew culture the heart was thought of as the center of thinking and willing as well as of feeling, and therefore as the source of moral and immoral behavior (Gen. 6:5; Jer. 5:23; Mark 7:21). To love God with all one's heart meant to let God direct one's thinking, dreaming, desiring, and willing. The author of Psalm 139, recognizing that loving God with all one's heart is not a simple possibility, begs, "Search me, O God, and know my heart; test me and know my thoughts. See if there is any wicked way in me, and lead me in the way everlasting" (vv. 23–24).

Nephesh, the Hebrew word in the commandment translated "soul," designated the vital principle in a living thing, its "life." This word probably underlies the use of "soul" (*psychē*) in Mark 8:35, correctly translated "life" ("For those who want to save their life will lose it"). To love God with all one's soul, then, means to love God more than one's own life. Although a literal demonstration of this is found only in martyrs, putting God before self is required of all.

The third phrase in verse 30, "with all your mind," does not correspond directly with anything in Deuteronomy 6:5. Perhaps Mark or his source felt that "heart" would not be perceived by Greek readers as including thinking and willing. In any event, the addition (or clarification) emphasizes that we are summoned to love God with our intellect. This by no means suggests that we are to sacrifice our intellect on the altar of religion. We are not asked to believe, for example, that God can make two plus two equal five. Love for God requires rather that we be honest thinkers, using our heads as well as we can, yet humbly, always recognizing the limits of human reason. As in the familiar hymn of Alfred, Lord Tennyson ("Strong Son of God"), we must pray:

> Let knowledge grow from more to more,
> But more of reverence in us dwell;
> That mind and soul, according well,
> May make one music as before.

"With all your strength" refers in the first instance to bodily power, and thus to the dedication of our hands, feet, eyes, ears, and mouth to the glorification of God. Ancient Jewish thinkers suggested that "strength" included economic power; to love God with all one's strength, accordingly, involves the dedication of wealth and material possessions. The wise and compassionate use of money glorifies God.

The most striking aspect of Jesus' response is that he refuses to limit his answer to the question asked. After naming "the first of all" he adds a second commandment, "You shall love your neighbor as yourself" (Lev. 19:18), and brackets the two together with the comment, "There is no other commandment greater than these" (v. 31). In this way Jesus teaches that it is not enough to love God; those who love God are obligated to love their fellow humans also. Implicit in this requirement is a statement about the nature of God; it is because God is compassionate that we are commanded to show compassion to one another. Further reflection on the relationship between these two commandments is found in 1 John 4: "God is love, and those who abide in love abide in God, and God abides in them. ... Those who say, 'I love God,' and hate their brothers or sisters, are liars. ... The commandment we have from him is this: those who love God must love their brothers and sisters also" (vv. 16, 20, 21).

Although John's emphasis lies on loving others within the faith community, "neighbor" clearly involves those outside as well, as made clear in the parable of the Good Samaritan (Luke 10:25–37). Indeed, Jesus taught that the neighbor includes even the enemy who mistreats and maligns: "But I say to you that listen, Love your enemies, do good to those who hate you, bless those who curse you, pray for those who abuse you" (Luke 6:27–28). This expansion of neighbor love to include enemies demonstrates that the love Jesus is talking about is not primarily *affection* (although this is by no means excluded) but *action*; to love the neighbor is to act magnanimously and compassionately. By the same token, love for God must be understood not primarily as a "warm, fuzzy feeling" but as a firmly held *commitment* to fulfill the demands of our relationship with God.

The phrase "as yourself" in verse 31 has prompted preachers to suggest that we cannot love others if we do not love ourselves. Although a healthy self-love is certainly to be encouraged, it is unlikely that the Hebrew commandment or Jesus had this in mind. Because the love commandment concerns behavior more than feeling, the phrase "as yourself" simply refers to the fact that it is normal for human beings to treat themselves well. And, despite the preachers' suggestion, it is possible even for those who hold a very low opinion of themselves to fulfill this commandment. Indeed, many have increased their self-esteem precisely through such obedience. Alcoholics who have lived with self-contempt for years discover through the recovery program of Alcoholics Anonymous that the best antidote to this crippling attitude is dedicated commitment to helping other alcoholics. By loving others they learn to love themselves.

The passage reaches its climax in verse 31. It is a little surprising that Mark extends the story to include a long response from the questioner and Jesus' reaction to the reaction. Coming at the conclusion of an extended series of hostile disputes, these verses serve to underline Jesus' superiority over his opponents. Even a scribe (the scribes have always appeared as antagonists; 2:6, 16) is compelled to acknowledge Jesus' wisdom. By echoing the prophets' conviction that love for God and neighbor is more essential to true religion than sacrifices (see Isa. 1:11–17; Hos. 6:6; Mic. 6:6–8), the scribe suggests that Jesus stands in the prophetic tradition. This acknowledgment places him "not far from the kingdom of God," which probably means that he must progress a little further toward true discipleship. Others, although remaining antagonistic, are silenced by Jesus' wisdom. They dare not challenge him with any more questions.

Although parallels to this passage are found in Matthew 22:34–40 and Luke 10:25–37, only Mark introduces the Great Commandment with the monotheistic creed of Judaism, "Hear, O Israel: the Lord our God, the Lord is one" (v. 29). Why? Perhaps the evangelist wanted to remind former pagans that, despite the honor bestowed on the risen Jesus (see my comments on the next passage), Christians do not worship him as a second god. Christianity is not another form of polytheism but an authentic development of the monotheistic faith of the Hebrew scriptures.

WHO IS THE MESSIAH'S FATHER?
Mark 12:35–37

> 12:35 While Jesus was teaching in the temple, he said, "How can the scribes say that the Messiah is the son of David? [36] David himself, by the Holy Spirit, declared,
> > 'The Lord said to my Lord,
> > "Sit at my right hand,
> > until I put your enemies under your feet."'
> [37] David himself calls him Lord; so how can he be his son?" And the large crowd was listening to him with delight.

"Son of David" served as a synonym for "Messiah" in first-century Judaism, because the end-time redeemer of Israel was normally thought of as a descendant of David, in accordance with such prophecies as Isaiah 11:1–5 and Ezekiel 34:23–34. Since Jesus did not rebuke Bartimaeus for

addressing him as "Son of David" in 10:47–48, it is puzzling that he seems
to deny the equivalence of the terms here. Is he really suggesting that the
Messiah will not be descended from David?

Some scholars have argued that the historical Jesus could not claim
David as his forefather, and that this passage reflects an attempt by Jesus
or his followers to defend his messiahship against the charge that his an-
cestry disqualified him. This is improbable. It is entirely unlikely that Jesus would have been crucified as "the King of the Jews" (15:26) if there
had been no basis for his alleged royal ambition. Since Paul makes little of
the Davidic descent of Jesus apart from a brief mention in Romans 1:3, it
is more likely fact than fiction.

Assuming, then, that Mark (and the historical Jesus) did not deny the
Messiah's descent from David, what is the point of this passage? Psalm
110:1 is cited in order to demonstrate that the title "Son of David" is
an inadequate and misleading description of the Messiah. Because "son
of ——" could identify quality of character as well as origin (for example,
"Sons of Thunder," Mark 3:17; "son of destruction," John 17:12), "Son of
David" suggested one who would establish a kingdom by courage, cun-
ning, and brute force, as had David himself. The psalm suggests that the
Messiah will be of a very different order.

Psalm 110, like other royal psalms (such as Psalms 2, 72, 89), originally
celebrated the coronation or other events in the life of actual kings of Israel and Judah. By the first century these psalms were regularly treated as
messianic prophecies. The book of Psalms as a whole was attributed to
David, but in the case of Psalm 110 the attribution is explicit in the su-
perscription "Of David. A Psalm." It was believed that David, as a scriptural author, was a prophet moved by the Holy Spirit, who prophesied
about the last days (Acts 2:30). Jesus here argues that, because David refers
to the future king as "my Lord," he acknowledges that his great successor
will be not only far greater but of a very different character.

By interpreting Psalm 110:1 as a reference to the Messiah, Jesus attributes to that figure a very passive role. Instead of leading his military
forces in the final battle against Israel's enemies, he sits at God's right
hand until God has subdued his foes. It is also interesting that this verse
speaks of subjugation, not destruction (compare Phil. 2:10–11). These two
features well suit the gentle Messiah who taught his followers to love their
enemies (Matt. 5:44; Luke 6:27–28).

Psalm 110:1 became the most important Old Testament verse for interpreting the meaning of Jesus. It is quoted or alluded to in the New Tes-

tament more often than any other passage in the Hebrew scriptures. Its language is taken up into the Apostles' Creed: "and is seated at the right hand of the Father." An allusion to this verse will reappear in Jesus' response to the high priest at his trial (14:62), prompting the verdict of blasphemy. It became for Christians an indispensable tool for interpreting the resurrection of Jesus (see Acts 2:32–36). The nonviolent Messiah had been vindicated against his enemies and elevated to the position of greatest honor at God's right hand.

This use of Psalm 110:1 constituted a first step along the path of christological reflection that led eventually to the doctrine of the incarnation and the Trinity. Underlying the title "the Son of God" is traditional messianic thought based on Nathan's prophecy concerning David's successor, in which God promises, "I will be a father to him, and he shall be a son to me" (2 Sam. 7:14). The title did not divinize the Messiah but merely identified him as God's special representative. In the light of Psalm 110:1, however, Christians understood the title as implying a unique relationship; of no other human being could it be said that he sat beside God as a Son with his Father. Although the Messiah was "descended from David according to the flesh," his true significance lay in the fact that he was uniquely God's Son (Rom. 1:3–4).

In Mark 12:35–37 Jesus makes no claim for himself, but readers of the Gospel know that he is the Messiah (8:29) and that he has been identified by a Voice from heaven as "my Son" (1:11; 9:7). These two identifications will be conjoined in the high priest's challenge, "Are you the Messiah, the Son of the Blessed One?" (14:61).

A WIDOW'S GENEROSITY
CONDEMNS GREEDY HYPOCRITES
Mark 12:38–44

12:38 As he taught, he said, "Beware of the scribes, who like to walk around in long robes, and to be greeted with respect in the marketplaces, 39 and to have the best seats in the synagogues and places of honor at banquets! 40 They devour widows' houses and for the sake of appearance say long prayers. They will receive the greater condemnation."

41 He sat down opposite the treasury, and watched the crowd putting money into the treasury. Many rich people put in large sums. 42 A poor widow came and put in two small copper coins, which are worth a penny. 43 Then he called his disciples and said to them, "Truly I tell you, this poor

widow has put in more than all those who are contributing to the treasury. ⁴⁴ For all of them have contributed out of their abundance; but she out of her poverty has put in everything she had, all she had to live on."

The preceding passage, 12:35–37, completes a long series of disputes of Jesus with various opponents in the temple. These last two paragraphs of the chapter contrast one group of opponents, "the scribes," with a poor widow who donates all she has to the temple.

Jesus' warning in verse 38 does not identify which scribes are being criticized. "Scribe" could designate a city clerk (Acts 19:35), a learned intellectual (1 Cor. 1:20), or an expert in the interpretation of the Jewish law. Because of the way the term is used in 2:16; 7:1, 5, we infer that it is legal experts of the Pharisaic tradition who are referred to here. Apparently some of these scribes were guilty of drawing attention to themselves by wearing distinctive clothing ("long robes"). They coveted deferential greetings and places of honor at synagogue services and banquets. Despite their thirst for honor, they behaved dishonorably, using their profession and status as means to defraud widows of their husbands' estates, perhaps by charging illegitimate fees or by abuse of trusteeship. To make matters worse, they cloaked their crimes in ostentatious religiosity. A few scholars have even proposed that the long prayers of verse 40 were offered in public as supplications for the very widows they were defrauding!

Unfortunately, the scribes attacked by Jesus had no monopoly on hypocrisy of this kind. In every age and every religion there are people who try to defuse suspicion concerning their private lives by a public show of religious piety. All too often in our own time religious leaders who condemn in the harshest terms the immorality of others are discovered to be guilty of the same sins. Now, as in Jesus' day, such hypocrites receive the greater condemnation.

The sin of defrauding widows was especially heinous, for a widow who had no close male relative was especially vulnerable to the unscrupulous. The testimony of women was not accepted in Jewish courts, according to the first-century historian Josephus. The widow of Jesus' parable in Luke 18:2–5 has no recourse except to pester a judge until he adjudicates her case simply to be rid of her.

In the second paragraph, attention shifts from the scribes' victimization of widows to a woman who may perhaps be one of their victims. Jesus sits in view of the treasury and its receptacles for freewill offerings as people from all walks of life make their donations for the support of the temple and its sacrifices. Rich people make substantial contributions. A widow donates two *lepta*, the smallest coins in circulation. It is estimated that their combined value was less than seven tenths of one percent of a *denarius*, the normal daily wage for an unskilled laborer (Matt. 20:2). What is remarkable about the widow's offering is that it is not just a portion of her limited resources but all that she has left. Mark is not concerned about how Jesus knew this (had he overheard something she muttered to herself?) or what the woman's motivation was (was hers a last act of desperation, by which she hoped to provoke God into rescuing her from starvation?). All emphasis falls on Jesus' declaration that the woman, whatever her reasons, has given more than any of the rich donors, because she gave not according to her means but beyond her means.

We must be careful not to infer that Jesus is commending the widow as an example to be followed. According to Mark 7:9–13, he emphatically rejected the Corban rule, which permitted an offering to God to be substituted for support of aging parents. Since in Mark's context Jesus has just roundly denounced those who deprive widows of their means of support, it seems hardly likely that he is here represented as happy to see a widow do this to herself by giving her all to the temple. Because he placed human need above religious observance (2:23–3:6), he would surely have regarded the widow's need as superseding the temple's, especially because the temple was destined soon to be destroyed (see 13:1–2).

The widow's suicidal gift is awe-inspiring, like the self-sacrifice of the martyr, but it is not to be encouraged. Within a century of Jesus' death some Christians sought martyrdom in order to make the greatest possible religious sacrifice. The church wisely condemned such behavior. Martyrdom was not to be avoided by cowardly renunciation of the faith, but neither was it to be pursued as a religious goal. The same advice applies to the economic martyrdom of the widow.

Even though the widow does not provide a model to be imitated, her generosity constitutes the starkest possible contrast to the despicable greed of prominent religious leaders who enrich themselves by taking advantage of vulnerable women.

11. Jesus Teaches About the Future
Mark 13:1–37

For modern readers chapter 13 is undoubtedly the most difficult section of Mark's Gospel. Many of its ideas are foreign to us. In an era of space exploration, it is hard to take seriously the prediction that the stars will fall from heaven (v. 25). The mysterious figure identified as "the desolating sacrilege" has little meaning for us. The notion of a divine timetable culminating in the return of Christ in glory is not easy for us to take seriously after two millennia of waiting.

Instead of rashly dismissing this chapter as irrelevant for contemporary Christianity, we must make every effort to grasp its basic message. Although the passage does indeed contain a number of predictions, some clear and others less so, the primary emphasis lies not on the predictions as such but on the imperatives that accompany them: "Beware . . . Do not be alarmed . . . Do not worry . . . Be alert . . . Keep awake!"

The early Christians for whom Mark wrote lived in constant danger of persecution for their faith (although seldom in the first century, apart from the brief firestorm in Nero's Rome, did persecution result in martyrdom). They eagerly awaited Jesus' return in glory to rescue them from a hostile world. The chapter addresses two of their primary concerns: When will our Lord come? What are we to do in the meantime? The answer to the first question is: His coming is certain, but only God knows when (v. 32). The response to the second question is twofold: Christians are to be constantly on guard against whatever might distract them from being faithful to Jesus, and are to proclaim his gospel everywhere.

JESUS PREDICTS THE DESTRUCTION OF THE TEMPLE
Mark 13:1–2

13:1 **As he came out of the temple, one of his disciples said to him, "Look, Teacher, what large stones and what large buildings!"** 2 **Then Jesus asked**

him, "Do you see these great buildings? Not one stone will be left here upon another; all will be thrown down."

Questions are often raised by scholars concerning the authenticity of various sayings in this chapter. It is argued that the Jesus we know from the other chapters was not much given to prophesying future events. It would be foolish, however, to assume that Jesus gave no thought to the future. If, as this book presupposes, Jesus did in fact regard himself as God's Messiah, yet foresaw his own violent death, he must also have anticipated God's vindication and thought about what would happen to his followers in the interim. Because Jesus was a child of his own day, it is probable that his thinking about the future was influenced by ideas from his environment regarding the "messianic woes" or "birthpangs" (v. 8) that would precede the victorious rule of the Messiah (see my comments below). Although it is possible that some sayings derive not from the earthly Jesus but from the risen Christ as mediated through a prophet (such as John of Patmos, who wrote the Revelation), there is nothing in the chapter that must be rejected as inauthentic because it contradicts teaching attributed to Jesus outside chapter 13.

Certainly little doubt attaches to the first prediction, which foretells the destruction of the temple. According to 14:58, *false* witnesses testified that Jesus said, "I will destroy this temple that is made with hands, and in three days I will build another, not made with hands." A modified version of this saying appears in Matthew 26:61, "I am able to destroy the temple of God and to build it in three days." No parallel is found in Luke's Gospel, but in Acts a similar statement is attributed to Stephen by his accusers: "We have heard him say that this Jesus of Nazareth will destroy this place" (Acts 6:14). Still another version is found in John 2:19 in connection with Jesus' cleansing of the temple: "Destroy this temple, and in three days I will raise it up." Although John suggests that Jesus was referring to his body (2:21), we are left with the impression that Jesus did in fact on some occasion utter a prophetic threat against the temple.

In Mark's context the occasion is supplied by the exclamation of an unnamed disciple, "Look, Teacher! What massive stones! What magnificent buildings!" (NIV). As reconstructed by Herod the Great at immense cost, the Jerusalem temple was one of the wonders of the ancient world. The enclosed site was four times as large as the sacred Acropolis in Athens, twice as large as the Roman Forum. Very impressive were the huge retaining walls that were erected in order to provide the large, level surface for the temple complex. One of the stones in the Western Wall (now known as "the Wailing Wall") is forty feet in length. Archeologists estimate that a still larger stone in the South Wall weighs over one hundred tons. Herod used so much gold in decorating the exterior of the buildings that, according to Josephus, the sight almost blinded spectators when the sun shone on it.

The temple's religious significance, of course, far outweighed its aesthetic value in the minds of Jews. It was of central importance as the location of God's presence with Israel (Deut. 12:5). During the catastrophic war with Rome, A.D. 66–70, the hope of the rebels for divine deliverance did not finally collapse until they saw the temple in flames. It is in light of this fervent belief regarding God's presence in the temple that we must assess Jesus' prophetic declaration that the temple was to be destroyed. If uttered publicly, as claimed by the "false witnesses" of 14:58, such a prophecy would have been regarded by the populace as an act of treason against God and Israel.

What prompted Jesus' prophecy? Some have argued that this was a purely political prognostication. After witnessing how revolutionary hotheads were trying to inflame resentment against Rome into a war of independence, Jesus could easily see that such a movement could end only in total disaster. Although political foresight ought not be denied to Jesus, it seems more likely that his prediction was evoked by religious considerations. Just as Jeremiah prophesied that the temple would be destroyed as punishment for Israel's sins (Jeremiah 7), so Jesus foresaw the razing of the temple as one scene in the end-time drama of divine rescue and retribution. The saying as preserved for us gives no hint of the reason for God's displeasure with the temple. It may have been general impenitence and lack of faith on the part of Israel that called forth Jesus' prophetic threat. On the other hand, it may well have been the refusal of the temple's priestly leadership to acknowledge his divinely authorized leadership (11:27–33) that prompted the prophecy.

In any event, the prophecy was not long in awaiting fulfillment. About forty years later, in August of A.D. 70, the temple buildings were set ablaze by the victorious Roman soldiers and were later razed to the ground.

THE COMING WOES
Mark 13:3–13

13:3 When he was sitting on the Mount of Olives opposite the temple, Peter, James, John, and Andrew asked him privately, 4 "Tell us, when will this be, and what will be the sign that all these things are about to be accomplished?" 5 Then Jesus began to say to them, "Beware that no one leads you astray. ⁶ Many will come in my name and say, 'I am he!' and they will lead many astray. ⁷ When you hear of wars and rumors of wars, do not be alarmed; this must take place, but the end is still to come. ⁸ For nation will rise against nation, and kingdom against kingdom; there will be earthquakes in various places; there will be famines. This is but the beginning of the birth-pangs.

⁹ "As for yourselves, beware; for they will hand you over to councils; and you will be beaten in synagogues; and you will stand before governors and kings because of me, as a testimony to them. ¹⁰ And the good news must first be proclaimed to all nations. ¹¹ When they bring you to trial and hand you over, do not worry beforehand about what you are to say; but say whatever is given you at that time, for it is not you who speak, but the Holy Spirit. ¹² Brother will betray brother to death, and a father his child, and children will rise against parents and have them put to death; ¹³ and you will be hated by all because of my name. But the one who endures to the end will be saved."

The prediction about the destruction of the temple prompts a twofold question on the part of the first four disciples (1:16–20): "Tell us, when will this be, and what will be the sign that all these things are about to be accomplished?" Some scholars argue that both questions are narrowly concerned with the fate of the temple; the disciples cannot be represented as asking about the other events that Jesus is about to announce. Because Mark clearly intends that verse 4 serve as the transition from the temple prophecy to the remainder of Jesus' teaching about the future, we must assume that he regards the disciples as asking about the whole chain of events of which the destruction of the temple is merely the curtain-raiser. While we look back on the Roman demolition of the temple as simply an isolated event in history, for early Jewish Christians it was a harbinger of the end. It must have been an almost automatic reflex for those who heard Jesus' horrifying prediction to ask, "What else? and when?"

Jesus refuses to respond to their questions directly. Instead of giving answers, he issues a warning against false Christs who may try to take advantage of the end-time excitement occasioned by the destruction of the temple. "In my name" seems to mean "claiming to be the Messiah." Less probable is the suggestion that these deceivers will claim to be Jesus, perhaps the reincarnation of the spirit of Jesus (compare the claim that Simon the magician is "the power of God that is called Great," Acts 8:10). In any event, the purpose of the warning is obvious; his followers are to remain faithful to *Jesus*, regardless of how impressive subsequent religious leaders may seem. What this implies for modern Christians is clear; ultimate loyalty cannot be granted to any pastor, priest, bishop, or evangelist. A religious leader is to be followed only to the extent that she or he follows Christ.

On the basis of various Old Testament prophecies, it was generally believed that there would be an increase of warfare in the time preceding the end. The forecast of wars and rumors of wars would therefore not have surprised Jesus' followers (vv. 7–8 seem to reflect Isa. 19:2 and 2 Chron. 15:6). More surprising would have been the admonition, "Do not be alarmed." The terror to which Jesus refers is not fear for one's safety in time of war, for these wars may occur at some distance, but rather the dread that the end-time terrors are arriving. Verse 7 assures the disciples that, although an increase of warfare is inevitable as God's purposes are being worked out, nevertheless wars do not signal the end. The same is true of earthquakes and famines. Although often regarded as end-time signs, they must not be so interpreted, because they belong only to the *beginning* of "the birthpangs" or messianic woes. In prophetic references to God's judgment, "birthpangs" usually refers to the terrible agony of childbirth, not to its joyful outcome (Jer. 4:31). The point seems to be that Jesus' followers must be prepared for an extended interim. The end will be delayed beyond the anticipated wars, earthquakes, and famines.

The first clause in verse 9 is undertranslated in the NRSV. The full force of the Greek is caught better by the KJV, "But take heed to yourselves." That is, the object of the verb "beware," the same verb as in verse 5, is not an external threat, such as deceivers or persecutors, but oneself! The warning may be paraphrased: "As for you, constantly be on guard against your own weakness. External events have no power to compel you to be unfaithful; disloyalty comes from within."

Although the theme of Jewish persecution of Christians appears repeatedly in Matthew, verse 9 is the only instance of the motif in Mark. From the book of Acts we know that Christian evangelists were frequently the objects of Jewish hostility. Paul himself testifies not only that he had personally persecuted the church "and was trying to destroy it" (Gal. 1:13; compare 1 Cor. 15:9; Phil. 3:6), but also that as a Christian he had five times received from the Jews the forty lashes minus one, and was frequently in danger from his own people (2 Cor. 11:24, 26). According to Acts 24–26 the apostle was made to stand before governors (Felix and Festus) and a king (Agrippa) and was destined to appear also before the emperor in Rome. We need not assume, however, that Mark 13:9 was created with Paul's case in mind. Jesus' knowledge of what happened to John the Baptist and what was certain to happen to him was sufficient to explain a prediction that his followers would suffer persecution of various kinds.

(It is, of course, possible that a less specific prediction from Jesus' lips is here embellished with details reflecting later experiences.)

In verse 11 Jesus assures the disciples that when they are called upon to make a public defense before a Jewish judicial body or a pagan ruler they need not be anxious about what to say because they will be prompted by the Holy Spirit. In 3:29 Jesus implied that his power to exorcise evil spirits derived from the Holy Spirit. Here he promises that the same power of God will provide persecuted followers with the right words of defense. This is Mark's only allusion to the role of the Spirit in the church.

Although persecution is a manifestation of opposition to God, it nonetheless fulfills a positive function in the divine plan. An Old Testament prototype is provided by the mistreatment Joseph received from his brothers, who sold him into slavery. At the end of the story, Joseph tells his brothers: "Even though you intended to do harm to me, God intended it for good, in order to preserve a numerous people, as he is doing today" (Gen. 50:20). Persecutions will provide occasions for witnessing to both Jews and Gentiles. A modern illustration was reported by a soldier. Returning tired and wet from a long march in the cold rain, he was disgusted by the sight of another private kneeling in prayer. Angrily he hurled his muddy boots at the object of his disgust and then sank into a deep sleep. The next morning he was astonished to find his boots, cleaned and polished, neatly placed by his bed. This so impressed him that he became a Christian.

Verse 10 continues this theme by announcing that the interim between "the beginning of the birthpangs" and "the end" must be extended precisely so that the gospel may first be proclaimed to "all nations," or, better, "all the Gentiles" (the usual New Testament meaning of the Greek phrase; see Rom. 1:5). It is often argued that this verse cannot be attributed to Jesus, for the hesitancy of the Jerusalem church to admit Gentiles (Acts 10:1–11:18) is incomprehensible if Jesus had so taught. Others counter that the reluctance involved not the admission but the status of Gentiles, that is, whether former pagans could join the church without becoming Jewish proselytes (in Acts 6:5, "Nicolaus, a proselyte of Antioch," a former pagan, is chosen for special service in the church). The Gospels preserve little of Jesus' teaching about the future of the Gentiles, but the saying in Matthew 8:11, responding to the faith of a Gentile centurion, indicates that he expected Gentiles to participate in God's kingdom. In this matter he shared a perspective found repeatedly in the book of Isaiah, especially chapters 40—66, that God's future plan for Israel includes Gentiles: "I will give you as a light to the nations, that my salvation may reach to the end of the earth" (Isa. 49:6; see also 42:6; 66:19). Further evidence of Jesus' openness to the future inclusion of Gentiles can be found in his teaching about the all-inclusive compassion of God (Matt. 5:43–48).

Preaching the good news will not protect Jesus' followers against the world's hatred, however. Verse 12, possibly a free paraphrase of Micah 7:6, expresses an expectation commonly found in Jewish writing about the evil days preceding God's final intervention; family loyalty will be dissolved. We must not assume that Mark includes this utterance as a fulfilled prediction; we have no evidence in the New Testament or elsewhere of early martyrdoms due to familial hatred. Indeed, apart from the execution of a considerable (but unspecified) number of Christians by Nero as scapegoats for the great fire in Rome in A.D. 64, there are remarkably few Christian martyrs in the first century. Undoubtedly, Christians were often hated by their relatives as apostates from the family's religious tradition (whether Jewish or pagan) and by their neighbors as disgusting "goody-goodies" (1 Pet. 4:4). The same, of course, is often true today, not only for new converts in non-Christian communities in Africa and Asia, but also for persons in nominally Christian homes who become "intoxicated with the gospel." Many a young person who has experienced God's call to full-time Christian service has been confronted with angry resistance from parents and siblings.

To the English reader, "the end" in verse 13b is the same expression as in verse 7, but this second instance lacks the definite article in the Greek. "To (an) end" is an adverbial idiom, which may mean either "completely" or "finally" (as in Luke 18:5) or "to the end." Both meanings may be intended in John 13:1, "Having loved his own . . . he loved them to the end/to the uttermost." Here in Mark the phrase is ambiguous. Since a prolonged interval prior to the end is anticipated, it is probable that some will die before the glorious day arrives. It will not be possible for such persons to endure *to the end*, but they will not be excluded from the kingdom if they persevere *to the uttermost*. There is no suggestion in this verse of salvation by works. Faithfulness is a necessary condition, but not the purchase price of admission to the Age to Come.

THE GREAT TRIBULATION
Mark 13:14–23

13:14 "But when you see the desolating sacrilege set up where it ought not to be (let the reader understand), then those in Judea must flee to the mountains; 15 the one on the housetop must not go down or enter the house to take anything away; [16] the one in the field must not turn back to get a coat. [17] Woe to those who are pregnant and to those who are nursing infants in those days! [18] Pray that it may not be in winter. [19] For in those days there will be suffering, such as has not been from the beginning of the creation that God created until now, no, and never will be. [20] And if the Lord had not cut short those days, no one would be saved; but for the sake of the elect, whom he chose, he has cut short those days. [21] And if anyone says to you at that time, 'Look! Here is the Messiah!' or 'Look! There he is!'—do not believe it. [22] False messiahs and false prophets will appear and produce signs and omens, to lead astray, if possible, the elect. [23] But be alert; I have already told you everything."

In this paragraph an answer is finally given to the disciples' question in verse 4, "Tell us, when will this be, and what will be the sign that all these things are about to be accomplished?" The sign, Jesus tells them, will be the appearance of "the desolating sacrilege" in a place "where [he] ought not to be." The mysterious phrase "the desolating sacrilege" is undoubtedly an allusion to Daniel. In each of three instances (Dan. 9:27; 11:31; 12:11) it refers to the horrifying desecration of the temple by Antiochus IV; on top of the great altar in Jerusalem the Syrian king erected a pagan altar on which pigs were sacrificed to Zeus. This diabolical affront to the God of Israel was seared into Jewish memory. In verse 14 Jesus (or a Christian prophet, if the prophecy is from a later date) predicts that God will destroy the temple in an act of revenge against a still more serious affront to his holiness; not a *thing* (a pagan altar) but a *person* will stand in the temple, claiming divine honors: "But when you see 'the abomination of desolation' usurping a place which is not his" (NEB; the NRSV incorrectly translates a masculine participle with a neuter subject, "it"). "Where he ought not to be" is to be understood as referring to the temple because of the background in Daniel and the reference to Judea later in the verse. Mark's parenthetical remark ("Let the reader understand") may be intended to draw attention to the fact that the Danielic prophecy has here been reinterpreted. Why does Mark not mention the temple explicitly? Prophecies of this kind are often couched in ambiguous or mysterious language. A second possibility is that when Mark wrote, the temple had already been destroyed by the Romans. If that were indeed the case (the date of Mark's writing is still disputed by scholars; see the Introduction), Mark may have removed an explicit reference to the temple, believing nevertheless that the promised sign would appear in the ruins of the holy place. Whatever the date of the Gospel, for Mark the ultimate affront to God's holiness still lies in the future, because for him the associated events depicted in the following verses have not yet occurred.

A possible parallel to verse 14 is found in 2 Thessalonians 2:3–4, "Let no one deceive you in any way; for that day will not come unless the rebellion comes first and the lawless one is revealed, the one destined for destruction. He opposes and exalts himself above every so-called god or object of worship, so that he takes his seat in the temple of God, declaring himself to be God." Although neither Mark nor Paul identifies this figure as "Antichrist," it seems likely that both are alluding to the Jewish conception of an ultimate opponent of God, who among Christians came to be known as "Antichrist" (1 John 2:18). There is no uniformity regarding details, but underlying all the Jewish and Christian allusions to this figure is the conviction that evil will become more rampant just prior to the end.

The warning to flee to the hills immediately without retrieving anything from one's house is not practical counsel concerning what to do if the Romans sack Jerusalem, but end-time advice based on the expectation that God will treat the demonized temple like Sodom and Gomorrah. These verses echo the angels' command to Lot in Genesis 19:17, "Flee for your life; do not look back or stop anywhere in the Plain; flee to the hills, or else you will be consumed." The woe of verse 17 (which, reversed, appears as a beatitude in Luke 23:29) and the suggestion that God be entreated not to schedule the flight in winter (when swollen streams would impede the escape) reinforce the frightfulness of the divine vengeance and the urgency of flight.

The motif of end-time flight is now combined in verses 19–20 with the motif of the Great Tribulation, as prophesied in Daniel 12:1 and echoed in the Dead Sea Scrolls: "And it shall be a time of distress for all the people redeemed by God, and among all their afflictions there will have been nothing to equal it from its beginning until its end in final redemption" (War Scroll i. 11–12). No details are provided regarding the suffering to be endured, but the severity of the tribulation is emphasized by the promise that the days have been shortened so that "the elect," those chosen for life in the Age to Come, may survive.

Because the Great Tribulation is followed immediately by Jesus' return in glory, there is danger that during this stressful period his followers will be deluded by persons who falsely claim to be the Messiah and by false prophets who allege that they can identify the real Messiah (vv. 21–22). Forewarned, Jesus' followers will be forearmed (v. 23).

The religious value of this paragraph lies not so much in the details of its predictions as in the faith clothed in the details. Pessimism concerning evil is strongly countered by optimism in God's power to redeem.

JESUS SPEAKS OF COMING AGAIN IN GLORY
Mark 13:24–27

13:24 **"But in those days, after that suffering,**
the sun will be darkened,
and the moon will not give its light,
25 and the stars will be falling from heaven,
and the powers in the heavens will be shaken.
26 Then they will see 'the Son of Man coming in clouds' with great power
and glory. 27 Then he will send out the angels, and gather his elect from the
four winds, from the ends of the earth to the ends of heaven."

Despite the very great importance to early Christians of Jesus' anticipated return in glory, or "second coming," the theme receives scant attention in Mark. In addition to this passage it appears only in 8:38 and 14:62. In all three passages Jesus refers to his future role by means of his mysterious self-designation, "the Son of Man." Because here and in 14:62 there is an obvious allusion to Daniel 7:13, "I saw in the night visions, and behold, with the clouds of heaven there came one like a son of man" (RSV), scholars have argued that "the Son of Man" was the title of a heavenly Messiah, an angelic figure whom God would send to judge the earth and rescue the righteous. After Jesus' resurrection, it is proposed, his followers identified Jesus with this figure, and "the Son of Man" became one of Jesus' messianic titles. Recent studies have challenged this hypothesis by showing that none of the Gospel authors treats the phrase as a messianic title. In Mark 2:10, 28, Jesus refers to himself in front of his enemies by means of this phrase, and no one in the narrative audience supposes that he is thereby claiming to be the Messiah. In Mark the phrase occurs most frequently in sayings in which Jesus speaks about his forthcoming passion (8:31; 9:9, 12, 31; 10:33–34, 45; 14:21, 41).

It is possible that the use of Daniel 7:13–14 as a prophecy of Jesus' coming in glory originated among Christians after Easter, as they searched the scriptures for texts that would help them understand the resurrection and confirm their hope in their Lord's return (see Rev. 1:7). Nevertheless, it would be foolish to deny the possibility that Jesus himself made use of the Danielic passage. If Jesus regarded himself as Messiah, yet recognized that it was probable that he would suffer a violent death, he must also have anticipated his future vindication by God, and Daniel 7:13–14 would have helped him to give shape to this hope.

Although our space-age minds balk at the prophecy that the sun and moon will cease to shine and the stars will fall from heaven, we must recognize that verses 24–25 are poetry, not prose. These lines reflect Old Testament passages such as Isaiah 13:9-10 and Joel 2:10-11, in which "the day of the LORD," the day of divine vengeance, is described. Remarkably, in this Markan passage the vengeful nature of the day of the Lord has been totally ignored. There is no mention here of the destruction or damnation of the wicked. Emphasis is placed entirely on the positive effects of Jesus' return "with great power and glory." At the command of the Messiah the angels will gather the elect, those whom God has chosen, from the most distant parts of the earth.

Mark includes no details regarding what will follow the joyful reunion of Jesus with his followers. We presume that, apart from the response to the Sadducees (12:25), the oral tradition of Jesus' sayings about the future contained no descriptions of life in the Age to Come. We should be grateful for this reticence. Jesus was content to leave the future in God's hands, and so should we!

Although we affirm our faith in the second coming of Christ whenever we recite the Apostles' Creed or the Nicene Creed, we tend to pay this doctrine little attention. This may be due in part to the fact that we are occasionally offended and embarrassed by the overemphasis it receives in some churches. We are repelled by those who seek to calculate the times in disobedience to verse 32. Nevertheless, we must not ignore such a significant element of our faith. Like the doctrine of the resurrection of the body, the doctrine of the second coming is not an optional feature, for the simple reason that, like the former, the latter is intimately related to our doctrine of God. The time of the second coming is none of our concern, and its nature is far beyond our mortal comprehension, but the conviction that it will occur is essential. It reminds us that our God is not an impersonal principle—the principle of vitality in the universe, for example—but the transcendent Creator who is also Lord of history. Whenever we pray "Thy kingdom come" we imply our expectation that Jesus will be reunited with all who honor him as Lord.

BEWARE, KEEP ALERT!
Mark 13:28–37

13:28 **"From the fig tree learn its lesson: as soon as its branch becomes tender and puts forth its leaves, you know that summer is near. 29 So also, when you see these things taking place, you know that he is near, at the very gates. 30 Truly I tell you, this generation will not pass away until all these things**

have taken place. 31 Heaven and earth will pass away, but my words will not pass away.

32 "But about that day or hour no one knows, neither the angels in heaven, nor the Son, but only the Father. 33 Beware, keep alert; for you do not know when the time will come. 34 It is like a man going on a journey, when he leaves home and puts his slaves in charge, each with his work, and commands the doorkeeper to be on the watch. 35 Therefore, keep awake— for you do not know when the master of the house will come, in the evening, or at midnight, or at cockcrow, or at dawn, 36 or else he may find you asleep when he comes suddenly. 37 And what I say to you I say to all: Keep awake."

The climax of chapter 13 has been reached in verses 26–27 with the promise of Jesus' glorious return. The concluding section, consisting of two short parables and associated sayings, is intended to assure readers that the second coming is indeed certain even though its date is unknown, and to exhort unceasing preparedness.

Whereas most trees in Palestine are green the whole year, the fig tree is deciduous. Its branches remain starkly bare until late in the spring, so that the appearance of fig leaves indicates that summer is not far off. On the basis of this simple observation of God's providential ordering of natural phenomena, Jesus assures the disciples that the sequence of events in God's salvation history is just as certain. "These things" refers not to the destruction of the temple (vv. 2, 4a) but to the happenings of verses 14–22. "He is near, at the very gates" (v. 29) is probably echoed in James 5:8–9, "for the coming of the Lord is near. . . . See, the Judge is standing at the doors!"

Verse 30 presents believers with a problem similar to that of 9:1 (see my comments on that verse). Jesus is represented as solemnly predicting that the end will come before the last of his contemporaries has died. Although it is probable that this deadline had not yet been confronted at the time Mark wrote, it is now evident that the prophecy was not fulfilled. Every attempt to avoid this conclusion by giving "this generation" a meaning other than the obvious one rescues Jesus from the charge of false prophecy only by attributing to him a pointless observation, "The human race [alternatively: Israel] will not pass away before I come again." If this Amen saying ("Truly" is a weak rendering of *Amēn*) is in fact authentic rather than the utterance of an early Christian prophet, it must be treasured as evidence of the true humanity of Jesus. However Christians understand the divinity of the Second Person of the Trinity, it is theologically imperative that the humanity of Jesus remain fully intact, and this means that it was possible for Jesus to be mistaken. That he did not claim absolute knowledge is evidenced by verse 32; it is improbable that anyone in the early church would have attributed to Jesus ignorance regarding the date of his return in glory, if Jesus had insisted that he possessed divine omniscience.

The nonfulfillment of the prophecy (whether it originated with Jesus or a post-Easter follower) must be taken as a sign of grace. God's patience has extended the time during which the gospel may be proclaimed and people may repent (see v. 10 and 2 Pet. 3:1–10). As Robert Gundry points out (*Mark*, 790), biblical prophecy is sometimes subject to delayed fulfillment or even nonfulfillment in accordance with God's larger plan. Although Jonah receives a divine commission to prophesy the destruction of Nineveh within forty days, the threat is withdrawn when the Ninevites repent, and only Jonah is disappointed at God's seeming inconsistency (Jon. 3:1–4; 4:1–3).

In the Markan context the saying of verse 31 serves to affirm the certainty of the prophecy of verse 30, but it may well have applied originally to Jesus' teaching as a whole. Even if he was mistaken about the nearness of the end, his words about loving one's enemies because of God's compassionate treatment of the undeserving (Matt. 5:38–48; Luke 6:27–36) will stand to eternity.

It has sometimes been objected that verse 32 contradicts verse 30; after claiming that the end will come within a generation, Jesus disavows any knowledge of the date. This misses the narrow focus of the second saying, which explicitly refers to "that day or hour." Although Jesus is sure that the end is near, he refuses to speculate concerning its precise timing, acknowledging that only God knows. Implicit in this disavowal is a warning to his followers to resist the temptation to calculate the times. It is surely an act of spiritual arrogance when Christians claim to know more than their Lord!

Whether verse 32 is an authentic saying of Jesus is uncertain, for nowhere else in Mark does he refer to himself as "the Son" (the closest parallel in the Synoptic Gospels is the saying about the mutual knowledge of the Father and the Son in Matt. 11:27; Luke 10:22). Even if the saying derives from an early Christian prophet, it reflects Jesus' intimate relationship with God as *Abba*, "Father" (see 14:36).

In a college course in which all grading is dependent on a final examination, there is a natural tendency for students to slack off until the end of the semester. A professor known to give "pop quizzes" may be heartily disliked (and avoided if possible!), but there is a greater likelihood of ongoing preparedness. The closing verses of the chapter address a similar problem. If the return of Christ is delayed, why not postpone total commitment to a later date? The little parable of the man who journeys afar is intended as a stern warning to Christians who are tempted to say to themselves, "Let us eat, drink, and be merry, and *tomorrow* we will be Christ's faithful disciples." Although each servant in the parable is given a specific task, we ought not to allegorize this detail, since there is no evidence that Mark has done so. All stress rests on the doorkeeper, who is strictly admonished to be on the watch at all times. A remarkable feature of the story is the warning that the master of the house may well return during the night (the four terms in v. 35 name the four three-hour watches into which Roman military tradition divided the night). Because a traveler returning home from a long journey would normally plan to arrive by daylight, the suggestion that he might appear at night underscores the necessity for constant preparedness.

In the context of Mark's narrative, the concluding admonition, "And what I say to you I say to all," can be understood as directed beyond the four disciples (see v. 3) to the twelve and the other followers of Jesus (see 10:32; 15:40–41; according to Acts 1:15, one hundred and twenty followers of Jesus were gathered in Jerusalem at the time of his death). There can be little doubt, however, that Mark intended his readers to feel included in the "all."

Centuries have passed, and it is much more difficult for modern Christians than for Mark's contemporaries to regard Jesus' return as imminent. The warning "Beware, keep alert" (v. 33) is still apt, however. Because we live constantly in uncertainty regarding the imminence of our own death, we know that the moment of ultimate accountability may come when we least expect it. Like the Gospel's first readers, we must strive to be constantly prepared, as proposed in a prayer designed to be read at funerals:

Eternal God, who commitest to us the swift and solemn trust of life; since we know not what a day may bring forth, but only that the hour for serving thee is always present, may we wake to the instant claims of thy holy will, not waiting for tomorrow, but yielding today.

12. Jesus' Last Days
Mark 14:1–15:47

From the very beginning of this book I have treated Mark as "a passion narrative with an extended introduction" (see the Introduction). The passion narrative in the broader sense of the term, which includes everything in Jesus' last week in Jerusalem, began with his triumphal entry in 11:1–11. Now at 14:1 the passion narrative in the narrower sense begins with the decision to have Jesus put to death. These two long chapters (14–15) report just three days in Jesus' earthly life, but they are obviously the most important three days for Christian devotion. They amplify what is narrated so succinctly by Paul in 1 Corinthians 15:3–4, "Christ died for our sins in accordance with the scriptures, and . . . was buried." At various points we will have occasion to note how Mark treats the events associated with the death of Jesus as happening "in accordance with the scriptures." By echoing passages from the Old Testament, Mark and other Gospel writers express their conviction that Jesus' death was not just another statistic in the unending saga of senseless deaths but the climactic event in the history of God's saving activity.

JESUS' ENEMIES PLOT HIS DEATH
Mark 14:1–11

14:1 **It was two days before the Passover and the festival of Unleavened Bread. The chief priests and the scribes were looking for a way to arrest Jesus by stealth and kill him; 2 for they said, "Not during the festival, or there may be a riot among the people."**

3 While he was at Bethany in the house of Simon the leper, as he sat at the table, a woman came with an alabaster jar of very costly ointment of nard, and she broke open the jar and poured the ointment on his head. 4 But some were there who said to one another in anger, "Why was the ointment wasted in this way? 5 For this ointment could have been sold for more than

three hundred denarii, and the money given to the poor." And they scolded her. ⁶ But Jesus said, "Let her alone; why do you trouble her? She has performed a good service for me. ⁷ For you always have the poor with you, and you can show kindness to them whenever you wish; but you will not always have me. ⁸ She has done what she could; she has anointed my body beforehand for its burial. ⁹ Truly I tell you, wherever the good news is proclaimed in the whole world, what she has done will be told in remembrance of her."

¹⁰ Then Judas Iscariot, who was one of the twelve, went to the chief priests in order to betray him to them. ¹¹ When they heard it, they were greatly pleased, and promised to give him money. So he began to look for an opportunity to betray him.

The story of Jesus' last three days begins very abruptly with a temporal reference. To modern readers it is misleading; in Jewish reckoning "after two days" meant "the next day" (note how resurrection "after three days" in Mark 8:31 is the same as "on the third day" in Matt. 16:21). Mark is telling us that the decision to have Jesus done away with was made on Wednesday, only one day before the Passover lambs were slaughtered in preparation for the annual seder meal (see v. 12). Although Passover, essentially a one-day observance, and the seven-day festival of Unleavened Bread had separate origins, they had been combined for centuries, except in one respect: Passover could be celebrated only in Jerusalem (Deut. 16:5–6), whereas it was possible for those who remained in their native villages to celebrate the festival of Unleavened Bread. The number of those who made the annual pilgrimage for Passover was immense; it is estimated that the number of persons in Jerusalem swelled to five times the normal population.

Although in the earlier chapters Pharisees are frequently mentioned as Jesus' opponents (in 3:6 they plot his destruction with the Herodians), they are nowhere mentioned in these final chapters. The archenemies responsible for Jesus' death are "the chief priests and the scribes," joined by "the elders" in the trial scene (v. 53; see also 14:43; 15:1), in accordance with the first and third passion announcements (8:31; 10:33–34; for notes on these groups, see my comments on 8:31). During the period in which the emperor appointed a Roman governor for Judea, the high priest was treated by the Romans not only as the head of the Jewish religion but also as the ethnic ruler of the Jewish population. He was assisted in this role by a council consisting of other chief priests, the scribes, and the elders.

No motive is suggested for the determination to put Jesus to death. The reader is expected to remember that the chief priests and scribes began to seek a way to get rid of him following his cleansing of the temple, "for they were afraid of him, because the whole crowd was spellbound by his teaching" (11:18). In the Fourth Gospel a political motive is attributed to the conspirators: "If we let him go on like this, everyone will believe in him, and the Romans will come and destroy both our holy place and our nation" (John 11:48).

The phrase "not during the festival" is misleading, for Jesus was in fact arrested at this time. There was no point in waiting until the festival was over, when Jesus would presumably be returning to Galilee with a crowd of other pilgrims. A proper understanding of the phrase is indicated by the word translated "by stealth," which could also be rendered "by connivance" or "by trickery." What Mark means is "not in the festal assembly." Their intention is to arrest Jesus at a moment when he is not surrounded by enthusiastic followers, for a riot would be sure to occur.

The solution to their problem is supplied almost immediately (either the same day or the next) by Judas Iscariot, who goes to the leaders with an offer to hand Jesus over to them ("betray" is an alternative translation of a verb that means "hand over" or "deliver up"). The third passion announcement now finds its fulfillment, "The Son of Man will be handed over to the chief priests and the scribes" (10:33). That is to say, it is not secret information (for example, that Jesus regards himself as the Messiah) but a person that Judas "betrays." Although Mark underscores his infamy by reminding us that Judas is "one of the twelve" (his appointment to this select group was reported in 3:19), he gives no hint of the informant's motive. Although money is mentioned in verse 11, it is not stressed, and it seems unlikely that a man who had left home and occupation to follow Jesus would be motivated by greed. Was he disenchanted with Jesus because of his refusal to assume the role of conquering king? Jesus' aversion to armed conflict must have been obvious from the beginning to all who heard him teach nonresistance and love of enemies (Matt. 5:38–48). Did he desperately hope to provoke Jesus—or God—into action by placing the Messiah in the hands of his enemies? We ask such questions, but Mark shows no interest in satisfying our curiosity, quite possibly because he does not know the answer. Judas's deed is evil, but evil is an unfathomable mystery, as Jeremiah testifies: "The heart is devious above all else; it is perverse—who can understand it?" (Jer. 17:9). The passage ends with Judas on the hunt for an opportune moment when he can turn Jesus over to his enemies in the absence of a crowd.

Between these two somber scenes of plotting and betrayal Mark places a starkly contrasting story of loving acceptance. Jesus is reclining (*not* sitting) at a banquet in Bethany in the home of Simon the leper (presumably his leprosy occurred either before or after this time). An unnamed woman approaches, breaks the neck of an alabaster jar, and pours out on his head all the perfumed oil it contains ("ointment" is an inappropriate translation, for in common usage it refers to a product that cannot be poured). Because she could be satisfied with merely breaking the seal, her destruction of the valuable container further emphasizes the fact that she is holding back nothing of the very expensive perfume that she is lavishing on Jesus. Some of the diners are righteously indignant at this extravagant waste of a precious commodity. Its sale could have produced for charity the equivalent of a year's wages (a denarius was the normal daily wage, according to Matt. 20:2). It was traditional in Jewish society to show special concern for the poor at Passover.

Jesus defends the woman's extravagance as "a good service" that has been performed in a timely fashion. His comment, "For you always have the poor with you" is not cynical but realistic. It is not just at Passover (or Thanksgiving and Christmas?) that one has the opportunity to contribute to the poor but every day, and the obligation is unceasing; but there are other good works that can be performed only at a specific time. The rabbis, debating whether giving money to the poor or burying the dead was the more important good work, determined in favor of the latter, for it had to be done at the right time and involved personal service, whereas giving to the poor did not. Jesus may be reflecting such a debate when he calls the woman's action "a good service" and suggests that she has prepared his body for burial. Although dining sumptuously, Jesus is very much aware that his death is imminent.

Wherever the gospel is proclaimed, Jesus declares, the woman's extravagant gift of love will be reported in memory of her. Those who are convinced that Jesus did not foresee an extended interim between his death and his return in glory regard it as unlikely that this is an authentic saying. If Jesus did consider himself God's Messiah (as this book holds), it is to be assumed that he expected his followers to tell his story after his death. He solemnly announces to her critics that this woman's devotion will be a part of that story.

Mark's narrative provides no motive for the woman's action. It is tempting to think of her as anointing Jesus as king, just as Samuel anointed Saul and David (1 Sam. 10:1; 16:13), but nothing in the story supports such a conjecture. It is unlikely that she intends to anoint his body for burial, for it is Jesus who justifies her deed with this explanation, and she presumably knows nothing of the plot to kill him. It is best to assume that her act expresses loving devotion.

Why was this woman so devoted to Jesus? Jewish women were not equal partners with their husbands, fathers, and brothers in synagogue and temple worship, nor were they encouraged to study scripture and religion. Although the evidence is admittedly slender, it appears probable that Jesus' public teaching was addressed to women as well as men (in 6:44 Mark specifies that the audience consists of men only, as if to suggest that women were normally included). Many of his healings involved women (1:30; 5:25–29, 41). In 15:40–41 we learn that some women traveled with Jesus in Galilee and that many others accompanied him to Jerusalem. It seems altogether probable that the fierce loyalty of so many women was prompted in part by the fact that Jesus took them seriously and included them as his students. In Luke 10:38–42 Mary assumes the posture of a disciple and is defended by Jesus for doing so.

It is striking that in the closing chapters of Mark the women play a much more positive role than the men. Whereas the male followers of Jesus turn cowards and disappear from the scene, the female disciples remain within sight of the cross (15:40), observe the burial (15:47), and visit the tomb (16:1–2). In this passage the contrast is starker yet; the woman's self-forgetful devotion shines all the brighter against the dark foil of Judas's infamous disloyalty.

The cultural subordination of women is lamentably still with us, even in the church. Such inequality is not to be tolerated. Women must not be kept waiting until Jesus' second coming to be given their rightful status among his followers!

JESUS AND HIS DISCIPLES CELEBRATE PASSOVER
Mark 14:12–21

14:12 **On the first day of Unleavened Bread, when the Passover lamb is sacrificed, his disciples said to him, "Where do you want us to go and make the preparations for you to eat the Passover?"** 13 **So he sent two of his disciples, saying to them, "Go into the city, and a man carrying a jar of water will meet you; follow him,** 14 **and wherever he enters, say to the owner of the house, 'The Teacher asks, Where is my guest room where I may eat the Passover with my disciples?'** 15 **He will show you a large room upstairs, furnished and ready. Make preparations for us there."** 16 **So the disciples set out and went to the city, and found everything as he had told them; and they prepared the Passover meal.**

17 **When it was evening, he came with the twelve.** 18 **And when they had**

taken their places and were eating, Jesus said, "Truly I tell you, one of you will betray me, one who is eating with me." [19] **They began to be distressed and to say to him one after another, "Surely, not I?"** [20] **He said to them, "It is one of the twelve, one who is dipping bread into the bowl with me.** [21] **For the Son of Man goes as it is written of him, but woe to that one by whom the Son of Man is betrayed! It would have been better for that one not to have been born."**

The central event of the annual Passover pilgrimage to Jerusalem was the consumption of a freshly slaughtered—and ritually sacrificed—yearling lamb or goat after sunset on the fifteenth day of Nisan, that is, the evening of the first full moon following the spring equinox. According to Deuteronomy 16:5–7, the Passover sacrifice could be offered and eaten only in Jerusalem. Since Jesus has been staying in Bethany (11:11–12; compare 11:15, 27)—that is, outside the ritual bounds of Jerusalem—it is necessary to find a location within the city for the sacred meal. (Because the Passover sacrifice was offered on Nisan 14, that is, prior to the first day of Unleavened Bread, which began at sunset, v. 12 seems to be in error; probably the daylight hours preceding the Passover meal were loosely referred to as the first day of Unleavened Bread, because all traces of leaven had to be removed before sunset and because Jews sometimes spoke of a "day" as consisting of all the waking hours, both before and after sunset.)

Jesus' instructions are reminiscent of the parallel in 11:2–3, where two disciples are dispatched to secure a colt for Jesus' entry into Jerusalem. Here it is tempting to suppose that Jesus has made prior arrangements and that the man carrying a water jar (men usually carried water in skins) is a secret sign that Jesus and his host have agreed upon in order to elude the attention of the authorities. Mark offers no support for such speculation, however. The high priests do not need to have Jesus or his disciples under surveillance, because Judas, their paid informant, has promised to deliver Jesus to them at an opportune time (vv. 10–11). Nor are we told who the householder is or why the large room is made available to Jesus. Was this the place where Jesus' followers gathered after Easter according to Acts 1:13, or the home of John Mark mentioned in Acts 12:12? Mark is not interested in such details. For the evangelist this little narrative serves to emphasize Jesus' clairvoyance; he already "sees" the large upper room and predicts in detail how his disciples will find it.

Jesus announces that the large upstairs room will be "strewn" (a more literal translation than "furnished") and ready. Although Jews sat at table for ordinary meals, at banquets it was customary to recline on rugs, cushions, or

couches and eat from low tables, in the Roman fashion. This was considered
a requirement at Passover, even for poor people, as a symbol of the freedom
God had conferred on Israel at the exodus. "Strewn" thus indicates that
there will be a sufficient number of cushions or mats for the diners. The
words "when they had taken their places" represent a verb that literally
means "while they were reclining" (for further evidence of this posture at the
Last Supper, see John 13:23, where the same verb is translated correctly).

The Passover meal has already begun when Jesus shocks his disciples
with the announcement that one of them will betray him. The phrase "one
who is eating with me" emphasizes the perfidy of the informant, because
eating together was a sign of friendship. Many see here an allusion to
Psalm 41:9, "Even my bosom friend in whom I trusted, who ate of my
bread, has lifted the heel against me" (which is explicitly quoted in the parallel in John 13:18). Although in all four Gospels the disciples are eager to
know the identity of the traitor in their midst, the secret is fully divulged
only in John 13:26. In Matthew 26:25 Judas asks, "Surely not I, Rabbi?"
and receives Jesus' indirect affirmation, "You have said so." Here in Mark
(as in Luke 22:23) there is no explicit reference to Judas. Instead, each of
the disciples asks, "Surely, not I?" The form of the question assumes that
the answer will be "No" and yet leaves open the possibility of an affirmative response. Perhaps Mark wants his readers to engage in some soul-
searching as they consider the capacity for evil that lurks even within those
who sincerely desire to follow Jesus.

In verse 21 "goes" may mean "goes to his death," but it more probably
means "goes into the hands of his enemies," for the focus of the saying is
on betrayal. "As it is written of him" constitutes a general reference to the
Old Testament, giving no hint about which texts are in mind. If Psalm 41:9
is echoed in verses 18–20, the reference may be to this verse. In any event,
the significance of the phrase is clear: Jesus' fate is not a meaningless accident of history but part of God's plan as revealed in scripture. In most English translations the wordplay in the original saying is obvious; twice "the
Son of *Man*" is contrasted with "the *man*." The self-designation "the Son
of Man" is used primarily in sayings in which Jesus speaks about his vocation and destiny (see my comments on 2:10). Although it is not a title by
means of which the meaning of Jesus is conveyed to his hearers, it does
point to his uniqueness in the divine plan; no other person—past, present,
or future—is identified in this way.

The implicit contrast is between Jesus, who fulfills scripture by willing
obedience to God's will, and Judas, who fulfills scripture by willful disobedience. It is a necessary characteristic of divine providence that God can

turn evil into good. This, of course, does not exonerate the evils we commit in our resistance to God's will. Of Judas it is said, "It would have been better for that man if he had not been born" (RSV). A similar sentiment is found in a saying about those who cause "little ones" to stumble (9:42).

The French deist Voltaire, who had little use for organized religion, is credited with saying, "God will forgive me, it's his trade" (*Dieu me pardonnera, c'est son métier*). God's readiness to forgive is a red thread running through both Old and New Testaments, but is never to be taken for granted. Divine mercy is not "money in the bank" to be squandered by deliberate choice of evil. God's fierce love holds us accountable for the injuries we inflict on others. "It is a fearful thing to fall into the hands of the living God" (Heb. 10:31).

THE LAST SUPPER
Mark 14:22–26

> 14:22 **While they were eating, he took a loaf of bread, and after blessing it he broke it, gave it to them, and said, "Take; this is my body."** [23] **Then he took a cup, and after giving thanks he gave it to them, and all of them drank from it.** [24] **He said to them, "This is my blood of the covenant, which is poured out for many.** [25] **Truly I tell you, I will never again drink of the fruit of the vine until that day when I drink it new in the kingdom of God."**
> [26] **When they had sung the hymn, they went out to the Mount of Olives.**

The sacrament of the Lord's Supper, the Eucharist, has become such a fixed part of the church's liturgy that it is difficult for us to read Mark's story of the founding experience without superimposing on it our own perspective. A second problem is that modern Christians are likely to be more familiar with Paul's tradition (1 Cor. 11:23–26) and thus to read Mark's version as if it coincided with Paul's. We must remember that by the time Paul wrote 1 Corinthians, this distinctive Christian celebration had become detached from its background in the Jewish celebration of Passover.

The Passover meal was a communal recollection of God's saving action in the exodus from Egypt. It was forbidden to celebrate in groups of fewer than ten persons, and often the groups were large. It was thus a liberation meal, and as such it was both a reenactment of the first Passover meal (Exod. 12:1–28) and an anticipation of the future liberation in God's end-time salvation. Messianic excitement grew in intensity at Passover, because of the belief that the Messiah would appear on the anniversary of the first liberation. Attributed to a first-century rabbi is the saying "On this night they were saved; on this night they will be saved." Perhaps Jesus' disciples, convinced that Jesus was the Messiah, fervently hoped that this would be the night when God would powerfully install Jesus as rescuer of his people, despite his predictions of suffering and death.

In Jesus' day the motif of liberation was underscored by the posture of the participants. Instead of sitting at table as for ordinary meals, the members of the Passover company reclined on cushions or mats in Roman fashion, as a reminder of their God-given freedom (see my comments on the preceding passage). The festal meal began with a cup of wine, the first of four to be consumed ritually during the course of the dinner. Over this the head of the company uttered a prayer that spoke of the sanctity of the occasion. (There is no mention of this first cup in Mark, but see Luke 22:17.) Next came the dipping of a vegetable into a bowl of salt water (v. 20; the NRSV inappropriately adds "bread"); this symbolized the crossing of the sea recounted in Exodus 14:21–22. Then a piece of unleavened bread, *mazzah*, reminiscent of the haste with which Israel left Egypt (Exod. 12:39), and a pungent vegetable, "bitter herb" (Exod. 12:8), symbolic of the bitterness of Egyptian slavery, were eaten. The main course followed, a roasted lamb or goat, which had been ritually sacrificed that afternoon in the temple; its blood had been thrown against the great altar by a priest, and portions of its fat had been burned on the altar. After this ("after supper," 1 Cor. 11:25) the second cup of wine was consumed, following which the head of the company told the story of the exodus and explained the symbolic meaning of each of the elements of the meal (Exod. 12:26–27). This second cup was accompanied by prayers for the future redemption of Israel. The third cup was followed by the grace after meals. After the fourth cup the Passover ritual was completed with the singing or reciting of certain psalms (v. 26).

Since by the time Mark wrote, the Lord's Supper had already been detached from the Passover, most of these details are omitted from his narrative, yet Jesus' words can be better appreciated against this background. As head of the Passover company, it was Jesus' responsibility to say the prayers and interpret the various actions. According to verse 22, Jesus took "a bread," that is, a flat *mazzah*, uttered the blessing (the NRSV rendering "after blessing *it*" is erroneous; Jews blessed God, not food), broke it, and interpreted the action. Imagine the astonishment of the disciples when Jesus, instead of reciting the usual interpretation of the *mazzah*, declared instead, "This is my body!" Because Mark adds no interpretive detail (contrast 1 Cor. 11:24), we must try to understand these words in terms of the Passover background. In a meal of liberation, celebrating the first redemption at the exodus and joyfully anticipating the final redemption at the coming of God's rule, Jesus announces, in effect: "As this bread has been broken, so will my body be broken in violent death, and God will use my death in his plan of redemption."

It was customary to use red wine at Passover, presumably in recollection of the blood sprinkled on the doorposts in Egypt so that God's avenging angel would "pass over" Israelite homes (Exod. 12:21–23). Although the phrase "the blood of the covenant" refers to the covenant at Sinai (Exod. 24:8), there was a tendency to combine the two references to blood, especially in view of the fact that the Sinai covenant was considered part of the exodus event taken as a whole. Again Jesus astounds his disciples with a startling interpretation of the red wine: "This is my blood of the covenant, which is poured out for many" (v. 24).

It is sometimes objected that Jesus could not have made such a statement, because the drinking of blood was exceedingly offensive to Jews. Because Jesus' blood is still coursing through his arteries in this narrative, however, it is clear that he does not intend his words to be taken literally. The red wine of Passover, he tells his disciples, is to remind them not of the blood of the first Passover lambs but of the new Passover sacrifice, the sacrifice of the Messiah's life, by means of which God will effect a new deliverance of his people (compare 1 Cor. 5:7). "For many," found also in 10:45, is a Semitic idiom found in Isaiah 53:11–12; it should be taken in an inclusive sense, "the many." Although Mark's cup saying does not include the adjective "new" (see Luke 22:20; 1 Cor. 11:25), the idea is surely implied, since Jesus is referring not to the exodus covenant but to a new covenant between God and his people, which will be sealed with the Messiah's blood. A "new covenant" is prophesied in Jeremiah 31:31–34.

The Amen saying of verse 25 ("truly" is a weak rendering of Jesus' characteristic *Amēn*, which opens an utterance instead of concluding it, as in normal usage) is associated by Luke with the first cup (Luke 22:18). Although the two versions differ in detail, both assert that Jesus will by no means drink wine again until the kingdom of God has come. The function of this saying is twofold: It reinforces the bread and cup sayings by stressing that for Jesus there will be no escape from a violent death, and it underscores the end-time perspective of the meal. This feature of the Last Supper receives special emphasis in the conclusion of Paul's report: "For as often as you eat this bread and drink the cup, you proclaim the Lord's death *until he comes*" (1 Cor. 11:26).

Although we often speak of the real presence of Christ in the Eucharist, in another sense the sacrament emphasizes the real absence of the church's Lord. Just as the Passover meal looks backward and forward, the Christian meal looks back to the cross as the crucial moment in salvation history and forward to the consummation of redemption in Jesus' glorious return to be with his people. Even though this future hope makes little sense to our scientifically trained thinking, it is a significant element of our Christian faith because it is integral to our doctrine of God. We confess that the Creator is also Lord of history, who will make an end just as he made a beginning. It is precisely because God is Alpha and Omega, both beginning and end (Rev. 1:8), that history is meaningful rather than a haphazard sequence of accidental events. There is, as Alfred, Lord Tennyson averred, "one far-off divine event, to which the whole creation moves" (*In Memoriam*, Conclusion, stanza 36).

As noted above, the Passover celebration ended with the singing of a hymn, that is, of one or more of the Hallel Psalms (Psalms 113—118). Jesus and his followers left the old city, but the Torah forbade them from returning to Bethany to sleep; Passover participants were required to remain in the Holy City until morning, in accordance with Deuteronomy 16:7. Because of the large number of pilgrims, however, the ritual boundaries of Jerusalem were extended to include the Mount of Olives as far as Bethphage. All four Gospels attest to this night journey to the Mount of Olives, but it is nowhere indicated whether or not Jesus expected to remain outdoors the whole night. At the Passover season it is usually too cold to sleep outside; the sleeping of the disciples in verses 37–41 is presumably "napping," not bedding down for the night.

PETER'S DENIAL IS PREDICTED
Mark 14:27–31

> 14:27 **And Jesus said to them, "You will all become deserters; for it is written,**
> **'I will strike the shepherd,**
> **and the sheep will be scattered.'**
> [28] **But after I am raised up, I will go before you to Galilee."** [29] **Peter said to him, "Even though all become deserters, I will not."** [30] **Jesus said to him, "Truly I tell you, this day, this very night, before the cock crows twice, you will deny me three times."** [31] **But he said vehemently, "Even though I must die with you, I will not deny you." And all of them said the same.**

Just as Jesus predicted betrayal by one of the twelve at the beginning of the Last Supper (v. 18), so now after the meal he prophesies the apostasy of the twelve as a group and of Peter, their leader, in particular. To early Christians it was very important that Jesus clearly foresaw the humiliations he was to suffer, not the least of which was the loss of faith in him on the part of his closest followers.

A comparison of English translations demonstrates the difficulty in finding the proper equivalent for the verb *skandalizō* (from which the English verb "scandalize" derives) as it appears in verse 27. The RSV and NIV agree in rendering the clause, "You will all fall away." The NRSV paraphrases, "You will all become deserters," taking the verb as an anticipation of verse 50, "All of them deserted him and fled." A very different understanding is reflected in the NEB, "You will all fall from your faith," modified in the REB to, "You will all lose faith." Underlying this Jewish-Greek verb (it was not used in normal Greek) is the Old Testament metaphor of the stumbling block, as it occurs, for example, in Psalm 119:165, "Great peace have those who love your law; nothing can make them stumble." A stumbling block is something that induces one to sin or lose faith, that is, to become unfaithful to God. The metaphor has appeared several times in this Gospel. In the interpretation of the parable of the Six Seeds we are told that the seed falling on rocky soil represents believers who apostatize ("stumble" or "fall away") when confronted with distress or persecution (4:17). At Nazareth Jesus' neighbors "stumbled" or "took offense" at him; that is, they refused to acknowledge that God was using Jesus as his special instrument (6:3; for other instances, see 9:42–47). This evidence suggests that here in 14:27 the metaphor refers to an action more catastrophic than cowardly flight; the disciples, who have dared to believe that God has been active in Jesus' ministry, will lose faith and become unbelievers.

In 1 Corinthians 1:23 Paul writes, "We proclaim Christ crucified, a stumbling block to Jews." To most Jews, the disciples included, the idea of a crucified Messiah constituted a contradiction in terms. The Messiah was expected to inflict suffering on the wicked, not experience it himself. Even though Jesus has repeatedly announced to the twelve his forthcoming violent death, it has been impossible for them to incorporate this teaching into their faith in him. Their superficial faith will be shattered by his passion, so that true faith in God's crucified Messiah can be awakened in them by the resurrection.

The inadequacy of the disciples' faith will be demonstrated by their running away, but this too will accord with God's plan, as prophesied by Zechariah 13:7. For Zechariah's imperative "Strike!" Mark substitutes "I will strike," in order to make more explicit the fact that God's plan underlies what will happen this night.

As in the three passion announcements (8:31; 9:31; 10:33–34), this prediction of the smiting of the shepherd (the shepherd is a common metaphor for the king; see especially Ezek. 34:23) is accompanied by a reference to the resurrection. The RSV/NRSV rendering "But after I am raised up" is to be preferred to that of the NIV, "But after I have risen." Although the verb can legitimately be translated in either way, the New Testament testimony as a whole is that Jesus did not stand up by his own power but that God raised him from the dead (Acts 3:15; Rom. 4:24; 1 Cor. 15:15). The promise that Jesus will go in advance of his disciples to Galilee—and, presumably, restore them to fellowship with himself there—will be echoed by the angel in 16:7. Even though the disciples will give up on Jesus, he will not give up on them.

Peter's protestation of undying faithfulness to Jesus, regardless of what the other disciples will do, gives greater force to Jesus' prediction of his threefold denial, which will be narrated in verses 66–72. In the next passage it will become clear that Peter's protestation is based on self-confidence, not confidence in God's power to strengthen him against temptation. While Jesus prays in Gethsemane, Peter sleeps.

If, as early tradition claims, the Gospel of Mark was written in Rome soon after Peter's martyrdom at the hands of Nero (see the Introduction), this passage must have had special poignancy for its first readers. Through his experience of Jesus' death and resurrection, the over-confident, superficial Peter had become a rock of faith (see Matt. 16:18), enabled by God's Spirit to take up his cross and follow the crucified Messiah.

A legend based on the late second-century *Acts of Peter* reports that Peter was on his way out of Rome in order to evade martyrdom when he was met by Christ, to whom he said, "Where are you going?" (*Quo vadis?*) Jesus responded, "I am going to Rome to be crucified." Puzzled, Peter asked, "Lord, are you being crucified again?" and received the response, "Yes, Peter, I am being crucified again." Through this encounter Peter found courage to return to Rome, where he was crucified upside down. Although this story is probably pure fiction, it testifies to the way in which the memory of Peter's courageous martyrdom continued to be cherished by believers.

JESUS PRAYS IN GETHSEMANE
Mark 14:32–42

14:32 **They went to a place called Gethsemane; and he said to his disciples, "Sit here while I pray."** 33 **He took with him Peter and James and John, and began to be distressed and agitated.** 34 **And said to them, "I am deeply grieved, even to death; remain here, and keep awake."** 35 **And going a little farther, he threw himself on the ground and prayed that, if it were possible,** the hour might pass from him. [36] He said, "Abba, Father, for you all things are possible; remove this cup from me; yet, not what I want, but what you want." [37] He came and found them sleeping; and he said to Peter, "Simon, are you asleep? Could you not keep awake one hour? [38] Keep awake and pray that you may not come into the time of trial; the spirit indeed is willing, but the flesh is weak." [39] And again he went away and prayed, saying the same words. [40] And once more he came and found them sleeping, for their eyes were very heavy; and they did not know what to say to him. [41] He came a third time and said to them, "Are you still sleeping and taking your rest? Enough! The hour has come; the Son of Man is betrayed into the hands of sinners. [42] Get up, let us be going. See, my betrayer is at hand."

This passage has a double focus: the faithfulness of Jesus and the unfaithfulness of his disciples.

As the spiritual descendants of the framers of the Nicene Creed, modern Christians believe that Jesus of Nazareth was the incarnation of God the Son, the Second Person of the Holy Trinity. This theological affirmation remains central and indispensable, but we must not forget that the Council of Nicaea also affirmed the full humanity of Jesus. He was not simply a divine visitor who wore the appearance of human flesh. Nor was he partly human and partly divine. However we define his divine origin, we must hold firmly to the conviction that his divinity did not compromise his humanity at any point whatsoever. If Jesus was not completely human, his death on the cross was a charade drained of theological significance.

The Gethsemane story is to be treasured as a necessary reminder of this fundamental truth. Here we see that Jesus was not God's robot, moving without question or emotion toward his death on the cross. From the first announcement of the passion in 8:31 he has been steadfastly pursuing the destiny of suffering ordained for him by God. In 14:21 he declares that God's plan has been foretold in scripture. Now we perceive that God's plan for the "ransom for many" (10:45) requires the willing cooperation of the human Jesus. For the moment the idea that everything is predestined is bracketed out; Jesus struggles with the possibility that he may resist the will of God. His obedience, like ours, is not automatic!

Those who assume that Jesus could not experience fear or anxiety, because he was God's Son, are compelled to reconsider their assumption by verses 33–34, where strong emotions are attributed to Jesus: "Horror and dismay came over him, and he said to them, 'My heart is ready to break with grief'" (NEB). Mark's startling language prepares us for his portrayal of Jesus throwing himself on the ground. Because Jews normally stood to pray (see Luke 18:11, 13), this indicates not a customary prayer posture but agonized pleading with God—"that, if it were possible, the hour might pass from him" (v. 35). Although the content of the hour is not specified, it is clear from the context that the phrase refers to the coming betrayal, desertion, condemnation, and crucifixion.

Jesus' prayer begins with *Abba*, an Aramaic word meaning "father," which was normally used only by little children, an affectionate term comparable to our "Daddy." It was rarely if ever employed before Jesus as a way of addressing God. His use of it is thus a sign of the special intimacy of his relationship with God. Proof of its significance is provided not only by its appearance here in a Greek Gospel but also by the fact that Paul twice uses the word when writing to a largely Gentile audience (Rom. 8:15; Gal. 4:6).

The cup that Jesus asks his Father to remove is the cup of death (see my comments on 10:38, where the metaphor also appears). Some scholars propose that in this case it refers also to the cup of God's wrath against sin (Isa. 51:17; Jer. 25:15). William Lane argues that in Gethsemane Jesus does not shrink from physical suffering but rather from the alienation from God that is implied in acceptance of the cup of God's vengeance—an alienation that will be reflected in the cry of dereliction in 15:34 (see Lane, *The Gospel According to Mark*, 516). Attractive though this suggestion is, it may say more than Mark intended. The passage presents Jesus as a healthy young person who wants to live, not die. He is by no means obsessed with a desire for martyrdom, like Bishop Ignatius of Antioch eighty years later, who prayed for the privilege of being the victim of Roman persecution. The significance of Jesus' forthcoming death is enhanced for us by the fact that he desperately wants to evade execution, if he can persuade God to alter the plan. Such an understanding is supported by Hebrews 5:7, which seems to reflect the Gethsemane tradition: "In the days of his flesh, Jesus offered up prayers and supplications, with loud cries and tears, to the one who was able to save him from death." The author of Hebrews interprets Jesus' death as a voluntary act of obedience to God's will: "Although he was a Son, he learned obedience through what he suffered; and having been made perfect, he became the source of eternal salvation for all who obey him" (Heb. 5:8–9; see also 10:5–10). Similarly, Mark presents the agony of Gethsemane as a testing of Jesus' willingness to conform his will to God's will. Although he begs his Father to allow him to live, he obediently submits, praying, "Yet, not what I want, but what you want."

At verse 37 attention shifts from Jesus' faithfulness to the disciples' unfaithfulness. Although he had commanded Peter, James, and John to stay awake while he prayed, they slept. While all three are guilty, Peter alone is rebuked. We are probably to see here a connection with the preceding passage, in which Peter rashly claims, "Even though all become deserters, I will not" (v. 29). The imperatives in verse 38, however, are plural, not singular. All are instructed to keep awake and pray; in this way they may be able to escape falling prey to temptation (does Mark intend the plural to take in his readers also?).

The conclusion of verse 38 is easily misunderstood. The words must not be seen as supporting the Gnostic dualism of a good soul or spirit in an evil body. "Flesh" represents the frailty and weakness of men and women apart from the empowerment of God (see Isa. 40:6, RSV: "All flesh is grass"). In this saying "spirit" represents the better self that is eager to do what is right, but which is constantly frustrated by the weakness that submits to temptation. We have here an anticipation of Paul's treatment of the human dilemma in Romans 7:19, "For I do not do the good I want, but the evil I do not want is what I do."

Jesus leaves the disciples and prays, "saying the same words" (v. 39). Although there is no mention of prayer between his second and third confrontations of the disciples in verses 40–41, we are surely meant to assume it. Thus Jesus prays three times while the three disciples sleep three times. There is undoubtedly an intended parallel with Peter's threefold denial of Jesus (vv. 30, 66–72). By staying awake and praying, Jesus has been prepared for his hour of trial. By sleeping, Peter has lost the opportunity of securing God's help at his time of testing.

Verse 42 gives Jesus' last word to his disciples in this Gospel. The imperatives "Get up, let us be going" express his readiness to meet his destiny. He will not wait for his betrayer to find him, but will advance to confront his enemies.

JESUS IS ARRESTED WITH JUDAS'S HELP
Mark 14:43–52

14:43 **Immediately, while he was still speaking, Judas, one of the twelve, arrived; and with him there was a crowd with swords and clubs, from the chief priests, the scribes, and the elders.** 44 **Now the betrayer had given them a sign, saying, "The one I will kiss is the man; arrest him and lead him away under guard."** 45 **So when he came, he went up to him at once and said, "Rabbi!" and kissed him.** 46 **Then they laid hands on him and arrested him.** 47 **But one of those who stood near drew his sword and struck the slave of the high priest, cutting off his ear.** 48 **Then Jesus said to them, "Have you**

come out with swords and clubs to arrest me as though I were a bandit? [49] Day after day I was with you in the temple teaching, and you did not arrest me. But let the scriptures be fulfilled." [50] All of them deserted him and fled.

[51] A certain young man was following him, wearing nothing but a linen cloth. They caught hold of him, [52] but he left the linen cloth and ran off naked.

Jesus' announcement of the betrayer's arrival (v. 42) is promptly fulfilled. Because Judas has already been identified as "one of the twelve" (v. 10; see also 3:19), the repetition serves to underline the heinousness of his disloyalty.

The character of the crowd armed with swords and clubs is not indicated for us. Mark is interested only in the fact that these men represent "the chief priests, the scribes, and the elders," the three constituent groups of the court that will condemn Jesus to death (14:53–65; 15:1). The same three groups were mentioned in the first passion announcement (8:31) and in the temple confrontation regarding Jesus' authority (11:27). The reference to "the slave of the high priest" (v. 47) suggests that the armed band sent out to capture Jesus consists not of temple police or any other constabulary (contrast the reference to "guards" in vv. 54, 65; see also John 7:32; Acts 5:22), but an irregular posse. We might even paraphrase "a band of thugs." Whatever the historical background, Mark does not want to present the event as a normal police action with a duly authorized arrest warrant. The verb translated "arrest" in verses 44 and 46 simply means "take hold of" (see 1:31; 3:21; 5:41; 9:27) and is so translated later in this passage (v. 51). It is also to be noted that Jesus is not known by sight to these men, although he must have been a familiar figure to the temple police (see v. 49); Judas must identify him for them.

In the last half of the passage Judas greets him as "Rabbi" (literally, "My great one"; the term at this time could be used of any religious teacher) and kisses him. Although it was normal for a disciple to kiss his teacher, it may have been insulting for an inferior to greet and kiss before being greeted by his superior. In any event, the kiss of Judas has become proverbial for the worst kind of disloyalty. Having completed his treachery, Judas disappears from Mark's story. The evangelist has no interest in reporting either the remorse or the death of Judas (see Matt. 27:1–10; Acts 1:18–19).

In Mark's narrative the kiss of the betrayer (together with its planning, v. 44) serves another purpose as well. It reinforces the point that the armed band is seeking Jesus only. We are hereby reminded that Jesus' enemies do not regard him and his twelve closest followers as the central cell of a revolutionary movement. No attempt is made to slaughter or capture the disciples. Consequently, the reader is led to infer that the flight of the followers in verse 50 is due to cowardice rather than to a direct threat to their lives. Their running away is also, of course, a fulfillment of Jesus' prediction in verse 27.

Mark tells us nothing about the man who cut off the ear of the high priest's slave except that he is one of the bystanders. Because the verb "stand by" is used frequently in these chapters with respect to nondisciples (14:69–70; 15:35, 39), it seems unlikely that Mark regards the sword wielder as one of the twelve (contrast Matt. 26:51, "one of those with Jesus," and Luke 22:50, "one of them"; in John 18:10, Simon Peter is the culprit). Moreover, there is no rebuke from Jesus, as is found in all the other Gospels. Instead, Jesus refers to the swords of his abductors. It is probable, therefore, that Mark means us to understand that in the confusion and darkness a member of the armed band, brandishing his weapon in a threatening gesture, has mistakenly wounded one of his fellows. Because the removal of an ear was sometimes used as a punishment of public disgrace, Mark may perhaps include the incident as symbolic of the disgraceful behavior of Jesus' enemies.

Jesus' words to the agents of his enemies in verses 48–49 constitute a taunt: "Is such a show of force necessary in order to capture an unarmed and peaceable teacher of God's ways? Am I a bandit? Why didn't you arrest me in the temple, where I taught daily?" Readers know, of course, why a temple arrest was not prudent; Jesus was there surrounded by supporters (see 11:18; 12:12, 37; 14:1–2). The word "bandit" prepares us for the anomaly that Jesus, the peaceful Messiah, will be crucified between two bandits (15:27). Jesus' reference to "the scriptures" is general; no specific passage is mentioned (but v. 50 refers back to v. 27, where Zechariah 13:7 was quoted). As in 1 Corinthians 15:3–4, the reference to "the scriptures" indicates that what is happening is in accordance with God's saving purpose.

The incident reported briefly in verses 51–52, which is found in no other Gospel, has greatly interested scholars ancient and modern. In the ancient church it was often proposed that the unnamed follower was the evangelist, John Mark, whose mother Mary had a house in Jerusalem (Acts 12:12; concerning the identity of the evangelist, see the Introduction). Although intrigued by this suggestion, modern scholars point out that nothing in the text itself supports the conjecture. There was no reason why the author could not have identified himself, or in some other way have indicated that he was an eyewitness. Puzzling is the fact that the young man is wearing only a linen loin cloth (which may have been used as sleepwear;

linen does not indicate wealth—contrast "fine linen" in Luke 16:19). Exercising their imaginations, some scholars have proposed that the young man's home was close by, and, awakened by the uproar in the garden, he had been drawn to the scene by curiosity. The verb "was following" need not mean that the young man was a follower of Jesus (the twelve have already disappeared in v. 50). Others suggest that the posse may have sought Jesus at Mark's home, and he has hastened to Gethsemane to see what will happen. Such guesswork leads nowhere. We can learn nothing more than what Mark tells us. The same is true of the suggestion regarding the symbolic significance of the little story. Because candidates for baptism were baptized naked in the early church, Mark's readers could perhaps have seen the young man as a new believer, ready to commit himself to faith in Jesus. His flight, however, does little to encourage such symbolism. Another suggestion notes the parallel with the young man dressed in a white robe in the empty tomb (16:5); the first figure represents Jesus' humiliation, the second his vindication. It is best to concede that Mark has provided us with no certain clue to his reasons for including the narrative.

JESUS IS TRIED BY THE HIGH PRIEST
Mark 14:53–65

14:53 **They took Jesus to the high priest; and all the chief priests, the elders, and the scribes were assembled. ⁵⁴ Peter had followed him at a distance, right into the courtyard of the high priest; and he was sitting with the guards, warming himself at the fire. ⁵⁵ Now the chief priests and the whole council were looking for testimony against Jesus to put him to death; but they found none. ⁵⁶ For many gave false testimony against him, and their testimony did not agree. ⁵⁷ Some stood up and gave false testimony against him, saying, ⁵⁸ "We heard him say, 'I will destroy this temple that is made with hands, and in three days I will build another, not made with hands.'" ⁵⁹ But even on this point their testimony did not agree. ⁶⁰ Then the high priest stood up before them and asked Jesus, "Have you no answer? What is it that they testify against you?" ⁶¹ But he was silent and did not answer. Again the high priest asked him, "Are you the Messiah, the Son of the Blessed One?" ⁶² Jesus said, "I am; and**

> **'you will see the Son of Man**
> **seated at the right hand of the Power,'**
> **and 'coming with the clouds of heaven.' "**

⁶³ **Then the high priest tore his clothes and said, "Why do we still need witnesses? ⁶⁴ You have heard his blasphemy! What is your decision?" All of them condemned him as deserving death. ⁶⁵ Some began to spit on him, to**

blindfold him, and to strike him, saying to him, "Prophesy!" The guards also took him over and beat him.

One of the worst slanders spawned by Christian anti-Semitism is the epithet "Christ-killers." All four Gospels testify to the fact that it was the Roman administrator Pontius Pilate who ordered the execution, and it was his soldiers, not Jews, who nailed Jesus to the cross. Despite this indubitable fact of history, the Gospel writers tell the story in such a way that a greater share of responsibility is attributed to the high priest and the highest court of the Jewish people. Pilate is portrayed as an unwilling accomplice in their scheme to get rid of Jesus (see 15:9–15). This view of Pilate does not conform with what Josephus tells us about this firm, sometimes obstinate, administrator. In Luke 13:1 we hear about "the Galileans whose blood Pilate had mingled with their sacrifices." It was on a political charge, namely, that Jesus claimed to be "the King of the Jews," that Pilate crucified him (15:2, 26). There need be little doubt, however, that the Jewish high priest and his associates played a significant role in bringing the case to Pilate. It was in their best interests to maintain the status quo of Roman rule. In their eyes Jesus constituted a threat to this policy. The Jewish people as a whole, of course, were not consulted on the matter and ought not be held responsible for the action of leaders who were not democratically chosen.

Although the political charge is certain, the Gospel writers were not content to treat the execution of Jesus merely as a blatant instance of political expediency. Faith demanded that the behavior of the Jewish leaders be treated theologically. Because Jesus was God's Messiah, rejection of him constituted rejection of God. That is, to the evangelists Pilate's role is less significant theologically, because he does not claim to believe in the God of Israel. Because the high priest and other members of the high court claim to believe, they are guilty.

Scholars have cast doubt on the historicity of the Jewish trial as depicted by Mark. On the basis of the rules of procedure recorded later in the Mishnah, it seems most unlikely that the Sanhedrin, the highest court in Israel, would convene (1) in the private residence of the high priest (v. 54), (2) at night, and (3) during the sacred night of Passover. (Perhaps to correct Mark, Luke 22:66 postpones the trial until the next morning and intimates that the court met in its normal location.) One may even wonder whether it would have been possible to bring together all seventy-one members of the court on this night when all were involved in separate celebrations of the Passover. On the other hand, it can be argued that this was an extraordinary case requiring the suspension of normal procedures, and that the members had been alerted in advance regarding the planned arrest.

A more serious question concerns Mark's report that the court found Jesus guilty of blasphemy. Although the noun, and the corresponding verb "blaspheme," could be used in a variety of situations, the crime of blasphemy was narrowly defined on the basis of two Old Testament texts: Exodus 22:28, "You shall not revile God," and Leviticus 24:16, "One who blasphemes the name of the LORD shall be put to death." It is obvious that Mark does not present Jesus as guilty of reviling the name of God. He is not guilty of the crime of blasphemy.

It is generally agreed that claiming to be the Messiah did not constitute blasphemy, although it may very well have appeared "blasphemous" (in the nonlegal sense) for a man to arrogate this honor to himself instead of waiting for God to designate him as such in a public way. Certainly, no New Testament writer regarded it as contrary to the Jewish law of blasphemy for Christians to proclaim that Jesus was Messiah (see Acts 4:5–21; 5:27–42). Some have proposed that, although the claim to be the Messiah was legally permissible, Jesus' positive response to the question "Are you . . . the Son of the Blessed One?" did constitute blasphemy, because "Son of God" connoted divinity. This conclusion is unjustified. Mark, like Matthew and Luke, understands "the Son of God" as a synonym for "the Messiah," on the basis of Nathan's prophecy to David (2 Samuel 7; see my comments on 1:11).

The remainder of Jesus' response to the high priest may very well have sounded blasphemous to Jewish ears. Jesus declares that his judges will see him ("the Son of Man" is Jesus' recognized self-designation; see my comments on 2:10) seated at the right hand of God, in fulfillment of the messianic prophecy of Psalm 110:1 (see Mark 12:35–37), and "coming with the clouds of heaven," as prophesied in Daniel 7:13 (see Mark 13:26). Although it is impossible to prove or disprove that Jesus said the words here attributed to him by Mark, we have no reason to doubt that he firmly believed that God would vindicate the rejected Messiah. These Old Testament texts helpfully communicate this expectation. Neither text, however, suggests that Jesus is "God the Son" as this was understood by later Christian theology. Nevertheless, the Christian claim that Jesus was seated at God's right hand, when taken literally, undoubtedly offended Jewish monotheists and was regarded as "blasphemous," although not legally so.

Because it is impossible to reconstruct the trial on the basis of independent records (references to Jesus' death in Jewish literature are late and legendary), it seems best on the whole to conclude that Jesus' appearance before the high priest constituted a pretrial hearing, on the basis of which a political charge was prepared for presentation to Pilate. Although what he said may have been heard as "blasphemous," it is unlikely that the high court found him guilty of a religious crime punishable by death. Neither Luke nor John mentions blasphemy in connection with the appearance before the Jewish authorities (see Luke 22:66–71; John 18:13, 19–24).

In Mark's account special attention is given to the "false testimony" that Jesus had publicly claimed, "I will destroy this temple that is made with hands, and in three days I will build another, not made with hands" (v. 58). Mark has already reported Jesus' prediction that the temple will be destroyed (13:2), but in the earlier passage there is no suggestion that Jesus himself will be responsible. Other versions of the saying concerning the temple are found in John 2:19, "Destroy this temple, and in three days I will raise it up," and Acts 6:14, "For we have heard him [Stephen] say that this Jesus of Nazareth will destroy this place." Despite all scholarly efforts, it is impossible to reconstruct the wording and meaning of the original temple saying, if such there was. It remains possible that Mark's assessment is correct; the version he reports was false testimony, that is, a deliberate misrepresentation of Jesus' prophecy regarding the temple's destruction. If Jesus did in fact promise that a temple not made with hands would replace the old, he may have referred either to the expectation that God would supernaturally create a temple for the new age (compare the new Jerusalem of Rev. 21:2) or that the followers of the Messiah would constitute a "living" temple (as in 1 Pet. 2:5).

Mark's references to false testimony in verses 55–59 emphasize that Jesus is innocent; no legitimate charge can be brought against him. In this connection it must be noted that the Pharisees, who are presented as the principal opponents of Jesus earlier in the Gospel, disappear from view in the chapters dealing with the final events of his life (their last appearance is in 12:13). Although it was reported in 3:6 that the Pharisees wanted to destroy Jesus because of his healing on the sabbath, there is not the slightest hint in any of the Gospels that Jesus was officially condemned as a sabbath violator. Nor is there any suggestion, despite Mark's parenthetical remark in 7:19 ("Thus he declared all foods clean"), that Jesus was perceived by his enemies as teaching that the food laws of the Torah should be abolished. It is not surprising, therefore, that none of the Gospels suggests that the Jewish authorities who denounced Jesus to Pilate found him guilty of encouraging Jews to abandon their observance of the law.

Because Jesus was a peaceful man who taught love of enemies (Matt. 5:38–48), not the violent overthrow of the Roman government, the political charge against him appears hollow. The authorities, both Jewish and Roman, well understood, however, that even a peaceful teacher can become a tool in the hands of fanatical followers. In John 6:15 we are told that the crowd who participated in the miraculous meal in the wilderness "were about to come and take him by force to make him king." Apparently the high priest and the Roman governor concurred that it was prudent to forestall such a possibility. According to John 11:47–50, Caiaphas the high priest was of the opinion that it was better for one man to die for the people rather than have the whole nation destroyed by the Romans.

In addition to this political motive, there were probably others as well. Although the narratives of chapter 12 concerning the "cleansing" of the temple and the subsequent disputes have been colored by Christian reflection, they witness to the fact that Jesus' independent and authoritative style provoked the religious leaders in the capital just as it had irritated the Pharisees in Galilee. Mark refers to their response as "jealousy" (15:10). Presumably he means that the leaders resented Jesus' popularity (11:18). From their perspective he was a troublesome meddler in their religious business and should be eliminated. The political charge facilitated his removal.

Concerning "the chief priests, the elders, and the scribes," see my comments on 8:31. The mistreatment of Jesus reported in verse 65 apparently conforms with the tradition that those guilty of serious transgression against the Torah should be treated with utter contempt (Num. 12:14; Deut. 25:9). The blindfolding suggests that those in charge of the prisoner played a malicious game of blindman's buff, in which Jesus was the victim. The taunt "Prophesy!" relates to his fame as a prophet (6:15; 8:28) and to the fact that some expected the Messiah to have prophetic powers (John 6:14–15). For Mark the irony is intense; the one so taunted as a false prophet has truly prophesied his ill-treatment (10:34).

PETER DENIES KNOWING JESUS
Mark 14:66–72

14:66 **While Peter was below in the courtyard, one of the servant-girls of the high priest came by. [67] When she saw Peter warming himself, she stared at him and said, "You also were with Jesus, the man from Nazareth." [68] But he denied it, saying, "I do not know or understand what you are talking about." And he went out into the forecourt. Then the cock crowed. [69] And the servant-girl, on seeing him, began again to say to the bystanders, "This man is one of them." [70] But again he denied it. Then after a little while the bystanders again**

said to Peter, "Certainly you are one of them; for you are a Galilean." [71] But he began to curse, and he swore an oath, "I do not know this man you are talking about." [72] At that moment the cock crowed for the second time. Then Peter remembered that Jesus had said to him, "Before the cock crows twice, you will deny me three times." And he broke down and wept.

The report of Peter's behavior at the high priest's mansion is hardly inspiring. The historicity of the incident can be assumed; it is unlikely that any Christian would have fabricated such an anecdote about Jesus' leading apostle. Because the passion narrative focuses on what happens to Jesus, we may appropriately ask why this unedifying story has been included at all—in all four Gospels, no less! There seem to be three main reasons for its importance.

First, Peter's cowardice provides a foil against which we can better appreciate Jesus' steady faithfulness to his Father's will (v. 36). Mark artfully sandwiches this story with the preceding one by means of verse 54; in this way he suggests that Jesus' trial and Peter's unofficial "trial" are contemporaneous. The parallel is reinforced by the threefoldness of the challenge each faces. In an upper room crowded with members of the high court, Jesus is confronted by the false testimony of many, a specific charge regarding the temple, and a direct question from the high priest (vv. 56, 57–58, 61), while below in the courtyard Peter is challenged three times by servants concerning his relationship to Jesus. While Jesus never falters in allegiance to his Father, Peter's loyalty to his master collapses, apparently out of fear for his life (see v. 31), although nothing else in Mark's passion narrative indicates that the authorities were trying to capture and execute Jesus' disciples. The threefoldness of the contrast harks back to Gethsemane, where Jesus prays three times and three times Peter is caught napping (vv. 32–42), despite Jesus' warning, "Keep awake and pray that you may not come into the time of trial." Now Peter denies Jesus once for each of his failures to pray in Gethsemane.

Second, Peter's behavior constitutes a negative example for readers of the Gospel. This is how Christians ought *not* to behave! Even in front of a female servant he plays the coward (in Jewish courts women were not permitted to give evidence). There is a progression in the expressions of Peter's disloyalty. In his first response he is merely evasive; he claims that he has no idea what the girl is talking about and moves away from the firelight to the shadows of the entryway. When she later identifies him to bystanders as one of Jesus' associates, he explicitly denies the truth of her accusation. Finally, when the bystanders insist that his Galilean accent marks him as a member of the group, he is not content simply to repeat his denial; he curses and utters an oath. The translation is perhaps misleading, for we often use the verb "curse" with the weakened meaning "use obscene or profane language." The Greek verb is formed from the noun *anathema*, which refers to the act of invoking injury or evil on someone. Verse 71 does not indicate the object of Peter's curse. Some scholars believe that the unexpressed object is Jesus, as in 1 Corinthians 12:3 ("Let Jesus be cursed!"). Early in the second century, Pliny, the Roman governor of Bithynia, acquitted persons charged with the crime of being Christians if they did homage to the gods and especially if they cursed Christ, which, he understood, genuine Christians could not be induced to do. Perhaps even in Mark's time persecuted Christians were invited to curse Jesus in order to escape further mistreatment. To do so, of course, would be to become guilty of apostasy. Whether or not Peter is here represented as cursing his master, his threefold denial of any relationship with Jesus renders him an apostate. He renounces his faith in Jesus! He also disobeys Jesus' teaching about not using an oath to certify the truth of a statement (Matt. 5:33–37; compare Matt. 23:16–22; James 5:12).

Third, Peter's sorry tale is included in the Gospels as a classic instance of the superabundance of God's grace. By rights the apostate Peter should have been removed from fellowship with Jesus and his followers after the resurrection, but his reinstatement is implied by the angel in 16:7, "But go, tell his disciples *and Peter* that he is going ahead of you to Galilee; there you will see him" (compare 14:28). Elsewhere in the New Testament we read of a special resurrection appearance to Peter (Luke 24:34; 1 Cor. 15:5; see also John 21). The book of Acts testifies to the powerful leadership exerted by the forgiven Peter.

We can safely assume that Mark does not intend that his readers conclude that they too can deny their Lord under pressure and expect to be restored as "easily" as was Peter. Because of Mark's emphasis on the death and resurrection of Jesus as God's saving act, it is likely that he regarded Peter's apostasy as cured only by the "ransom for many" (10:45).

Modern readers do not often experience the kind of persecution that would pressure them to deny their faith. Wherever Christians are in a minority, however, there is a constant temptation to keep the light of faith hidden under a bushel. During the communist regime in eastern Europe, Christians suffered severe discrimination in education and the workplace. Young people often had to make a difficult choice: If they insisted on retaining membership in the church, they could be denied a high-school graduation diploma and be prevented from pursuing professional employment. Many chose to be loyal to the church and paid dearly. With the collapse of communism, it now seems easier to be Christian, but only because the pressures are subtler, as in western democracies. Many Christians in America forefeit a promotion or lose a job because loyalty to Jesus impels them to "blow the whistle" on unethical practices. Such courage is gained by keeping one's eyes fixed steadily on the faithful Jesus, not the weak-kneed Peter.

PILATE ORDERS JESUS' EXECUTION
Mark 15:1–15

15:1 **As soon as it was morning, the chief priests held a consultation with the elders and scribes and the whole council. They bound Jesus, led him away, and handed him over to Pilate.** [2] **Pilate asked him, "Are you the King of the Jews?" He answered him, "You say so."** [3] **Then the chief priests accused him of many things.** [4] **Pilate asked him again, "Have you no answer? See how many charges they bring against you."** [5] **But Jesus made no further reply, so that Pilate was amazed.**

[6] **Now at the festival he used to release a prisoner for them, anyone for whom they asked.** [7] **Now a man called Barabbas was in prison with the rebels who had committed murder during the insurrection.** [8] **So the crowd came and began to ask Pilate to do for them according to his custom.** [9] **Then he answered them, "Do you want me to release for you the King of the Jews?"** [10] **For he realized that it was out of jealousy that the chief priests had handed him over.** [11] **But the chief priests stirred up the crowd to have him release Barabbas for them instead.** [12] **Pilate spoke to them again, "Then what do you wish me to do with the man you call the King of the Jews?"** [13] **They shouted back, "Crucify him!"** [14] **Pilate asked them, "Why, what evil has he done?" But they shouted all the more, "Crucify him!"** [15] **So Pilate, wishing to satisfy the crowd, released Barabbas for them; and after flogging Jesus, he handed him over to be crucified.**

Pontius Pilate was apparently so well known to Mark's readers that he felt it superfluous to identify him. Yet he was by no means an important figure in Roman history. Nothing is known about his career apart from his stint as prefect of Judea. He is depicted as a harsh and insensitive administrator by two Jewish authors of the time, Philo and Josephus, but his tenure of ten years or more was not especially tumultuous and was longer than that of any of his predecessors or successors. It is his role as judge of Jesus of Nazareth, however, that has endowed him with lasting fame. The Roman historian Tacitus reports nothing about Pilate except for the single fact that "Christus, from whom their [the Christians'] name is derived, was executed at the hands of the procurator Pontius Pilate in the reign of Tiberius." His name is recalled whenever the Apostles' Creed is recited: ". . . suffered under Pontius Pilate."

As Roman prefect, Pilate was not only chief administrator of his province but also supreme judge, with the power to pass and implement capital sentences. If we had only the report of Tacitus, we would assume that Jesus was brought before Pilate on a capital charge and that the Roman judge issued a guilty verdict. The Gospels, however, tell the story in such a way that responsibility is transferred from Pilate to the chief priests and other members of the Jewish court. Mark even neglects to mention Pilate's death sentence, reporting only the consequence, namely, "he handed him over to be crucified" (v. 15). The purpose of this omission is apparently to subordinate the political charge of 15:2 to the religious charge of 14:64. Jesus is crucified, Mark wants us to know, not because he is guilty of a political crime against Rome, but because of the hostility of the Jewish religious authorities.

Although history is overlaid with theology in Mark's telling of the story, it is not fiction that he is writing. The crime of which Pilate found Jesus guilty is specified in the inscription placed on the cross, "the King of the Jews" (v. 26). Because Pilate was firm in dealing with threats to Roman rule (Luke 13:1), we can assume that his failure to search out and destroy Jesus' followers indicates that he did not really regard Jesus as a revolutionary, but rather as a religious fanatic who could be used by rebels if he were not safely put out of the way. Mark is therefore not far from the truth in his claim that Pilate found Jesus innocent of the charge brought against him (v. 14, "Why, what evil has he done?"). There is also no reason to doubt the report that Jesus was brought on Pilate's attention by Jewish religious leaders. Pilate's paid informers were undoubtedly too busy keeping an eye on genuine revolutionaries like Barabbas and his associates to be concerned about the Galilean holy man who publicly taught that taxes should be paid to Caesar (12:17). Jesus' prophetic act of cleansing the temple would have been of no interest to the Romans, but we can readily believe that it excited the animosity of the chief priests, who resented his interference in their affairs (11:15–18).

The early morning consultation, which concludes the all-night session of the council, is apparently devoted to a determination of the political charge against Jesus that will be brought to the prefect. Mark gives no details; they must be inferred from Pilate's abrupt question "Are you the King of the Jews?" Luke fills out the accusation "We found this man perverting our nation, forbidding us to pay taxes to the emperor, and saying that he himself is the Messiah, a king" (Luke 23:2). Jesus' response to Pilate is carefully evasive; "You say so" neither affirms nor denies the truth of the charge. He cannot say "Yes," because he is not "the King of the Jews" as Pilate understands the phrase. Neither can he say "No," because as the one whom God will install as the Messiah he is in some sense already the King of Israel (see my comments on 11:1–11). By his response Jesus makes Pilate an unintentional witness to his true status.

After the chief priests have vigorously prosecuted their case against the prisoner, the Roman judge invites him to present his defense. Jesus silently declines. He knows that no word of his will convince his enemies to drop their charges. Moreover, he has already prayerfully determined in Gethsemane to accept the cup of suffering presented to him by his Father (14:36). What is now happening to him is in fulfillment of his own prediction in 10:32–34. From this point on he will say nothing until the final cry of dereliction in verse 34. Although Mark makes no allusion to the text, Christian readers are reminded of Isaiah 53:7, "He was oppressed, and he was afflicted, yet he did not open his mouth; like a lamb that is led to the slaughter, and like a sheep that before its shearers is silent, so he did not open his mouth." The amazement of Pilate is appropriate to the narrative; the prefect is unaccustomed to prisoners who refuse to attempt a defense, even when it is entirely futile. At the theological level, the amazement is intended to quicken our awe at Jesus' silent submission to suffering on our behalf.

The historicity of the Barabbas incident is vehemently debated by scholars. Some regard the alleged annual amnesty as the figment of Mark's imagination. The practice is nowhere mentioned by Josephus or Roman sources and seems improbable. Why would the prefect release a convicted terrorist who is likely to rally others to the revolutionary cause? On the other hand, there are recorded instances in the ancient world in which one or more prisoners were released at a festival as a conciliatory act. Because Passover celebrated liberation from slavery in Egypt, it is possible that this custom predated the Roman occupation of Palestine and was continued simply because it was too well established to be abandoned without public outrage (note the wording in John 18:39, "*You* have a custom that I release someone for you at the Passover").

Mark refers to "the insurrection," as if it were well known to his readers. Josephus, who reports many incidents of revolutionary activity, writes nothing about Barabbas or a notable insurrection at this time. It may have been a relatively minor event. Since Barabbas is in custody but has not yet been crucified, it can be inferred that the insurrection is of very recent occurrence. Perhaps the two bandits crucified with Jesus (v. 27) were Barabbas's co-conspirators.

The crowd who come to make sure that Pilate observes the tradition of releasing a prisoner at Passover apparently have no particular candidate in mind. Because the famous teacher from Galilee was tried secretly during the night, they are unaware that he is a possible candidate until Pilate proposes him. Jesus' enemies are determined that their plans will not be foiled by a fickle public, so they prompt the crowd to call for the release of Barabbas. Since Barabbas is described by Mark not as a common murderer but as a patriotic revolutionary, he is presumably a hero in the eyes of the crowd, so that little persuasion is needed. For Mark the scene is important for reinforcing the fact that Jesus is innocent of the political charge; he is rejected by the very people who clamor for the release of a certified revolutionary.

Because "Barabbas" is a surname, originally meaning "son of the father" or perhaps "son of our teacher," he undoubtedly had a given name. According to many manuscripts of Matthew 27:16–17, he was called "Jesus," that is *Yeshua* in Aramaic. This was a common name among Jews at the time, which is not surprising, for it is equivalent to "Joshua" (this Old Testament figure is referred to as "Jesus" in the KJV of Acts 7:45 and Heb. 4:8). It is probable that the name was dropped by many scribes because it was repugnant to them that Barabbas the murderer should bear the precious name of Jesus. Whether the name also stood in the original text of Mark must remain a matter of conjecture. If such were the case, the irony would be even stronger, for a popular etymology connected *Yeshua* with the verb "save" (Matt. 1:21). In any event, we may say that *at the theological level* the crowd is offered a choice between two kinds of salvation: the do-it-yourself "salvation" of human violence, represented by Barabbas, and the salvation effected by God through Jesus (10:45; 14:24). The Son of God is rejected in favor of the revolutionary hero.

We may properly suspect that for theological reasons Mark has diminished the historical role of Pilate and overemphasized the role of the raucous crowd. The issue of blame is important for us because of the unhappy role it has played in the horrible history of Christian anti-Semitism. Matthew furthers Mark's exoneration of Pilate by having "the people as a whole" assume full responsibility for the crime of executing the Son of God: "His blood be on us and on our children!" (Matt. 27:25). Haters of the Jews have used the alleged crime of "deicide" as an excuse for arson, plunder, and murder. One weapon against anti-Semitism is truth; it was not the Jewish crowd but the Roman governor who crucified Jesus. Whatever his motives, Pilate *was* responsible.

The scene concludes with Pilate having Jesus flogged, as was normal prior to crucifixion. In this frightful punishment, the prisoner was stripped and beaten with leather lashes to which pieces of bone or lead were attached. Often the flesh was flayed to the bone, and frequently the prisoner died prior to crucifixion. It is sometimes suggested that this was "merciful," in that it accelerated the death of crucified victims, who might otherwise survive the torture for several days. In contrast to some later reports of Christian martyrdoms, this terse report provides no descriptive details concerning the flogging inflicted on Jesus. We should be grateful for Mark's reverential reticence.

JESUS IS RIDICULED BY PILATE'S SOLDIERS
Mark 15:16–20

> 15:16 **Then the soldiers led him into the courtyard of the palace (that is, the governor's headquarters); and they called together the whole cohort.** [17] **And they clothed him in a purple cloak; and after twisting some thorns into a crown, they put it on him.** [18] **And they began saluting him, "Hail, King of the Jews!"** [19] **They struck his head with a reed, spat upon him, and knelt down in homage to him.** [20] **After mocking him, they stripped him of the purple cloak and put his own clothes on him. Then they led him out to crucify him.**

The Roman prefect of Judea resided in Caesarea. Because of the danger of increased unrest caused by masses of pilgrims, it was common for the governor to move to Jerusalem at Passover. He was accompanied by army units that supplemented the regular garrison in the Antonia, a castle situated at the northwest corner of the temple mount (see Acts 21:31–34). His temporary residence in Jerusalem, like his permanent administrative quarters on the coast (Acts 23:35), was called the praetorium. This was not the Antonia but, according to recent scholarship, the palace of the Hasmoneans, not far from the southwest corner of the temple complex.

The cohort attending Pilate was probably not part of a legion, all members of which were Roman citizens, but a unit of the auxiliary forces, recruited from the local population. Because Jews were excused from military service on religious grounds, the soldiers involved in the execution of Jesus were probably Gentiles from somewhere in Palestine or Syria. On the other hand, if the Italian Cohort mentioned in Acts 10:1 was already stationed in Caesarea, there may have been Roman citizens among them.

A cohort numbered from six hundred to a thousand men, but it is not necessary to assume that an entire cohort accompanied Pilate to Jerusalem.
There may also be a measure of exaggeration in Mark's report that the soldiers in charge of Jesus were able to call together all the members of the unit.

The "purple cloak," while clearly parodying the royal purple of the emperor and client kings, was probably a soldier's red cloak. The thorny
crown need not have been intended as an instrument of torture, but
merely as another attempt at parody; emperors and client kings were often depicted on coins wearing a wreath of leafy twigs. The thorns may
have been pointed outward to represent the radiate crown of divine kingship. "Hail, King of the Jews!" probably apes the salutation addressed to
the emperor. In verse 19 the farce turns nastier, as the soldiers beat their
prisoner on the head with a stick (the underlying Greek word can be used
not only for a pliable reed but also for a rigid rod) and show their utter
contempt by spitting on him.

Throughout this scene Jesus remains entirely passive. He accepts scorn
and humiliation without a word of retaliation. Persecuted Christians were
later encouraged to take Jesus as their model of nonretaliation: "For to this
you have been called, because Christ also suffered for you, leaving you an
example, so that you should follow in his steps. . . . When he was abused,
he did not return abuse; when he suffered, he did not threaten; but he en-
trusted himself to the one who judges justly" (1 Pet. 2:21, 23; compare
Matt. 5:39; Rom. 12:17).

For Mark and his readers, ancient and modern, this scene is heavy with
irony. The humbly silent man, whose kingship the soldiers mock, is king
indeed! Gentiles who ridicule him as king of the Jews will discover that he
is King of kings and Lord of lords (Rev. 17:14; 19:16).

JESUS IS CRUCIFIED
Mark 15:21–32

15:21 **They compelled a passer-by, who was coming in from the country,
to carry his cross; it was Simon of Cyrene, the father of Alexander and Rufus. 22 Then they brought Jesus to the place called Golgotha (which means
the place of a skull). 23 And they offered him wine mixed with myrrh; but he
did not take it. 24 And they crucified him, and divided his clothes among
them, casting lots to decide what each should take.**

**25 It was nine o'clock in the morning when they crucified him. 26 The in-
scription of the charge against him read, "The King of the Jews." 27 And with
him they crucified two bandits, one on his right and one on his left. 29 Those**

who passed by derided him, shaking their heads and saying, "Aha! You who would destroy the temple and build it in three days, [30] save yourself, and come down from the cross!" [31] In the same way the chief priests, along with the scribes, were also mocking him among themselves and saying, "He saved others; he cannot save himself. [32] Let the Messiah, the King of Israel, come down from the cross now, so that we may see and believe." Those who were crucified with him also taunted him.

[Please note that other ancient authorities include verse 28.]

Although the death of the Messiah is the climax toward which Mark's narrative has been building since 8:31, the crucifixion itself is reported with surprising brevity. No details are given concerning the pounding of nails, the excruciating pain, the incredible thirst. Apart from his mute refusal of myrrhed wine in verse 23, Jesus does nothing and says nothing until the final cry of dereliction in verse 34. The narrator says not a word about Jesus' unflinching courage and unwavering faith. This is in sharp contrast with earlier stories about Jewish religious martyrs. In 2 Maccabees 6–7 the victims make stirring declarations of their faith in God before they die. Whereas the martyrdoms are reported in such a way as to kindle faith and religious loyalty, this story has a very different function. The dying Jesus is not portrayed as a model of courageous faith to be imitated but as a unique instance in the history of God's saving activity. Implicit in the narrative is the conviction that the silent Jesus is offering his life as a ransom for many (10:45), in obedience to his Father's will (14:36).

Instead of focusing on the victim, the narrative emphasizes the audience. The first witness of the crucifixion to be mentioned is Simon the Cyrenian. Cyrene was a major city in North Africa (modern Libya), with a large Jewish population. We are not told whether he was in Jerusalem as a pilgrim or as an immigrant. Acts 6:9 reports that Cyrenians were prominent in the Synagogue of the Freedmen. Because Mark identifies Simon by mentioning the names of his sons, it is probable that these were Christians who were known to his readers, either in person or by reputation. In Romans 16:13 Paul sends greetings to "Rufus, chosen in the Lord," but unfortunately it cannot be demonstrated that this was Simon's son. A fascinating inscription in a first-century burial cave east of the Jerusalem temple, used by Cyrenian Jews, reads "Alexander, son of Simon." Both names were common, however, and the identity of this Alexander with the one mentioned by Mark must remain nothing more than an intriguing possibility.

Roman law permitted soldiers to impress civilians to carry burdens (the same technical term is used in Matt. 5:41). In this case the burden is the horizontal beam to which Jesus will be affixed before it is placed on the top of a post permanently installed in the ground (to form a T). Victims were normally required to carry the cross beam themselves. One suspects that Jesus was so weakened by the brutal flogging that he was incapable of bearing the burden, but Mark carefully omits any comment on the need for Simon's help. He does not want to make the degradation of Jesus a theme of his story.

Active but silent members of the audience are the soldiers, who are mentioned, however, only by means of indefinite verbs ("they compelled," "they brought," "they offered," "they crucified . . . and divided"). The executioners address no words to Jesus and make no comments about him. They take him outside the city to a rocky spur overlooking a garden (see "Golgotha," *Anchor Bible Dictionary*, vol. 2:1071–73; John 19:20; Heb. 13:12), over which the Basilica of the Holy Sepulchre is now built. The name "Golgotha" (later latinized as "Calvary"; see Luke 23:33, KJV) derived either from the shape of the hill, or, more probably, from the fact that it was "bald," that is, barren of vegetation. Although later rabbinic sources tell us that it was the custom of prominent women to offer drugged wine to condemned prisoners to reduce their suffering, the sequence of Mark's indefinite verbs suggests that in Jesus' case the soldiers perform this service, perhaps in mockery of his alleged royal status, for myrrhed wine was regarded as a treat. In any event, Jesus refuses to diminish his awareness by taking a drug.

The execution proper does not even get a sentence by itself; "And they crucified him" is only the first clause of a sentence devoted to the division of Jesus' personal belongings. Presumably these included an outer garment, a tunic, sandals, head covering, and belt. By custom and law these became the property of the executioners. Men were normally crucified naked, but it is possible that the Romans yielded to Jewish sentiment by allowing Judean victims a loin cloth. Christians came to see in the soldiers' appropriation of Jesus' clothing a fulfillment of prophecy: "they divide my clothes among themselves, and for my clothing they cast lots" (Psalm 22:18; John 19:24). Although this perception may lie beneath the surface of Mark's narrative, he makes no point of it, and there is no reason whatsoever to suspect that this detail of the passion narrative was fabricated on the basis of the psalm.

It was common practice among Romans to specify the crime of a prisoner being executed by placing a placard on the cross or hanging it from the neck of the victim. In Mark's narrative the crime is tersely stated: "The King of the Jews." In Matthew 27:37 this is expanded to "This is Jesus, the

King of the Jews," and in Luke 23:38 we read, "This is the King of the Jews." In John 19:19–22 the chief priests quarrel with Pilate over the wording of the inscription, "Jesus of Nazareth, the King of the Jews." To their demand that it read instead "This man said, I am King of the Jews," Pilate curtly responds, "What I have written I have written." Probably Mark's brief version is the earliest and is authentic. It is most unlikely that an early Christian would have fabricated such a title for Jesus. As we can observe in verse 32, "King of Israel" was the Jewish way of referring to the Messiah. Although Pilate did not regard Jesus' alleged royal pretension as a serious threat to Roman rule in Palestine, he undoubtedly concurred with the chief priests that Jesus' popularity with the masses could be misused by revolutionaries (see John 6:14–15 and my comments on Mark 15:1–15).

All four Gospels report that Jesus was crucified between two other men. Whereas Luke 23:32–33 identifies them simply as "criminals," Mark (followed by Matt. 27:38) calls them "bandits," a term used by Josephus as a designation for the revolutionaries whose activity led to the war against Rome in A.D. 66. Since Roman law did not employ crucifixion as the punishment for violent robbery, Mark is probably using "bandits" in the same way as did Josephus. It is a fair guess that the two men were involved in "the insurrection" with Barabbas (15:7). Although Mark does not develop the point, his readers must have seen great irony in the fact that "the King of the Jews," who had shown himself to be "Prince of Peace" (Isa. 9:6) by teaching the love of enemies (Matt. 5:43–48), had two violent men as his "retinue" in death. In the phrases "one on his right and one on his left" we may hear an echo of the request of James and John in 10:37. Because they were not able to drink his cup, they have fled, and in their places on right and left are two cruel men, who join Jesus' enemies in ridiculing him (v. 32, NIV: "Those crucified with him also heaped insults on him").

Although they are participants in the drama, no lines are given to Simon, the soldiers, or the bandits. Now center stage is taken by two groups who have speaking parts. The first group consists of those "passing by." Because they collectively say the same thing, like the chorus in a Greek tragedy, the designation of them as a succession of individual passersby is not entirely apt. This has suggested to interpreters that Mark is indicating an allusion to Lamentations 2:15, "All who pass along the way clap their hands at you; they hiss and wag their heads" as well as the more obvious prophecy in Psalm 22:7, "All who see me mock at me; they make mouths at me, they shake their heads" (see also Psalm 109:25). The taunt itself echoes the *false* testimony at the Jewish trial (14:57–58), but it is now assumed by the passersby to be *true*.

The chief priests and the scribes, the primary enemies of Jesus throughout the passion narrative (11:18; 14:1), make their final appearance in the role of the second group of speaking spectators. Their utter contempt is demonstrated by the fact that they do not deign to address Jesus directly but instead speak of him to one another. Sarcastically, they suggest that if only Jesus will validate his supernatural authority as God's Messiah by removing himself from the cross, they will be glad to believe in him. In the words "He saved others" we should see a reference to statements in the first part of the Gospel that use the Greek verb "save" with the meaning "heal" (5:23, 28, 34; 6:56). His healing powers, they assert, cannot rescue him from death by crucifixion.

Although the taunts of these two groups of spectators are delivered at the foot of the cross, they became a continually repeated experience for Jewish Christians. Other Jews challenged them with the question: How can a *crucified* man possibly be the Messiah? As Paul, the converted persecutor testifies, "Christ crucified" was "a stumbling block to Jews and foolishness to Gentiles." Only by means of the resurrection did Jesus' followers come to see in the crucified Messiah "the power of God and the wisdom of God" (1 Cor. 1:23–24).

Mark's reference to "those who passed by" may echo not only Lamentations 2:15 but also the haunting question of Lamentations 1:12, "Is it nothing to you, all you who pass by? Look and see if there is any sorrow like my sorrow." In the chapel of Victoria College in Toronto there is a huge oil painting of the crucifixion. On the left the three crosses are boldly depicted in all their horror. On the right is a stream of people dressed according to the fashions of the nineteenth century. Most of the men and women are laughing and talking, paying no attention whatsoever to the dying man on the central cross. A newsboy shouts out his headlines, which he obviously considers more important than what is happening beside him. A bishop pompously walks by, oblivious to Jesus, conscious only of his own importance. In the stream of human traffic there is one person, a fashionably dressed matron, who has caught a glimpse of the Crucified. On her face is a look of momentary horror, but the movement of her body is away from the cross, not toward it. Those who pass by do not want to consider the sorrow of the man from Nazareth.

Readers of Mark's story become spectators of the event—hostile, indifferent, or irresistibly drawn into the dramatic action. Some find it utter foolishness to make so much fuss over the death of one man when there is so much suffering in the world. Others are awed by the power of God and the wisdom of God (1 Cor. 1:24).

THE DEATH OF JESUS
Mark 15:33–41

15:33 **When it was noon, darkness came over the whole land until three in the afternoon.** [34] **At three o'clock Jesus cried out with a loud voice, "Eloi, Eloi, lema sabachthani?" which means, "My God, my God, why have you forsaken me?"** [35] **When some of the bystanders heard it, they said, "Listen, he is calling for Elijah."** [36] **And someone ran, filled a sponge with sour wine, put it on a stick, and gave it to him to drink, saying, "Wait, let us see whether Elijah will come to take him down."** [37] **Then Jesus gave a loud cry and breathed his last.** [38] **And the curtain of the temple was torn in two, from top to bottom.** [39] **Now when the centurion, who stood facing him, saw that in this way he breathed his last, he said, "Truly this man was God's Son!"**

[40] **There were also women looking on from a distance; among them were Mary Magdalene, and Mary the mother of James the younger and of Joses, and Salome.** [41] **These used to follow him and provided for him when he was in Galilee; and there were many other women who had come up with him to Jerusalem.**

In Mark's telling of the story all the taunting occurs in the morning. At noon, when the sun is at its highest point, there is sudden darkness that lasts until three in the afternoon. During these three hours nothing happens. Although the soldiers and the spectators have not left the scene, they are silent and invisible. All wait passively for the end to arrive.

There is no point in trying to explain the darkness as the result of a solar eclipse, which would be impossible when the Passover moon was full, and which in any case would last only a few minutes. Some have proposed that the darkness was due to a severe sandstorm, but no hint of this can be found in the narrative. It is best to conclude that, whatever the origin of the tradition, for Mark the darkness is not a natural phenomenon but one created by God. Unfortunately, the evangelist provides no clue concerning the theological significance of the darkness, with the result that there have been innumerable suggestions. Mark's Gentile readers may have been reminded of the Roman tradition that the sun was darkened when Julius Caesar died. The Jewish philosopher Philo believed that a solar eclipse announced the death of a king or the destruction of a city. Another suggestion is that God darkens the scene in order to spare Jesus from the gloating gaze of his enemies. On the whole it seems more probable that Mark's perspective on the darkness accompanying the crucifixion was influenced by the use of this motif by the Hebrew prophets. In the prophetic books of the Old Testament, darkness often symbolizes God's anger at sin

(Jer. 13:16; Ezek. 32:8; Joel 2:2, 31). Amos declares that "the day of the LORD," anticipated by many as a time of rejoicing, will be darkness, not light, because it will be the day of God's judgment of Israel (Amos 5:18–20; compare 8:9, "I will make the sun go down at noon").

At three in the afternoon, precisely at "the hour of prayer" (Acts 3:1), when a lamb was offered as a whole burnt offering to God on the high altar in the temple (Exod. 29:38–41), the darkness was suddenly pierced by a loud shout from the dying Messiah: "Eloi, Eloi, lema sabachthani?" These words represent an Aramaic translation of Psalm 22:1, "My God, my God, why have you forsaken me?" This "cry of dereliction," as it is regularly called, has puzzled and troubled interpreters in every age. Indeed, Luke apparently found it so troubling that he omitted it and put in its place the much more edifying last word "Father, into your hands I commend by spirit" (Luke 23:46).

Did Jesus really believe that God had abandoned him? Various attempts have been made to soften this impression. Occasionally it has been proposed that this word from the cross is not authentic, but rather fabricated by Mark or his source. It is very difficult, however, to believe that any early Christian would have voluntarily attributed such a troubling saying to Jesus. Another suggestion is that in quoting the first verse Jesus was alluding to the psalm as a whole, which ends on a very positive note. This, too, is a very improbable solution, especially in view of the narrative context. The bystanders do not hear the shout as a positive declaration of faith but as a call for help. It is best to assume that this anguished cry is authentic, and that it expressed the extremity of Jesus' suffering. Worse by far than the excruciating physical agony was the feeling that his Father in heaven, whom he addressed familiarly as *Abba* (14:36), had left him to die alone. This by no means suggests that Jesus died a broken and disillusioned man. His reproach, like Job's (see, for example, Job 9:22–24), must be seen not as the utterance of one who has given up believing in God but as the expression of a profound faith that is being tested to the uttermost. Like his prayer in Gethsemane, Jesus' cry from the cross is a salutary reminder to Christians of his genuine humanity. His divinity must not be conceived in such a way that his shout from the cross becomes mere play-acting (see my comments on 14:32–42).

Because the feeling of separation from God is one of the consequences of sin, Christians have regarded the cry of dereliction as a sign that Jesus, sinless though he was, bore the punishment that we merited. We cannot fathom the mystery of the atonement. Paul resorts to the language of paradox: "For our sake he made him to be sin who knew no sin, so that in him we might become the righteousness of God" (2 Cor. 5:21). In the same passage, however, Paul reminds us that Jesus was not actually separated from God in the agony of crucifixion, for God was directly participating in the event: "In Christ God was reconciling the world to himself, not counting their trespasses against them" (2 Cor. 5:19).

Because "Eloi" and "Elijah" are similar, some of the bystanders think that Jesus is calling upon Elijah to rescue him. Because Elijah had not died but had been taken directly to heaven (2 Kings 2:11), it was widely believed that, like an angel, he could come to an individual's aid. The offer of sour wine (an inexpensive thirst-quencher popular with soldiers and laborers) is not intended as a humane gesture but as a means of prolonging Jesus' agony a little longer, in order to mock his futile call for Elijah's help. Mark does not tell us that Jesus drank the wine; a better translation of the relevant clause would be "and he tried to give it to him to drink" (compare NIV: "offered it to Jesus to drink"). Indeed, it has been proposed that in Mark's view Jesus is already dead when the attempt is made, because verse 37, translated literally, can refer to the great shout of verse 34: "But Jesus, having cried out with a loud voice, expired." In any event, nothing new is added by the second shout. In both instances the loudness of the utterance is probably intended by Mark as a sign of supernatural power. In contrast with normal victims of crucifixion, whose strength is so drained that they can barely whisper before sinking into unconsciousness, Mark's Jesus remains fully aware, and, drawing on the power that has enabled him to perform miracles, dies with a mighty shout.

Because the verb translated "breathed his last" in verses 37 and 39 literally means "blow out," it has recently been suggested that the splitting of the temple curtain was caused by a miraculous wind coming from Jesus' mouth (see Gundry, *Mark*, 970). Most interpreters prefer to understand the miracle as effected directly by God, taking "was torn in two" as a "divine passive," that is, as a reverential avoidance of naming God as the one responsible for the action. Mark explicitly notes that the curtain was split from top to bottom, that is, without human help. When understood in this sense, the splitting of the curtain represents heaven's response to the crucifixion of the Son of God. Mark provides no clue, however, regarding the significance of the event. The central shrine in the temple complex had two great curtains. One hung at the main entrance and could be seen even at a distance as it billowed in the wind. The second separated the main room of the temple, the Holy Place, from the Holy of Holies beyond it. This second curtain is of theological significance to the author of Hebrews, who represents Jesus as our great high priest who has provided a new access to God by himself going beyond the curtain on our behalf (Heb. 6:19–20; compare 9:3). Later the same author uses the curtain allegorically as a reference to Jesus' physical death (10:20). Mark, however, does not indicate which curtain he has in mind or what theological significance he finds in the event. Does he regard the split curtain as a portent of the destruction of the temple or as a sign that Gentiles will obtain free access to God? These and other suggestions are mere guesses. It is best to content ourselves with the observation that Mark presents the occurrence as a heavenly portent that dramatically acknowledges the death of the Messiah. It is not just one of many would-be kings who has died on the cross but the Son of God.

This nonverbal declaration is given explicit confirmation in the words of the Gentile executioner: "Truly this man was God's Son!" His confession, echoing the voice from heaven at Jesus' baptism, "You are my Son, the Beloved; with you I am well pleased" (1:11), ties the end of Mark's story to its beginning and marks its climax. From the evangelist's perspective, Jesus is not the Messiah *despite* the crucifixion (which to nonbelievers constituted indisputable proof that he was not) but in a very real sense *because* of it. By his willing acceptance of a shameful and painful death, he fulfilled the role God had predestined for the Messiah (see 8:29–31).

Undoubtedly, Mark saw great irony in the fact that this verbal confirmation of Jesus' status came not from one of his own people but from a pagan. Although there is not the slightest suggestion that the centurion subsequently became a Christian (in this case one would expect Mark to name him; compare 15:21), he nevertheless symbolizes the vast number of Gentiles who would come to see in the crucified Jesus "the power of God and the wisdom of God" (1 Cor. 1:24).

The final group of spectators is mentioned only after the death has been reported. Women who traveled with Jesus in Galilee (compare Luke 8:2) and many others who adhered to his movement and who accompanied him on his last pilgrimage to Jerusalem have been watching and waiting through these long hours. Whereas the male followers of Jesus are nowhere in sight, the women have remained loyal. Three are mentioned by name, because they will be the witnesses of the empty tomb (16:1). Two of the three will also witness the burial and thus authenticate that Jesus was truly dead, truly buried, and truly resurrected.

Little is known of Mary of Magdala (a fishing town near Tiberias), except for Luke's report that she had been exorcized of seven demons (Luke 8:2). In each of the Gospels she appears as the leading witness of the resurrection (see also the longer ending of Mark, 16:9). It is only in later legend that Mary is identified with the sinful woman of Luke 7:36–50 and portrayed as a repentant harlot. The identity of the second woman, "Mary the mother of James the younger and of Joses," is uncertain. Some scholars maintain on the basis of Mark 6:3 that this is the mother of Jesus, arguing that James is referred to as "the small one" to indicate that he is Jesus' younger brother. Others believe that it is unlikely that Mark would fail to note that this was Jesus' mother, and therefore conclude that another woman is meant. Nothing at all is known about the identity of Salome. Matthew substitutes "the mother of the sons of Zebedee" (Matt. 27:56), but this need not mean that he thinks that Zebedee's wife is called Salome. She reappears in 16:1 but nowhere else in the New Testament.

JESUS IS BURIED
Mark 15:42–47

15:42 **When evening had come, and since it was the day of Preparation, that is, the day before the sabbath,** [43] **Joseph of Arimathea, a respected member of the council, who was also himself waiting expectantly for the kingdom of God, went boldly to Pilate and asked for the body of Jesus.** [44] **Then Pilate wondered if he were already dead; and summoning the centurion, he asked him whether he had been dead for some time.** [45] **When he learned from the centurion that he was dead, he granted the body to Joseph.** [46] **Then Joseph bought a linen cloth, and taking down the body, wrapped it in the linen cloth, and laid it in a tomb that had been hewn out of the rock. He then rolled a stone against the door of the tomb.** [47] **Mary Magdalene and Mary the mother of Joses saw where the body was laid.**

The burial of an executed criminal was by no means an automatic event in the ancient world. According to Roman custom the corpses of crucified persons remained on their crosses for days, to suffer decomposition and attacks from predatory birds. Eusebius, an early church historian, reports that the bodies of the Christian martyrs of Lyons were exposed in this way for six days and were then burned to prevent burial.

In Palestine, Roman custom and Jewish law came into conflict. Deuteronomy 21:23 strictly forbids the practice of extended exposure of criminal corpses: "his corpse must not remain all night upon the tree; you shall bury him that same day, for anyone hung on a tree is under God's curse. You must not defile the land that the LORD your God is giving you for possession." Jewish sources tell us that special burial places were provided for those executed for grievous offenses against God's law, such as blasphemy and idolatry. Such persons were not to receive an honorable burial, but it was essential that they not remain unburied. Burial of a stranger was considered one of the greatest of pious acts (Tob. 1:17–19). Josephus tells his pagan readers that Jews bury even their enemies.

The extent to which Romans gave in to Jewish sentiment in the matter of the burial of crucified criminals is not clear. It is quite conceivable that the occupying power deemed it wise to yield on the point, especially at Passover. On occasion such corpses may have been disposed of "dishonorably" in a mass grave.

Evidence in support of John's report that crucifixions were sometimes brought to a speedy conclusion by breaking the legs of the victims (John 19:31–32) can perhaps be seen in the recent discovery of the skeletal remains of a first-century crucifixion victim in a tomb near Jerusalem. The left leg was cleanly broken, the right thoroughly splintered, probably from the same blow (see "Crucifixion, Method of," *Interpreter's Dictionary of the Bible*, suppl. vol., 199). This evidence is not conclusive, of course, for the legs may have been broken days after the victim's decease to facilitate removal of the body.

The Roman emperors insisted that those executed for treason should not be given an honorable burial, so that they might not be viewed as heroes to be emulated. Because Jesus was executed as "the King of the Jews," his case was subject to this rule, whether or not Pilate regarded him as truly guilty of the crime. It is for this reason that it took some daring on the part of Joseph of Arimathea to request permission to bury Jesus. He ran the risk of being suspected by Pilate of being a member of the Jesus movement. Pilate would undoubtedly have denied the request if it had come from a known follower of Jesus.

Each of the other Gospels embroiders the picture of Joseph of Arimathea that we find in Mark. Luke 23:50–51 relates that he was a member of the Sanhedrin who had not agreed with the court's action against Jesus. According to Matthew 27:57 and John 19:38, he was a disciple of Jesus. Recent scholarship finds Mark's portrayal of Joseph more probable. It was precisely because he had no connection with Jesus and had in fact concurred in the guilty verdict (Mark 15:64 insists that the verdict was unanimous) that this pious Jew was given permission for a dishonorable burial of the criminal's corpse. This conclusion is supported by the fact that Mary Magdalene and Mary the mother of Joses, two close followers of Jesus, are not presented by Mark as assisting Joseph in the disposal of Jesus' body but merely as spectators (v. 47). Further confirmation may be seen in Acts 13:27–29, which suggests that the persons who condemned Jesus and asked Pilate to have him killed were also responsible for his burial. Although Mark and his readers may have assumed that Joseph washed the corpse, this is not made explicit. Nothing in the brief report emphasizes that Joseph gave Jesus an "honorable" burial. The linen cloth was necessary from a Jewish point of view to cover Jesus' nakedness. The tomb was probably an opening in the side of the old quarry below Golgotha (see my comments on 15:22). The opening had to be closed with a rock to prevent stray dogs from entering.

The fact that Joseph's name is remembered, however, suggests that there may be anachronistic truth in the claim of Matthew and John that Joseph was a disciple; he may later have become a member of the Jerusalem church. In any event, his pious act in burying their master was gratefully remembered by Jesus' followers.

The burial of Jesus is mentioned as an article of faith both in 1 Corinthians 15:3–5 and in the Apostles' and Nicene Creeds. The burial confirms that Jesus truly died and that his resurrection was therefore genuine, not the resuscitation of a drugged or comatose victim of crucifixion. Mark tells us that Jesus' body did not simply disappear (perhaps into a mass grave with the bandits crucified with him) but was placed in a tomb under the watchful eyes of two trustworthy women whose names he can recount, who were thus able to certify that the corpse was no longer there two days later.

13. The Empty Tomb
Mark 16:1–8

16:1 **When the sabbath was over, Mary Magdalene, and Mary the mother of James, and Salome bought spices, so that they might go and anoint him. ² And very early on the first day of the week, when the sun had risen, they went to the tomb. ³ They had been saying to one another, "Who will roll away the stone for us from the entrance to the tomb?" ⁴ When they looked up, they saw that the stone, which was very large, had already been rolled back. ⁵ As they entered the tomb, they saw a young man, dressed in a white robe, sitting on the right side; and they were alarmed. ⁶ But he said to them, "Do not be alarmed; you are looking for Jesus of Nazareth, who was crucified. He has been raised; he is not here. Look, there is the place they laid him. ⁷ But go, tell his disciples and Peter that he is going ahead of you to Galilee; there you will see him, just as he told you." ⁸ So they went out and fled from the tomb, for terror and amazement had seized them; and they said nothing to anyone, for they were afraid.**

Mark's Easter story is probably the least read and least appreciated of all the Easter stories in the New Testament. The reason is obvious. There is no encounter between the risen Jesus and any of his followers. The Gospel ends with the failure of the women, the only witnesses, to report the emptiness of Jesus' tomb and the message of the angel. Mark's story of Jesus' ministry, passion, and resurrection terminates abruptly with fear, flight, and silence.

This conclusion was so dissatisfying to ancient readers that two separate endings were supplied by scribes who copied the manuscript. The longer of these became widely accepted as a part of the Gospel and appears in many translations as verses 9–20. The best ancient manuscripts of the Gospels, however, do not contain either the short or the long ending. Eusebius, a church historian of the fourth century, testified that in his day the most accurate copies concluded with verse 8.

Did Mark intend to end his Gospel in this way? This question is vigorously debated. Many scholars insist that Mark must have included a fulfillment of the prediction of 14:28 (which is emphasized by repetition in
16:7): "But after I am raised up, I will go before you to Galilee." The last
page of the Gospel, it is argued, must have broken off the scroll before further copies were made, but probably after Matthew used Mark as the
source of his stories about the appearance of Jesus to the women in
Jerusalem and to the disciples in Galilee (Matt. 28:9–10, 16–20).

Other scholars urge that Mark had good reasons for ending his Gospel
with the fear of the women. There was no need to supply stories about the
risen Jesus, because such stories were well known to his Christian readers.
The resurrection of Jesus has been anticipated frequently, beginning with
the midpoint of the Gospel (8:31; 9:9, 31; 10:34; 14:28). Since readers are
expecting to find an appearance story as the climax of the Gospel, however, why would Mark refuse to provide it? The proposed explanation is
theological. Mark, it is suggested, was convinced that some Christians
were focusing so much attention on the glory of the resurrected Christ
that they were forgetting that discipleship means following the crucified
Jesus. Those who make Easter rather than Good Friday the focus of their
religious devotion are in danger of succumbing to a religiosity that is essentially selfish. It is not from the wondrous victory of the Resurrected but
from the humiliating defeat of the Crucified that we learn to humble ourselves, deny ourselves, and consider the needs of others above our own (see
8:31–37).

It is relatively unimportant which side we choose in this debate, however. Even if Mark's writing originally included resurrection appearances,
it is clear that it would remain a passion Gospel. The Easter narratives,
however powerful in themselves, would not erase the profound impression made on the reader by the persistent emphasis on Jesus' dying, which
dominates the narrative from 8:31 on.

To some readers the story of the empty tomb sounds like a pious fraud.
They may have little difficulty believing that Jesus' immortal soul survived
the death of his body and that his disciples felt his spiritual presence with
them, but they find the story of the resuscitation of his body totally incredible. We must remember that the story was no more believable in the
first century than in our own day. It must have seemed as ridiculous as
some of the tall tales that are presented as "news" in our supermarket
tabloids. If Jesus' disciples, despite disillusionment over his failed messiahship, had decided to honor the memory of their martyred teacher by

teaching what he taught, there was certainly no point in fabricating the improbable report of the empty tomb, which could only repulse potential adherents. Moreover, no Jewish follower of Jesus would have made up the story as we have it, for women were not regarded as credible witnesses in Jewish courts. The story is told in a simple, restrained fashion, without any defensive attempt to make it less incredible than it is.

Although the bodily resurrection of Jesus is by no means comprehensible as an event in human history, historians must address the probability that his corpse disappeared. Jews venerated the graves of their prophets and martyrs, but there is no record of early Christians venerating Jesus' grave. Indeed, its exact location seems to have been quickly forgotten. The proclamation of the resurrection of the crucified Messiah was apparently regarded by the religious authorities in Jerusalem as troublesome nonsense (Acts 4), yet they did not expose the fraud by producing Jesus' remains. Instead, the rumor circulated that the body had been stolen (Matt. 28:11–15), a rumor that was still alive a century later in the time of Justin Martyr.

The empty tomb narrative is not primarily about Jesus. It is essentially a story about God. For this reason it is more believable to Pinchas Lapide, an orthodox Jewish rabbi, than to those Christians who have difficulty believing that God actively intervenes in human affairs. In this book *The Resurrection of Jesus: A Jewish Perspective*, Lapide argues that the God whose mighty acts are described in the Hebrew scriptures was fully capable of raising up the prophet Jesus of Nazareth.

Seen in this light, the resurrection of Jesus must be regarded as God's comment on the crucifixion. The cry of dereliction of 15:34 receives its response on Easter morning. God did not abandon his Messiah! The resurrection serves as divine authentication of Jesus' ministry and of his obedient submission to suffering (14:36). If Jesus' body had moldered in the grave, that is, if God had been silent and absent, it is probable that Christianity would have remained a minor movement in Judaism, decreasing in numbers and vitality as the memory of Jesus faded. It was the incomprehensible Easter event that transformed the disciples from disheartened adherents of the repudiated Messiah to confident heralds of God's mighty act in the life, death, and resurrection of Jesus.

As Mark tells the story, the empty tomb is discovered by the same three women whom he has named as witnesses of Jesus' death (15:40), two of whom are explicitly identified as witnesses of the exact location of the burial (15:47; regarding their identities, see my comments on 15:40). Their visit to the tomb is not undertaken in order to complete the burial; Mark and his readers probably assumed that the corpse had been washed and anointed with oil before being wrapped in the linen shroud. They bring aromatic oils or perfumes to pour on Jesus' body, not for the purpose of embalming but simply in order to bestow special honor on his remains.

The women are astonished to discover that the huge slab of rock, which was placed at the entrance to the tomb, has been moved aside and that the body has been removed. By whom? Grave robbers? Enemies? Someone who transferred the corpse to another grave (John 20:2, 15)? Mark does not pause to consider such questions. Because the reason for the disappearance of the body is by no means self-evident, a divine revelation is needed. This is supplied by an angel. Mark calls him a "young man," but the fright of the women signals that he is no mortal but a heavenly messenger. Although modern readers are inclined to be skeptical about angelic apparitions, early Christians apparently had little difficulty with such reports. Angels are mentioned frequently not only in the New Testament but also in the Dead Sea Scrolls and other contemporary Jewish literature. The angel assures the women that Jesus' body has not been stolen; it has been resurrected by God. The NRSV translation in verse 6, "He has been raised," is much preferable to that of the RSV and NIV, "He has risen." The New Testament as a whole affirms that Jesus' resurrection was not automatic, that is, he did not get up of his own accord, but was raised by the direct intervention of God (Acts 2:24; Rom. 10:9; Gal. 1:1).

Mark's terse narrative does not develop the implications of this revelation. If it is not simply a matter of Jesus' righteous soul being in the hand of God (compare Wisd. of Sol. 3:1) but of his body being resurrected, the Easter event is an anticipation of the final resurrection of the dead (see 1 Cor. 15:20–21) and is thus the beginning of a new era.

No appearance of the risen Jesus is reported, but Mark leaves his readers in no doubt that such an appearance will occur. Jesus' own promise of 14:28 is reaffirmed by the angel: "But go, tell his disciples and Peter that he is going ahead of you to Galilee; there you will see him, just as he told you" (v. 7). Peter receives special mention, presumably because of his apostasy at the home of the high priest (14:66–72). The cowardice of the eleven disciples will be overcome by the postresurrection reunion. In Galilee, where it all began, they will begin again to follow Jesus.

The response of the three women is terror, flight, and speechlessness. Mark surely does not mean to suggest that this is the end of the matter. Somehow the news must be reported, for otherwise Jesus' sure prophecy of a reunion with the disciples cannot be fulfilled. The witnesses' silence must be temporary. The threefold reaction of the women dramatically represents the proper human response to the incredibly powerful activity of God. If the disciples were frightened by Jesus' stilling of the storm (4:40–41), by this walking on the sea (6:50–51), and by the transfiguration (9:6), how much more should the women be overcome by religious terror when they are confronted by the awesome event of the resurrection! In this powerful conclusion to his Gospel, Mark impresses upon the reader that the raising of Jesus is not an everyday event like the survival of a righteous soul but rather the world-shattering, world-remaking intervention of God the creator.

LATER ENDINGS APPENDED TO THE GOSPEL
Mark 16:9–20

The Shorter Ending

> And all that had been commanded them they told briefly to those around Peter. And afterward Jesus himself sent out through them, from east to west, the sacred and imperishable proclamation of eternal salvation.

The Longer Ending

> 16:9 Now after he rose early on the first day of the week, he appeared first to Mary Magdalene, from whom he had cast out seven demons. 10 She went out and told those who had been with him, while they were mourning and weeping. 11 But when they heard that he was alive and had been seen by her, they would not believe it.
> 12 After this he appeared in another form to two of them, as they were walking into the country. 13 And they went back and told the rest, but they did not believe them.
> 14 Later he appeared to the eleven themselves as they were sitting at the table; and he upbraided them for their lack of faith and stubbornness, because they had not believed those who saw him after he had risen. 15 And he said to them, "Go into all the world and proclaim the good news to the whole creation. 16 The one who believes and is baptized will be saved; but the one who does not believe will be condemned. 17 And these signs will accompany those who believe: by using my name they will cast out demons; they will speak in new tongues; 18 they will pick up snakes in their hands,

and if they drink any deadly thing, it will not hurt them; they will lay their hands on the sick, and they will recover."

[19] **So then the Lord Jesus, after he had spoken to them, was taken up into heaven and sat down at the right hand of God.** [20] **And they went out and proclaimed the good news everywhere, while the Lord worked with them and confirmed the message by the signs that accompanied it.**

The existence of two different endings for Mark in ancient Greek manuscripts and early translations indicates that neither is original. Each was added because scribes found Mark's conclusion in 16:8 too abrupt. The first of the two rounds off the Gospel by declaring that the women eventually obeyed the angel's command and that Jesus himself commissioned the worldwide mission of the disciples. The author of this ending may or may not have been aware of Matthew's commissioning narrative (Matt. 28:16–20).

The longer ending (vv. 9–20) was probably not written specifically for its present function, for it does not fit neatly with the preceding verses. It may have been created as a brief summary of the Easter stories in all the Gospels. The first verses (9–10) refer to the story in John 20:1–18, although verse 11 seems to reflect rather the disbelief of Luke 24:11. Certainly verse 12 echoes Luke's story of the appearance on the road to Emmaus (Luke 24:13–33), although, again, the motif of disbelief (v. 13) is missing from the Lukan narrative. Verse 14 does not correspond closely with any of the New Testament stories, but verse 15 parallels the Great Commission in Matthew 28:18–20. The reference to Jesus' ascension in verse 19 may draw on Luke 24:50–51. The remaining verses do not correspond with anything in the Gospels, but may echo stories in Acts about exorcisms (8:7; 19:12), speaking in tongues (2:1–13; 10:46), and Paul's survival of snakebite (28:3–6). There is no New Testament parallel to drinking "any deadly thing" (v. 18). It must be emphasized that these lines about handling poisonous snakes and drinking poisonous liquids are not scriptural. They do not belong to the authentic Gospel of Mark, and therefore are not part of the biblical canon. They should not be taken as authorization of aberrant practices that disregard the clear biblical injunction: "Do not put the Lord your God to the test" (Deut. 6:16; Matt. 4:7; Luke 4:12).

When the four Gospels were first put together into one book, *The Gospel*, with four large chapters ("According to Matthew," etc.), Mark may have been placed last, because it was shortest and written by a non-apostle (Matthew and John were regarded as the works of apostles).

There are early manuscripts of the Gospels in which John occurs in second position and Mark at the end. If this was the earliest ordering of the Gospels, the longer ending may have been appended to Mark at the time the fourfold Gospel was created. In this case its purpose was not only to solve the problem of Mark's abrupt ending but to provide a suitable epilogue to all four Gospels, for it seems to contain parallels to the other three.

Works Cited

Anchor Bible Dictionary, ed. D. N. Freedman. 6 vols. New York: Doubleday, 1992.

Davies, W. D. *The Setting of the Sermon on the Mount.* Cambridge: Cambridge University Press, 1964.

Gundry, Robert H. *Mark: A Commentary on His Apology for the Cross.* Grand Rapids: Wm. B. Eerdmans Publishing Company, 1993.

Hooker, Morna D. *The Gospel According to Saint Mark.* Peabody, Mass.: Hendrickson Publishers, 1991.

Interpreter's Dictionary of the Bible, eds. George A. Buttrick and Keith Crim. 4 vols. and Supplementary Vol. New York and Nashville: Abingdon Press, 1962, 1976.

Lane, William L. *The Gospel According to Mark.* Grand Rapids: Wm. B. Eerdmans Publishing Company, 1974.

Lapide, Pinchas. *The Resurrection of Jesus: A Jewish Perspective.* Minneapolis: Augsburg Publishing House, 1983.

Manson, T. W. *The Teaching of Jesus.* Cambridge: Cambridge University Press, 1939.

For Further Reading

Achtemeier, Paul J. *Mark.* Proclamation Commentaries. 2d ed. Philadelphia: Fortress Press, 1986.

Guelich, Robert A. *Mark 1–8:26.* Word Biblical Commentary. Dallas: Word Books, 1989.

Kingsbury, Jack D. *The Christology of Mark's Gospel.* Philadelphia: Fortress Press, 1983.

Nineham, D. E. *Saint Mark.* Pelican Gospel Commentaries. Baltimore: Penguin Books, 1963.

Williamson, Lamar. *Mark.* Interpretation: A Bible Commentary for Teaching and Preaching. Atlanta: John Knox Press, 1983.

Please note that the following abbreviations are also used throughout the text:

KJV, *King James Version* (Nashville, Tenn.: Thomas Nelson Inc., Publishers, 1982)

NEB, *The New English Bible* (Oxford University Press & Cambridge University Press, 1970)

NIV, *New International Version* (Grand Rapids, Mich.: Zondervan Bible Publishers, 1984)

REB, *The Revised English Bible* (Oxford University Press & Cambridge University Press, 1989)

RSV, *Revised Standard Version* (New York: Division of Christian Education of the National Council of the Churches of Christ in the U.S.A., 1973)

TEV, *The Good News Bible* (New York: American Bible Society, 1976)

Printed in the United States
29467LVS00005B/103-111